J. Smith

WORTHY IS THE LAMB

Worthy Is the Lamb

AN INTERPRETATION OF REVELATION

by
Ray Summers
CHAIRMAN, RELIGION DEPARTMENT
BAYLOR UNIVERSITY
WACO, TEXAS

BROADMAN PRESS
Nashville, Tennessee

Copyright, 1951
BROADMAN PRESS
Nashville, Tennessee

4213-14
ISBN: 0-8054-1314-6

Printed in the United States of America

To
ELDRED DOUGLAS HEAD
My teacher
My fellow worker
My friend

Preface

Preachers of the gospel are either naturally endowed with or acquire early in their ministry a healthy curiosity. Perhaps this quality is nowhere better reflected than in a course of study in a theological seminary. To such reflection the author of this work owes a debt of gratitude for having brought to his attention the acute need for just such a study as is presented in this work. Particularly should appreciation be expressed to the class in New Testament 7 for the summer session of 1941. It was during that eight weeks' study in the book of Revelation that the determination was made to pursue this study. In the years that have followed the class has been given once or twice every session, and out of this "laboratory" has come this work. The views have been subjected to the consideration of hundreds of students. The result has been both gratifying and stimulating.

The purpose in this study is twofold: First, to study the historical background of the book of Revelation. Through the inspiration of the Holy Spirit this book was given by a man to men. To both it must have had a meaning as it found them in their life situation. To get the meaning, we must understand that life situation. Throughout this work the starting place for interpretation is the Christian people of Asia Minor in the last decade of the first century A.D. I do not believe that any interpretation of Revelation can be correct if it was meaningless and if it failed to bring practical help and comfort to those who first received the book. To start from any other viewpoint is to follow the road which leads away from the truth of the book rather than the road which reveals the marvelous message of truth here given to troubled hearts. The second purpose of this study is to apply our knowledge of the background of the book in the interpretation of the book. We are to apply this knowledge to know what the book meant for those who first received it and, in consequence, what it means to us today. It is the view of this writer that both meanings are the same.

Many limitations have presented themselves in the course of this research. The study of apocalyptic literature is voluminous. For the present purpose it has been necessary to limit the consideration to the apocalyptic literature which may have influenced the writer of Revelation; i.e., Jewish apocalyptic. There are many places where one feels a temptation to turn aside for lengthy discourse on obviously false interpretations of frequently perverted passages in the book, but limitation of space forbids one's yielding. For the most part the interpretation here presented is positive rather than negative. It has been necessary, too, to avoid lengthy polemics and try to present the book as it must have been understood by those who first received it.

Many books have been consulted in the course of the years which have gone into this study. To all of them acknowledgment should be made. A bibliography is given to indicate the most helpful works. Of these, the ones which have been leaned on most heavily are indicated in the footnotes. Perhaps others used and not indicated will be apparent to the reader who has devoted much reading to the hundreds of volumes printed on Revelation. If so, I regret the oversight in the acknowledgment due. One unconsciously absorbs much which he later uses without ability to give credit where credit is due.

The title chosen, *Worthy Is the Lamb,* presents the central idea of the book. It is God's redeeming Lamb who dominates the lives of his people and the activity of this book. He is the One who is finally and completely victorious over the forces which try to destroy the work and the people of God. When the curtain falls on the last scene of this marvelous drama, the reader is overcome with the emotion which leads him to bow his head in reverence before God and join Handel in his soul-stirring chorus, "Worthy is the Lamb that was slain and has redeemed us to God by his blood, to receive riches and honor and glory and power."

RAY SUMMERS

Fort Worth, Texas

Contents

Introduction

Neglected, misunderstood, and grossly perverted, the book of Revelation stands quite alone in the New Testament. Most readers have been content to pass it by with the attitude, "No one understands it anyway." For many others it has had a peculiar fascination. For some the fascination has been from a religious motive; for others the fascination has been from the viewpoint of curiosity. There has been such a profusion of conflicting opinions about the meaning of the book that many have despaired of ever securing a comprehensive interpretation. It has been used extensively by individuals and groups who have found that they could prove almost anything by manipulation of the symbols contained in it. For this reason their attention has been centered upon Revelation as the basis for strange systems of interpretation. This policy follows an error related to one of the basic principles of interpretation: The obscure passage should be interpreted in the light of the clear passage. To take the opposite method is to tie one's hands from effective work in interpretation.

One has only to examine the multitudinous books written on Revelation to find the book pitifully mistreated at the hands of those who have not informed themselves on the possible meaning of the book for those to whom the Lord first gave it. Even among those who have made such effort to inform themselves there rages such controversy that many thoughtful men have abandoned the search for the truth of the book.

Facing this condition, two paramount questions confront us. Shall we abandon one of the books of our New Testament canon? There are many of us who believe that the Holy Spirit not only inspired the writing of the books of the Bible but that he also preserved them for the use of men. Believing this, we cannot consider the abandonment of the book the proper attitude for sincere Christians to take.

We cannot agree with Martin Luther, who at one time refused to have the book in his canon because, in his opinion, it was impossible to understand it. Since the Holy Spirit inspired its writing and through his own processes preserved it for us, it must have some meaning for men of all ages—those who first received it and those who read it in every generation. Surely we are not to abandon it.

The second question has to do with our study of the book. If we do not see fit to abandon it, is it not our duty before God and a confused world to seek earnestly to find the true meaning of the book? To most Christians Revelation is a closed book. Some help they find in the messages to the seven churches in the opening chapters. In time of sorrow they find comfort in the beautiful language of chapters 21–22. But the section from chapter 4 through chapter 20 leaves them wandering in a hopeless maze. Some others have gone to the opposite extreme. They have sought to interpret all the details of the perplexing visions in such way as to unfold all the pages of the future. Time after time they have worked out a chronology which has included the date for the end of the present age. Each time their date has come and gone and left their prophecies unfulfilled. Surely their errors serve as a warning against such purpose and procedure. Such a system only leaves the average reader mystified.

The purpose of this work is to present a method of approach by which the reader may come a little closer to the problem of the exegesis of Revelation. It is our purpose to determine the fundamental truths underlying this strange book. We are to determine the meaning of the book for those who first received it, the suffering Christians of Asia Minor, and the consequent meaning by application to conditions of our own day.

In the discussion which follows we will consider the nature of apocalyptic literature. Since Revelation falls within this distinctive body or type of literature, we cannot ignore the general nature of such works. The conditions out of which such works grow will be studied along with the characteristics of all apocalyptic literature.

The next step will be a survey of the methods of interpreting the book of Revelation. These fall into four general classes, with the method suggested in this work as a possible fifth method. This fifth method is the one presented as the one closest to the truth, but an apropos warning is suggested by Wishart,[1] who feels that every presentation of Revelation should be prefaced by some such warning as, "Let him who is without his favorite speculation cast the first stone!"

Proceeding from this point, the historical background will be treated in intense fashion. This will include a discussion of all matters relative to authorship, date, recipients, and occasion as they touch the interpretation of the book. The book reflects an attitude of faith in God and his purpose which is unsurpassed in the New Testament. This reflection can best be understood when we know the condition of the original readers of the book. The aim of this work, then, is to present a consistent interpretation of the book as a whole, keeping in mind that the chief aim is to bring out the spirit of confidence in the living, victorious, redeeming Lamb who moves with majestic step through this climactic revelation from God. This Lamb-Christ who was victorious over the chaotic world conditions of the first century will be victorious over similar conditions in every other century until "the kingdom of the world is become the kingdom of our Lord, and of his Christ: and he shall reign for ever and ever."

[1]C. F. Wishart, *The Book of Day* (New York: Oxford Press, 1935), p. vii.

PART ONE

THE HISTORICAL BACKGROUND

CHAPTER I

The Nature of Apocalyptic Literature

The book of Revelation belongs to a special class of writings known as apocalyptic. There is a certain amount of obscurity about such literature. Some readers frankly neglect Revelation because of this seeming obscurity. It is far better to recognize that in this type of writing we have an unveiling of a message. This unveiling comes only as we search diligently the writer's purpose and method of making that purpose known. The Greek word ἀποκάλυψις is a compound word which means "an unveiling." The purpose of the writer was not to cover up his message but to make it increasingly vivid by "unveiling" through signs and symbols. This type of literature is one of the most familiar types of religious thinking. While other religions have their apocalyptic side, this place of apocalyptic literature in religion has been especially notable in Judaism. For that reason, and because of its connection with Christian literature, the discussion of apocalyptic literature here will be confined largely to Jewish work.

I. Jewish Apocalyptic Literature

After the great period of Old Testament prophecy closed, the Jews fell into difficult times. "It was such troublous times as these that gave birth to apocalyptic literature."[1] This is a series of pseudepigraphic works which appeared during the period between 210

---

[1] C. H. Allen, *The Message of the Book of Revelation* (New York: Abingdon-Cokesbury Press, 1939), p. 15.

B.C. and A.D. 200. They have many features in common, the most prominent thing being the use of "vision" as a literary device by which to introduce their conceptions.

1. The Background of Apocalyptic Literature

When the Jews returned from Babylon to Palestine, though surrounded by heathen of various creeds, they were strongly monotheistic. There was little attempt to molest the Jews so long as the Persian influence with its near-monotheistic Zoroastrianism held sway. With the coming of the Greek power a different state of affairs emerged. The calm contempt of the Greek culture influenced the whole people and seduced many of them into disloyalty to the religion of their fathers. While many in political circles tended thus to be seduced into idolatry, there was a large class utterly uninfluenced by Hellenic culture. No small portion of this class hated fanatically all tampering with their religion and all apostasy of their fellow Jews. As the years passed, this feeling became intensified. Gradually all those who shared this feeling were drawn together. It was but natural that out of this movement would come expressed desires for release from the undesirable conditions. In this group were many mystics who felt the personal power of Deity. As is natural with mystics, their feelings led them to see visions and dream dreams. These visions and dreams pointed always to a glorious day of release from the darkened conditions of the fateful present.

Political events always aided these tendencies. This is reflected even in the days of Daniel when visions were given which assured the ultimate vindication of God's people and the establishment of an eternal kingdom with God as its Ruler. When the Jews came under the reign of Antiochus Epiphanes (175-164 B.C.), they experienced the darkest days they had known since the period of the Exile. He saw that the best way to destroy their national life was to uproot their religion. He prohibited, on pain of death, the observance of their religious rites and set up the image of a heathen god in their Temple. The persecutions under Antiochus Epiphanes led not only to the revolt under the Maccabees but also to the release of another series of apocalyptic visions and hopes from the mystics of the day.

The next political event to cause conditions calling for apocalyptic literature was the iron fist of the Romans under Nero and Domitian. This is reserved for subsequent discussion.

2. Conditions out of Which This Literature Grew

It is readily seen that troublous times gave birth to apocalyptic literature. Trial, suffering, sorrow, and near-despair furnished the soil in which this type of writing grew. Written in days of adversity, this form of expression always set forth the present as a time of great persecution and suffering, but, in glorious contrast, the future as a time of deliverance and triumph. This was expected to come through the intervention of God in human affairs, bringing judgment to the unrighteous powers and setting up his own government. In days of such extreme difficulty as is here pictured, men were prone to doubt and compromise, and in some cases to apostatize. The purpose of these writings was to stress the virtue of loyalty and to stimulate faith by showing in vivid fashion the certain overthrow of evil and final victory for God's righteous cause. The writers of apocalyptic books performed an invaluable service in encouraging faith and loyalty under such conditions.

Often one is led to question as to why literature is presented in such a cryptic manner as characterizes apocalypses. The answer to such a question is seen in the fact that this literature was written in dangerous times. The personal safety of both writer and reader was endangered if the persecutors understood the true meaning of the book. For this reason the message of the apocalypse was written so as to conceal and to reveal—to conceal the message from the outsider but to reveal its message to the initiated.[2] Thus, this kind of writing is to be found in the Old Testament after Israel passed under the heel of foreign domination. It is found in the New Testament in the most dangerous days faced by Christianity during the first century.

Revelation is rightly placed in this class of literature. In many ways it differs from Old Testament and noncanonical apocalyptic,

---

[2] Cf. Allen, Dana, Wishart, Beckwith, *in loco*.

but it cannot be understood apart from these modes of thought and expression. An understanding of this type of literature is essential to a right understanding of Revelation. It may well be added that in placing Revelation in this type of literature, most of which lies outside the canon of Holy Scripture, we do not detract from its practical value or its canonical character. The superiority of Revelation from a theological point of view does not place it in a different literary category from the corresponding noncanonical works.

This study reveals the truth that apocalyptic literature grew out of dangerous and trying days. This within itself furnishes a long step in the direction of understanding the work. It is, however, only one in a long series of steps necessary to the understanding of this type of literature.

3. Comparison of Prophecy with Apocalyptic

It has been observed previously that apocalyptic followed prophecy. It is a mistaken idea, however, that the two are one and the same. They are alike in many ways touching their general fields, but they are quite different when it comes to a specific application of method to field. They differ both in matter and in form.

(1) Differences from prophecy in *content.*—The predictive element is present in apocalypses, as in prophecy, but it is more prominent and relates to longer periods and involves a wider grasp of the condition of the world at large. Alike in prophecy and apocalypse there is reference to the coming of the Messiah, but in apocalyptic writings the references are wider and the messianic hope more defined. In the prophets and psalmists the Messiah had mainly to do with Israel. He would save his people. He would die for them. His people would all be righteous. All this applies to Israel. There is little if any imperial outlook. In the apocalypses the imperial outlook is prominent. Beginning with Daniel, we find mentioned the establishment of a worldwide kingdom of which there would be no end.[1] This idea reaches the acme of apocalypse in Revelation when we find "the kingdom of the world is become the kingdom of our Lord and of his Christ" (11:15).

[1] Cf. Daniel 2:44.

6

While the prophet was primarily one who spoke "for God," a preacher of righteousness who used prediction either as a guarantee of his divine mission or as an exhibition of the natural result of rebellion against God's righteous laws, to the apocalyptist prediction was the main thing. In the typical apocalypse there is very little exhortation.

The scope of apocalyptic is incommensurably greater than that of prophecy. Prophecy dealt with the past in an incidental way and devoted itself to the present and the future as the two of them grew out of the past. On the other hand, apocalyptic took within its scope things past and present even though its main interest was in the future. While the common man looked at the surface, the writer of apocalyptic tried to get behind the surface, to delve to the bottom of the essence of things and find their real significance. With this in view the apocalyptist frequently sketched the whole course of world affairs with a view to presenting the ultimate complete triumph of righteousness over evil.[4] Apocalyptic was the first type of literature to grasp the great idea that all history is a unity—a unity following naturally as a corollary of the unity of God.

Prophecy and apocalyptic differ essentially in their views on eschatology. Eschatology of the prophets dealt almost exclusively with the destiny of Israel *as a nation,* and the destinies of the Gentile *nations,* but it had little message of light or comfort for the individual beyond the grave. According to Charles,[5] we owe every advance beyond this conception to apocalyptic. This great authority lists the following as permanent contributions of apocalyptic: (1) The doctrine of a future blessed life springs not from prophecy but from apocalyptic; (2) The doctrine of a new heaven and a new earth is derived from apocalyptic; (3) The doctrine of a catastrophic end of the world comes from apocalyptic.

From this study it is readily observed that prophecy and apocalyp-

---

[4] Cf. R. H. Charles, *Religious Development Between the Old and the New Testaments* (New York: Henry Holt and Co., n.d.).

[5] R. H. Charles, *A Critical History of the Doctrine of a Future Life in Israel, in Judaism, and in Christianity* (2d ed.; London: Adam and Charles Black, 1913), p. 178. In subsequent footnotes this book will be designated by its shorter title, "Eschatology."

tic are kindred though different types of thought and literature from the viewpoint of content.

(2) Differences from prophecy in *form*.—In the literary form employed there are marked differences between prophecy and apocalyptic. Both make use of vision, but in prophecy in the more restricted sense of the word these visions are as a rule implied rather than described. Although Isaiah calls much of his prophecy "vision," yet in only one instance does he describe what he sees. The only instance in which he describes what he sees (chap. 6) is not at all predictive; the objective is exhortation. In the case of apocalypses the vision is the vehicle by which the prediction is conveyed. In Ezekiel there are visions, but only one of these, "the valley of dry bones" (chap. 37), is predictive. In prophecy the symbols used are always natural; in apocalyptic, they are largely arbitrary. A good contrast is seen here between Ezekiel and Daniel. Ezekiel's vision of the dry bones naturally suggests death. The reader feels that the process by which they are revived is the natural course which would be taken in such an event. But what is told in Daniel relative to the he goat has no natural reason for the changes which take place, only a symbolic one. The weird, the gorgeous, the unreal, or the terrible features of the vision described in apocalyptic are thrown into all the higher relief by the boldness of the narrative. This constitutes a great difference between prophecy and apocalyptic from the viewpoint of literary form. Apocalyptic has a form as well as a purpose all its own.

4. Summary of the Main Noncanonical Apocalypses

In the times of distress men of vision often ventured to peer into the secrets of heaven and wrote accounts of their visions for the admonition and encouragement of their contemporaries. A piece of literature thus produced was called a Revelation, or, to use the Greek equivalent, an ἀποκάλυψις. These writings were very popular among both Jews and Christians. Examples of this work may be found in Daniel, Ezekiel, Isaiah, and Joel. Several Jewish apocalypses which never found a place in the canon of the Old Testament were highly prized and widely used by both Jews and Christians. Because of their importance in the realm of apocalyptic literature, a brief survey of each will be made here.

(1) *The Book of Enoch.*—This book, sometimes called 1 Enoch, is perhaps the most important of the noncanonical apocalypses. In its present form it appears to be a composite containing several different apocalypses which were written during the second and first centuries B.C. These writings, pseudonymously ascribed to the patriarch Enoch, represent the attempts of different authors to help their contemporaries by disclosing to them the content of numerous visions dealing with a wide variety of subjects.

In its present arrangement, which is probably the form in which it was read by early Christians, the book begins with Enoch's declaration that his eyes had been opened by God. An angel showed him a vision and then explained everything to him in order that he might record the revelation, not for those of his own generations but for a remote age yet to come. The first thing to be revealed was the fact that the Holy Great One was to come to execute judgment upon all and to destroy all the ungodly. This was to be a time of trembling for sinners, but the righteous had nothing to fear because they would find God's mercy and would be established in everlasting joy and peace all the days of their life. The fate of the fallen angels is described along with the place where they dwell in eternal imprisonment. Enoch visited Sheol in this vision, observing the throne of God situated on one of seven magnificent mountains. He was permitted to see the tree of life prepared for the enjoyment of the righteous after the final judgment. He then returned to earth and gazed upon Jerusalem, situated upon the holy mountain where joys awaited the faithful, and beyond it he saw the accursed valley where sinners were to be punished in the sight of the righteous.

The content of the second vision is disclosed in a series of parables, each concerned mainly with the impending destruction of evil and the triumph of righteousness. The first parable opens with a description of the coming judgment when sinners shall be judged and driven from the face of the earth. Enoch is sure that it would have been better for them if they had never been born. In contrast to this the dwelling place of the righteous is seen to be a place of blessedness

9

under the wings of the Lord of Spirits. The writer is quite overcome by the glory of the scene as he beholds the majesty of the Lord of Spirits who knows before the world was created what is to be forever from generation to generation. In the presence of God stand thousands of thousands and ten thousand times ten thousand angelic beings. The elect among men are given mansions in heaven, but sinners who deny the name of the Lord of Spirits are dragged off to punishment.

This same theme is carried out in the second parable. Destruction is decreed for sinners who will be permitted neither to ascend into heaven nor to dwell upon the earth. Presently God will send his Messiah to execute judgment and put down the kings and mighty ones from their seats. In the interim the righteous are being slaughtered, but their prayer for vengeance will not be in vain. The fountain of righteousness is inexhaustible, and the coming judgment to be inaugurated with the advent of the Son of man will mean a complete vindication of the righteous. The dead also will be raised to share the blessings of the new age.

The final scene of this second parable is the attack of heathen powers upon the Messiah and his righteous companions. The Parthians and Medes will be incited by evil angels to break forth as lions and wolves among the flocks. They will invade Palestine, but their attack will come to naught. Upon arriving before Jerusalem they will be smitten by a mania for self-destruction. This slaughter will rage until dead bodies are innumerable; all their hosts will be swallowed up in Sheol while the righteous gaze in safety upon the destruction of their enemies. After this all the Jews of the Dispersion will return in triumph to Jerusalem, brought there in a single day by the winds of heaven.

The third parable also depicts the final judgment to be enacted by the Messiah. It begins with rich blessings pronounced upon the saints, who are promised an eternal life of righteousness in the presence of the Lord of Spirits. Terrible retribution is to overtake sinners, particularly kings and those who exalt themselves among men. As the Messiah sits in judgment on his throne, the word of his mouth slays all sinners and unrighteous ones who are before him. They are the objects of his vengeance because they have oppressed his children. The righteous are incited to rejoice over this destruction of these who feel the wrath of the Messiah. In contrast to this, the righteous shall abide eternally with God and with the Son of man they shall eat and lie down and rise up forever and ever.

The third main division of Enoch gives information about the heavenly bodies. The changes of the moon, the length of the lunar year, the action of the winds, and other natural phenomena are regarded as means of determining God's will with reference to man's sin and the moral order. The apocalyptist believes that the phenomena of nature and the activities of man are so inseparably linked together that man's sin seriously affects the welfare of the physical world, hence the coming change in the moral order involves a corresponding change in the whole material universe. The deeds of sinners result in such perversions of nature's powers that the years will be shortened; fields will lack fertility; rains will be withheld; the moon will be irregular in its appearing; the sun will deviate from its course, and the stars will forsake their accustomed orbits. Guided by an angelic interpreter, Enoch observes the laws of these luminaries and thereby acquires a knowledge of events throughout the history of the world unto eternity when the new creation is accomplished.

A fourth section of the apocalypse of Enoch contains an account of two dream-visions, disclosing the course of history from the Flood down to the coming of the Messiah. The account follows history down to about 150 B.C. where it takes on apocalyptic characteristics. The Gentiles are to make a final assault upon the Jews. The fallen angels and other wicked ones are to be judged and condemned to the fiery abyss. Jerusalem is to be supplanted by a newer and greater city. All Gentiles left upon the earth are to submit to the Jews. The righteous dead will be raised, the Messiah will appear, and the New Kingdom will be established.

The closing chapters of Enoch are miscellaneous in content. In general they stress the rewards in store for the righteous and the adversities awaiting the wicked. After repeated blessings on the righteous and doom upon the wicked, the book closes with an admonition to future generations not to pervert the author's visions but to write down truthfully all his words in all languages.

This book was popular among the early Christians who found consolation in its repeated promises of deliverance for the persecuted righteous people of God. It stressed the necessity of faithfulness on the part of the righteous in times of sore affliction. It pictured the triumphant glory of the heavenly Messiah descending to the earth. It forecast the complete destruction of demonic powers, expressed a firm belief in the resurrection of the dead, and awaited the final revelation of a new heaven and a new earth. A knowledge of the book gives an excellent background for the understanding of Revelation.

(2) *The Assumption of Moses.*—This work appeared early in the first century A.D. It takes the form of an address delivered to Joshua by Moses before the departure of the latter from the earth. In content it is a revelation of the history of Israel from Moses' day until the advent of the Messiah. Its purpose is to protest against the diversion of Israel's interests into political channels and to encourage piety while awaiting the intervention of God on behalf of the righteous. The writer, like his contemporaries John the Baptist and Jesus, had no sympathy with the Zealots' ambition to instigate a revolt against Rome. On the contrary, he encouraged an attitude of patient endurance even to martyrdom, confident that God in his own time would vindicate the righteous.

The description of the events attending the end is characteristic of this type of Jewish literature. The Heavenly One will arise from his throne and he will go forth with indignation and wrath because of the wickedness of men. The earth shall tremble; the high mountains shall be made low, and the hills shall be shaken and fall. The sun shall be turned to darkness; the moon shall give no light but shall be turned wholly into blood. The stars shall be disturbed. The sea will retire into the abyss, and the rivers shall be dried up. The eternal God will appear to punish the Gentiles and destroy all their idols. Israel shall be happy when she looks upon her enemies in Gehenna. She shall rejoice and give thanks to her Creator.

(3) *The Secrets of Enoch.*—This work, also known as 2 Enoch, is another apocalypse which appeared in the first part of the first century A.D. It purports to disclose secrets which God revealed to Enoch. As the seer was led through the various heavens he saw wondrous things, including punishment imposed upon sinners and the blessings awarded the righteous. In paradise he found beautiful trees above which towered the tree of life yielding all manner of fruits. The garden was kept by hundreds of angels who sing praises to the Lord with never-silent voices. Such is the eternal inheritance of the righteous, who upon earth have endured all manner of offense from those that exasperate their souls but who have walked without fault before the face of the Lord.

The abode of the wicked was also seen by the seer. It was a terrible place filled with all manner of tortures and enshrouded in cruel darkness. Its only light was the murky flames that shot aloft from the fiery pit in which sinners were suffering their punishment. Every form of suffering was there. Fearful and merciless angels, equipped with angry weapons, added to the terrors of the place. Such were the torments in store for those who upon earth had dishonored God by their evils.

Upon arriving in the tenth heaven, Enoch found himself in the presence of God, who gave him instruction regarding the creation of the world. Each day of creation represents a thousand years of duration, so that at the end of seven thousand years a new and eternal world is to appear. The present age will close with a great judgment, after which there will be neither months nor days nor hours, but one eternal aeon to be inherited by the righteous. They will live eternally there and will never again experience labor, nor sickness, nor humiliation, nor anxiety, nor need of violence, nor night, nor darkness, but great light.

After learning this divine wisdom, Enoch was sent back to earth for thirty days to instruct his children in the secrets of heaven and to urge upon them the importance of living in the fear of the Lord. During this thirty-day stay upon the earth he wrote three hundred and sixty-six books for the instruction of his sons. After this he was caught up again to the highest heaven to dwell with God.

(4) *The Book of Baruch.*—This work, also known as 2 Baruch, purports to record the visions experienced by Jeremiah's scribe, Baruch, soon after the first destruction of Jerusalem by Babylon's King Nebuchadnezzar. It appears evident that the writer lived in the Roman period and wrote to comfort the Jews in the latter part of the first century A.D. sometime after the destruction of Jerusalem in A.D. 70. The book, like other apocalypses, shows that even though sinners may seem to be temporarily triumphant, the righteous are admonished to persist in piety, knowing that God in his own good time will come to their assistance, bestow upon them a glorious reward, and mete out terrible punishments to their enemies.

Baruch is represented as remaining among the ruins of Jerusalem when the captives were carried off to Babylon. While asleep he had a vision of a proud cedar tree symbolizing the haughty Roman Empire. God interprets the vision showing Baruch the course of history up to the coming of the Messiah. The seer is informed that the Babylonian Kingdom is to be succeeded by the dominion of the Persians, who in turn are to be subjugated by the Greeks. Lastly a fourth kingdom, the Roman, will arise. Her power will be harsh and evil far beyond that of her predecessors. Though exalting itself above the cedars of Lebanon, the Roman Empire will ultimately be brought to a sudden and inglorious end by the advent of the Messiah. This heavenly Prince will slaughter the Roman host, saving alive the last emperor only. He shall be bound and carried to Mount Zion. The Messiah shall convict him of all his impieties and shall gather and set before him all the works of his forces. He shall then be put to death, and God's chosen people shall be protected.

After much fasting, Baruch is favored with further revelations concerning the coming golden age of the messianic rule. As this event draws near the terrors of the last times increase, but the righteous who survive will be fittingly rewarded, and those who have died will be restored to life. The earth shall restore the dead in the same form as it received them. Judgment follows the resurrection. Sinners are consigned to torment, while the righteous shall be given a splendor surpassing that of the angels. In this faith the pious sufferers are to await expectantly the day of their deliverance.

(5) *The book of IV Ezra.*—This book, like Baruch, was produced out of calamities that overtook the Jews in the last part of the first century A.D. The book describes seven visions of Ezra in the time of the Exile, but the grief of Ezra over the destruction of Jerusalem by Babylon is a literary device for expressing grief over the havoc recently wrought by the Romans in the Holy City. Ezra asks why Israel, whom God has chosen, should be permitted to suffer so severely at the hands of sinners. In answer to this question an angel assures Ezra that God's love for Israel has not in the least abated but that his designs for the world are too comprehensive and far-reaching to be readily grasped by mortals. God's plan embraces a glorious ultimate deliverance for his people. This present evil world must continue until God's appointed time for intervention. Increase of agonies should give cheer and courage, since the acceleration of distress brings near the impending catastrophic end. As the end approaches, all nature will be out of harmony. The sun will appear at midnight, and the moon will shine at noon. Blood will seep from wood, and stones will speak. Fish in the sea will die. Volcanic eruptions will occur. Ignorance will prevail, and sin will have the upper hand.

The second and third visions of Ezra deal with the same problem. He receives assurance that this present evil world is fast hastening to an end. A new age, to be created by God himself, is held in store for the faithful. When wickedness has reached its climax, the New Jerusalem will be revealed. Righteous Israel shall dwell with the Messiah in perfect bliss for four hundred years. At the end of this period all will die, the Messiah included, and creation will return to the silence of primeval chaos. Then will follow the new creation; the dead will be raised; the righteous will receive their rewards in paradise; the wicked will be delivered to punishment in Gehenna.

The fourth vision reveals the glories of the heavenly Jerusalem prepared for the righteous. This vision was given especially to Ezra to assuage his sorrow.

The fifth vision portrays the downfall of Rome. The seer beholds a monstrous eagle with many wings and three heads, typifying the Imperial Roman power. While Ezra gazes upon this creature, a lion symbolizing the Messiah appears upon the scene and pronounces the early destruction of the eagle. Thus the Jewish seer is firmly convinced that he stands at the end of the age when the downfall of haughty Rome is imminent. In this conviction he occupied common ground with his contemporary John, who for very different reasons predicted an equally sweeping destruction of the Roman Empire. The pious Jews are not to lose heart since God's plan involves the early destruction of Roman rule and the establishment of a messianic regime.

Such, briefly, is the content of apocalyptic writing among the Jews. The persistence of those Jewish revelations attests the popularity and value of this type of literature for people of that age. When the Christian apocalyptist John held out to his suffering companions the hope of the destruction of Rome and the victory of God's cause, he was following a well-beaten path leading past many familiar landmarks. In confidently resorting to apocalyptic imagery for a solution of his difficulties he was moving in an atmosphere thoroughly congenial to many Christians, acquainted as they were with these Jewish antecedents of their own religion.

II. Characteristics of Apocalyptic Literature

The task of classifying the many characteristics of apocalyptic literature seems almost endless. Some authors give a general classification to cover all such literature. Others give characteristics of Jewish apocalypses alone. Still others list the characteristics of Revelation, the New Testament apocalypse. There appear to be almost as many different classifications of characteristics as there are interpretations of the book; and these are legion. The classification followed here is largely arbitrary. The main effort is to indicate all the major characteristics as they would touch Revelation.

1. Apocalyptic was always possessed of a *historical* significance. There was ever some critical historical situation with which it was connected. Elements of this historical situation are represented by the imagery of the book. Knowledge of the historical situation out of which the apocalyptic work grew greatly facilitates interpretation.

This cannot be done with perfect assurance in all cases, but the evidences favor the Domitianic persecution as the background of Revelation.

The truth is self-evident that a knowledge of the historical situation lends much aid in determining the correct interpretation. It has been observed previously that the main purpose of apocalyptic literature was to bring comfort, assurance, and courage in difficult days. To know the days concerned is to know the courage needed and to understand better the message employed to bring this courage. To ignore the historical situation is to ignore the main piece in the jigsaw of interpretation.

2. Generally, apocalyptic literature is of *pseudonymous* authorship. The writers of these books generally wrote in the name of some great man of the past, Enoch, Abraham, or Moses, rather than in their own names. Undoubtedly different reasons led to this procedure, which today is rather difficult to understand in spiritual men with an earnest message. To the writer there was doubtless nothing unethical in such a course of action, since they used so much from early sources that in many cases they were giving credit where credit was due. Then, too, the Hebrew writer was almost wholly devoid of the pride of authorship and showed no jealousy as to his literary rights. He was little concerned as to his personal fame; his sole object was the service of God and the well-being of the nation.

Another reason for this method has been suggested by Charles[6] after a study of all the Jewish apocalyptic literature in connection with the conditions and attitudes behind it. When the law reached supremacy among the Jews, it left no room for prophecy of any kind since it claimed to be the complete revelation of God. When the idea of an inspired law—adequate, infallible, and valid for all time—had become an accepted dogma for Judaism, as it became in the post-Exilic period, there was no longer room for an independent representative of God to appear with God's message.

Proceeding from this basis, Charles indicates that the prophet who released a prophecy under his own name after the time of Ezra and Nehemiah could not expect a hearing. Against the reception of

[6]Charles, *Eschatology*, pp. 200 f.

false truth the Law stood in the way unless the book containing it came under certain great names of the past. Against the claims and authorities of such names the official representatives of the Law were in part reduced to silence.

Legalism, becoming absolute, determined henceforth the character of Judaism. Prophecy and apocalyptic, which had exercised a determining influence in many of the great crises of the nation and had given birth to and shaped the higher theology of Judaism, were driven from their positions of secondary authority and either banished absolutely or relegated wholly into the background.

All Jewish apocalypses, therefore, from 200 B.C. onward were of necessity pseudonymous if they sought to exercise any real influence on the nation. For the Law was everything; belief in inspiration was dead amongst them, and their canon was closed. Charles holds that this did not hold true with reference to the apocalypse of the New Testament, as will be indicated in the discussion of authorship of the book of Revelation.

Allen[7] suggests yet a third reason for the advisability of concealing the authorship of apocalyptic literature. This reason is a very personal one with the writer of the books in question. It has been observed previously that the books of this type were free to prophesy doom upon the political power then in control. Anonymity might have led to investigations or might have brought punishment upon some supposed writer if the book fell into the hands of authorities; but if they thought it to have been written by some author who lived long ago, there was nothing they could do but endeavor to suppress it since the author was beyond their power. At first glance this may appear to be an unworthy motive, but when all the circumstances are considered, including the good accomplished by a work which could not otherwise be available to the people, criticism fades.

3. A third characteristic of apocalyptic literature is the presentation of the message through *visions*. This method was often used by the prophets, but in apocalyptic writings it became the chief method of expressing truth. These visions vary from scenes in heaven to scenes on earth. They abound in heavenly messengers or angels

------

[7]Allen, *op. cit.*, p. 18.

who are God's agents in the securing of his revelation to the seer.

There has been an abundance of discussion as to whether or not the writers actually saw the visions they describe. Some incline to the view that the writer saw the truth to be conveyed and then out of experience, conditions, and available literature he formed the images and visions used. Scholars are of divergent opinions on the matter. All agree that the most important question is the religious value of the teaching and not the form used in presenting the truth.

A close study of the New Testament apocalypse leaves a strong impression that the visions recorded were objectively real to John. This impression comes from the nature of the symbols and figures in the course of the visions as well as from references in which John seems to make a direct claim that the visions were objective.[8] Perhaps it is a matter of little importance. Objective or subjective, they present the same truth.

The highly elaborate vision is the most distinctive feature in the form of apocalyptic literature. The subject matter is attributed to a special revelation, commonly given in visions, ecstasies, or raptures into the unseen world. The vision or rapture in apocalyptic writings is a literary form wrought out with great fulness of details, often with strange symbolism and with fantastic imagery. It is this mode of unveiling hidden things in these writings that has given them the name apocalyptic.

4. As a fourth characteristic of apocalyptic literature, we find a *predictive* element. A review of the conditions out of which this type of literature grew will indicate the truth that the future is dealt with in apocalyptic. As has already been observed, apocalyptic was the word for a dark day and condition. It pictured the present as a time of evil, turmoil, persecution, upheaval, but the future was predicted to be a glorious period of vindication, triumph, and freedom from all the handicaps which beset us here. Thus it is noted that the prediction of the future is general, in the main, and deals with the character of events rather than the details. Caution should be observed and dogmatism avoided at this point in the interpretation.

5. One of the main characteristics of apocalyptic is the use of *sym-*

---

[8]Cf. Revelation 1:1, 12; 4:1; 5:1-2, 11; 22:8-9, and many others.

bol. Among writers of this type of literature there was developed an elaborate system of cryptic symbols and figures of speech for the expression of spiritual ideas. The writer was faced with the task of seeing the invisible, painting the unpaintable, and expressing the inexpressible. The writing is therefore full of imagery and symbolism which are hard to understand, and which make the task of the modern interpreter far removed from those conditions exceedingly difficult. Symbolism is a system in which qualities, ideas, principles, etc., are represented by things concrete. These symbols have a meaning for the initiated but are hopeless jargon to one unacquainted with such terms. Richardson[9] calls attention to a man who was in prison because he had "bumped off a bird in Alabama" and to the fact that the "soup" which a safe-cracker would use would hardly be fit to serve as a dinner course. These are illustrations on a very low level of symbolic language—language with a double meaning. The apocalyptic writers by compulsion of the unsympathetic and often hostile environment in which they and their readers lived developed a system of symbols, figures, and codes for comparatively safe communication. Thus, one cannot interpret symbols as one would interpret prose where the meaning lies on the surface.

The writer employs the symbols as a method of communicating his thoughts to those who were familiar with the process and at the same time concealing his ideas from those outside this circle. The symbols are often arbitrary rather than natural, as were the illustrations used by the prophets. The meaning of the greater part of the symbols is clear, but there are some symbols in the interpretation of which there is much room for diversity of opinion. About these symbols one cannot afford to be dogmatic. It appears that the wise thing to do in interpreting symbols is to follow the proper method of interpreting parables—find the central truth which is being portrayed and let the details fit in in the most natural way.

One of the main usages of symbol in this literature is found in the symbolism of numbers. Even a casual reading of the Revelation impresses one with the frequent recurrence of certain numbers. This

---

[9] D. W. Richardson, *The Revelation of Jesus Christ* (Richmond: John Knox Press, 1939), p. 20.

same thing is true in the other literature of this class. Because of this fact, it appears wise to include a discussion of the symbolism of numbers in this discussion. Most of the discussion which follows on this matter is a summary taken from Wishart[10] with occasional references to other works.

The symbolism of numbers: The inner significance of numbers was a kind of device which always had fascination for the Oriental mind. In that early day, when language was primitive and the vocabulary meager, one Hebrew word sometimes was compelled to do duty for a score of diverse meanings. Under such conditions men came naturally to use numbers as we use words. They were the symbols of moral or spiritual truth. A certain number would suggest a definite concept. The conceptions arose quite naturally through certain primitive associations. Just as the sound of a given word by long habit calls up the corresponding idea, so a certain number, by acquired association, called up a definite concept. Such numbers become symbols and cannot be read with the literal exactness that we employ when interpreting mathematical formulae.

After this fashion men saw a single object and came to associate with the number "1" the idea of unity or independent existence. It stood for that which was unique and alone. This word does not appear symbolically in the book of Revelation. It is, of course, at the base of other numbers that do appear—some frequently.

Amid the dangers of primitive life, with a fear of wild beasts, or of hostile attack by his enemies constantly before him, man gained courage in companionship. Two were far stronger and more effective than one. Thus the number "2" came to stand for strengthening, for confirmation, for redoubled courage and energy. There was a symbolic significance in the fact that Jesus sent his disciples forth two by two. Two witnesses confirmed the truth, and their testimony which otherwise would have been weak was made strong. Always this number meant augmented strength, redoubled energy, confirmed power. So in the book of Revelation[11] the truth of God is confirmed by two witnesses who are slain and rise again and ascend

---

[10]Wishart, *op. cit.*, pp. 19–30.
[11]Cf. Revelation 11:3–12.

to heaven. This symbolizes a strong witness which prospers then seems to be beaten to earth only to rise again to heavenly triumph. Likewise[12] there are two wild beasts mutually confirming and supporting each other as they wage war against the cause of righteousness. They present a formidable foe. But over against them God has a "twofold" instrument of warfare—the conquering Christ and the sickle of judgment. These prove to be too great for the two beasts to defeat. Thus, symbolically, we see the cause of righteousness triumph over evil.

Wishart suggests that man found in his primitive home the divinest thing that life had to offer him—father love, mother love, filial love. He found God reflected in the interplay of love and kindness and affection in his own household and began to think of the number "3" as a symbol of the divine. In his more thoughtful moments he carried that idea back into his conception of God. For this reason, doubtless, there appear glimmerings of a Trinity not only in the theology of the Hebrews but in the dreams of the Greeks. The divinest thing in life was "3" and the divine origin of life was "3." Here in the ultimate world ground were father love, mother love, and child love. Here, too, were the glimpses of the great mysteries which we express in the terms "Father," "Son," and "Holy Ghost." Three came to carry the thought of the divine.

When man went outside his home and looked about him, he had no conception of the modern world as we know it. No Copernicus had ever opened his eyes to the vast significance of the universe. To him the world was a great flat surface with four boundaries, east and west and north and south. There were four winds from the four sides of the earth. There were four angels, he thought, to govern the four winds. In the town he placed himself within the limit of four walls. Thus when he thought of the world he thought in terms of four. Four became the cosmic number. In Revelation there appear four living creatures symbolical of the four divisions of animal life of the world. There are four horsemen symbolical of the destructive powers of the world at war. The world in which men lived and worked and died was conveniently symbolized by "4."

[12] Cf. Revelation 13:1 ff.

Next, man turned from the study of his home and the world about him to study himself. Perhaps our decimal system arose from the intensive study by a man of his own fingers and toes. That was a crude and cruel age where many were maimed and crippled through disease, accident, or warfare. A perfect, full-rounded man was one who had all his members intact. So the number "5" doubled to "10" came to stand for human completeness. The whole duty of man was summed up in "10" commandments. The picture of complete power in government was that of a beast with ten horns. In Revelation the dragon,[18] the first beast,[14] and the scarlet beast[15] have ten horns each, and in the case of this last beast the ten horns are called ten kings—complete world power as it appeared to belong to Rome with her provincial system. As a multiple, "10" occurs also in many of the higher numbers of Revelation; "70" = a very sacred number, "1000" = ultimate completeness—completeness raised to the nth degree, etc.

When man began to analyze and combine numbers, he developed other interesting symbols. He took the perfect world number "4" and added to it the perfect divine number "3" and got "7," the most sacred number to the Hebrews. It was earth crowned with heaven —the four-square earth plus the divine completeness of God. So we have "7" expressing completeness through union of earth with heaven. This number runs throughout the book of Revelation. There are seven Spirits, seven churches, seven golden candlesticks, seven stars, seven sections to the book, each, save the last, divided into seven parts. The sacred number, multiplied by the complete number "10," resulted in the very sacred "70." There were seventy members of the Jewish high court, Jesus sent out seventy prepared workers. In a sweeping figure he presented the idea of an unlimited Christian forgiveness when he told a disciple to forgive his brother seventy times seven.

In the field of multiplication, "4" was multiplied by "3," and the resultant "12" became a well-known symbol. In Hebrew religious

[13] Cf. Revelation 12.
[14] Cf. Revelation 13.
[15] Cf. Revelation 17.

thought it was the symbol of organized religion in the world. There were twelve tribes of Israel, twelve apostles, twelve gates to the Holy City in Revelation. This number was reduplicated to 144,000 when the writer of our Apocalypse wanted to picture the security of a perfect number sealed from the wrath of God visited upon the world.

In the realm of division the perfect number "7" was cut in half. The resulting "3½" came to express the incomplete, that which was imperfect. It symbolized restless longings not yet fulfilled, aspirations unrealized. When the writer of apocalyptic wished to describe that condition, when he found it necessary to picture the world waiting for something which had not arrived, when he saw men in despair and confusion seeking for peace and light, he used "3½." This takes several forms: "3½," "a time, times, and a half time," "forty-two months," "1,260 days,"—all have the same meaning. In Revelation two witnesses preached "3½" years—an indefinite time; the court of the Temple was trampled by the ungodly "3½" years; the saints were persecuted forty-two months; the church was in the wilderness "1,260 days." Always "3½" or its equivalent stood for the indefinite, the incomplete, the dissatisfied; but in it all were the hope and patient waiting for a better day when truth would be delivered from the scaffold and placed on the throne usurped by wrong.

One last number must be treated in this study of symbolism. To the Jew the number "6" had a sinister meaning. As "7" was the sacred number, "6" fell short of it and failed. "Six" was the charge that met defeat, with success just in its grasp. It had within it the stroke of doom. It had the ability to be great but failed to measure up. It was for the Jew what "13" is for many today—an evil number. Some buildings skip from floor twelve to fourteen because thirteen is a bad rental proposition. Many hotels have rooms 12, 12A, and 14, but no 13, because no one wants to sleep in that room. It is possible that the dread of this number goes back to a night when thirteen men broke bread at the same table. From that room went one to commit the blackest betrayal in history and one to make the supreme sacrifice of history. Thus "6" was an evil number for the Jews. It is important to keep this in mind when we come to the number "666" in Revelation.

From this observation of the symbolic use of numbers, it follows that the numbers which occur in the book of Revelation cannot be understood with real numerical value, nor even as round numbers. They are purely symbolic, and we must discard our mathematical ideas and seek to discover their symbolic significance. A large part of the unscriptural dispensationalism of the past and present is based upon a false view of the value of the numbers employed by the writer.

Apart from this symbolism of numbers in Revelation, there is an abundance of other figurative language. Many objects are used symbolically. Birds, beasts, persons, cities, elements of nature, weapons, qualities (light, darkness, etc.), precious stones—all these and many others are made to serve the writer's purpose as he gives to us his picture book of the triumph of righteousness over evil. "In this weird world of fantasy, peopled by a rich Oriental imagination with spectral shapes and uncouth figures, where angels flit, eagles and altars speak, and monsters rise from sea and land—in a world of this kind many Asiatic Christians of that age evidently were at home, and there the prophet's message had to find them."[16] One cannot possibly approach the true interpretation of Revelation if he ignores this central characteristic.

6. The *dramatic* element, one of the most effective instruments of any writer, serves as another characteristic of apocalyptic. One of the chief purposes of apocalyptic literature was to make the truth taught as vivid and forceful as possible. Frequently the figures are presented for the purpose of adding vividness to aid in creating the desired impression. The details are of significance only from this viewpoint and are not to be pressed.

This principle is true of many of the visions and figures in the book. It makes its vivid and dramatic impression upon the reader by means of the grotesque and terrific symbols. Rivers of blood; hailstones weighing one hundred pounds; a dragon so large he knocks

---

[16]James Moffatt, *The Expositor's Greek Testament* (Grand Rapids: Wm. B. Eerdman's Publishing Company, n.d.), V, 301.

down a third of the stars when he lashes with his tail; Death riding a horse, with the Grave following behind; a woman, with the moon as a dress and the sun as a footstool; animals with many heads and horns; a dragon that casts from its mouth a river of water to destroy a woman who is flying through the air; a dragon, a beast, and a false prophet, each of which vomits up a frog which joins in gathering an army—all these are symbolical, but they are more than just symbols. They are exaggerated symbols for the purpose of a dramatic effect. The meaning of the figure is to be discerned by viewing it in broad perspective as a whole and not by trying to determine the meaning of each minute detail. One must not become so interested in the actor that he forgets the plot and its meaning.

This survey of the characteristics of apocalyptic literature helps us to see at once that we are not dealing with ordinary literature and hence cannot use ordinary methods of interpretation. This literature is thus written to unveil its message. This message can only be unveiled to us when we rightly interpret the symbols as they were related to the background of the book and as they conveyed their message to those who first received the book. Its meaning for them is its meaning for us. Therefore, we must find that meaning to know the application of the book today.

CHAPTER II

Methods of Interpreting The Book of Revelation

The interpretation of the book of Revelation depends entirely upon the method of approach. In the progress of Christian history there have been many methods of interpretation followed. Some have approached the book with the idea that it reveals all the future of history from the New Testament time to the consummation of the age. Others have supposed it to reveal the history of the apostasy of the Roman Catholic Church. Still others find nothing of abiding worth in the book and look upon it as a collection of early Christian myth with no significance for our day. Another group has sought to point out in the book principles of action on the basis of which God deals with man through all ages. Then some have sought to find the meaning that this book had in the day of its origin and to determine by application of that meaning its significance for every other generation.

> Learned works on this remarkable portion of the inspired volume do, indeed, abound. . . . But the views of the writers (Expositors of Revelation) are so utterly conflicting . . . that the student of them soon finds himself driven to take from each whatever of useful suggestions he may find there, and then proceed independently in his search for the meaning and lesson of the book.[1]

---

[1]Justin A. Smith, *An American Commentary on the New Testament* (Philadelphia: The American Baptist Publication Society, 188, reprinted, 1942), VII, Part III, 4.

It is the purpose of this section of study to sift these various methods, classify them, determine the weak points and strong points of each with a view to finding the correct approach to the book.

I. THE FUTURIST METHOD

This often used method of interpretation regards Revelation as almost wholly eschatological, dealing with the events of the end of the world. Such a view looks upon the cryptic symbols as a means of revealing the end of the age, the coming of the Lord, the millennial reign with the saints on the earth, the loosing of Satan, the second resurrection, and the final judgment. The view has been held by many sincere, devout Christians. They look upon the book as a volume of unfulfilled prophecy. From chapter 4 to the end of the book we have recorded events that are to be fulfilled in the future and closely connected with the second coming of Christ. Because of many natural desires to know the future, many have been far more interested in "the last things" than in present conditions with God's plan and purpose in this age of need.

> To some the book becomes largely a problem of celestial mathematics; and they are more concerned with the calculating of time charts than they are of securing social and economic and political righteousness for their immediate neighbors.[2]

The futurists hold that the events from chapter 4 to 19 are to take place within the brief space of seven years. This period of tribulation is interpreted to be the seventieth week mentioned in the familiar prophecy of Daniel 9:24–27, which seventieth week they regard to be separated by many centuries from the other sixty-nine and to come in at the close of the Christian Era.

Most futurists are literalists in their interpretation of Revelation. They stay as close as they can to literalism and see very little that is symbolical in the book. Examples of this literalism may be noted. In

---

[2]Richardson, *op. cit.,* p. 43.

the eleventh chapter the Temple is measured. Futurists hold that this is the Temple in Jerusalem and that it will be rebuilt before the end of the age. In the same chapter we find the symbols of two witnesses. The futurists hold that this is not a symbol but a prophecy concerning two great prophets who will make their appearance near the end of the world. Futurists also hold that the numbers in Revelation have to do with mathematical values and not symbolical representation. These are only a few examples of their literalism.

Another distinguishing mark of the futurists is their belief in the coming of a personal Antichrist. They interpret that the beast of Revelation is a personal wicked secular or ecclesiastical ruler who will be in power in the last days. This Antichrist is most often identified by this group with the "man of sin" of 2 Thessalonians 3.

Most of the futurists are millennarians in their theology. They hold that after the Lord is revealed from heaven at his second coming, the general judgment will not take place at once. Rather there will be a resurrection of the righteous and after that a reign of Christ with his saints on the earth for one thousand years. Not all futurists are millennarian. One of the outstanding futurists in regard to Revelation is Abraham Kuyper. In one of his works[3] he sets out a futuristic interpretation of the book. In another[4] he tears millennialism to shreds.

Pieters[5] divides the futurists into two groups. One group he calls the "Darbyite dispensationalists." The view held by this group originated with John N. Darby, the founder of the Plymouth Brethren. The most distinctive doctrine in their sytsem is their view of heaven and the Christian church. They hold that Jesus came to establish a visible rule on this earth and that John the Baptist had this in mind when he preached that the kingdom of heaven was at hand. Jesus set out his standards for this kingdom, but the Jews rejected him

---

[3]Abraham Kuyper, *The Revelation of St. John,* trans. John Kendrik de Vries (Grand Rapids: William B. Eerdman's Publishing Company, 1935).

[4]Kuyper, Chiliasm, *The Doctrine of Premillennialism,* trans. G. M. van Pernis (Grand Rapids: Zondervan Publishing House, 1934).

[5]Albertus Pieters, *The Lamb, the Woman, and the Dragon* (Grand Rapids: Zondervan Publishing House, 1937), pp. 56–60.

and his plans. The offer was then withdrawn, and the kingdom was postponed until the second coming. As a parenthesis in history Christ established his church. The church is not a fulfilment of the Old Testament. It is temporary and will come to an end at the "rapture," which is the sudden miraculous removal of all true believers to meet Christ in the air when he comes again. This "rapture" will not be visible to the world at large. The public part of the second coming of Christ will take place seven years later and is called "the Revelation." The seven-year period mentioned corresponds to the seventieth week of Daniel. The sixty-nine weeks closed with the first coming of Christ (his birth), but when the Jews rejected Christ prophetic time ceased and does not begin again until the "rapture." During the seven-year period Antichrist will rule. The Jews who have been restored to Palestine will make a covenant with him for the restoration of their worship. The Temple will be rebuilt at Jerusalem, the scattered tribes regathered, and the sacrificial system reinstituted.

In Ezekiel 40:1 and 44:31, we find a full description of the Temple and its courts. A building such as Ezekiel describes has never been built. According to Revelation there will be no temple in the New Jerusalem. Therefore, reasons the futurist, Ezekiel must be describing a temple which will be used on earth during the millennium. It is clear that it does not belong on the "new earth" because the land in which it is located is bounded by the sea and waters flow from it into the sea, but in the "new earth" (Revelation 21:1) there is no sea.[6] Such is the procedure of the literalist! Larkin continues to relate the sacrifices which will be carried on in this Temple. There is to be a daily morning offering but no evening offering. There will be burnt, meat, drink, sin, peace, and trespass offerings. Two feasts will be observed: Tabernacles and Passover, but there will be no Passover lamb offered since Jesus fulfilled that.

After three and one-half years Antichrist will break faith with the Jews. This will be followed by great tribulation and suffering on the part of those who have become believers since the "rapture."

---

[6] Clarence Larkin, *The Book of Revelation* (Philadelphia: Mayer and Lotter, 1919), pp. 180–191.

Antichrist will demand that he be worshiped, and the refusal of Christians and good Jews will bring about this great tribulation. Most of the events of Revelation chapters 4 to 19 will take place during this period, and when the Christians are just about over-whelmed, Christ will come to their rescue and overthrow Antichrist at "Armageddon." He will then establish his earthly kingdom and reign with his saints for a thousand years. He will be the Chief Ruler, and each follower who has been faithful will be given cities to rule over in proportion to his faithfulness, just as Jesus promised in the parable of the pounds (Luke 19:11–26).[7]

It is readily observed that in this amazing interpretation the book of Revelation for the most part has nothing to do with those who first received the book, for any who have used it, or for any of those who will use it up to the time of the last three and one-half years before the Lord's return. Thus the book has no word for the Christian church in its dangers, conflicts, and triumphs. The entire system appears to be unscriptural and unsound. This is a prevalent method of interpretation at the present time. It is the method set out in the Scofield system and taught in most of the nondenominational churches of the present day.

There is the second group of futurists who reject this dispensationalism. They hold to a future view of Revelation but deny the distinction between the "rapture" and the "Revelation." They believe that all believers pass through the great tribulation. Frost[8] is one of this group. He believes that Babylon will be rebuilt and that the personal Antichrist will rule. He holds that not many years remain before this end-time appears. He does not hold that all the events in Revelation must take place in the space of seven years.

Many objections to the futurist method of interpretation have been cited. These are objections to the method itself and not just objections to one of the two views which have been presented. The following objections represent the case for the opposition.

---

[7]Larkin, *op. cit.,* p. 183.

[8]What is here said is condensed from Pieters' discussion (*The Lamb, the Woman, and the Dragon,* p. 60) of the following book: Henry Frost, *The Second Coming of Christ.*

1. Objections to the Futuristic Method

(1) It is inconsistent with the statement made by John that the events predicted were in the main to come to pass soon. "The revelation of Jesus Christ which God gave to him to show to his servants what things it is necessary to come to pass shortly" (1:1). This literal translation includes two words which are of great importance at this place. δεῖ is an impersonal Greek verb which involves a moral necessity. "It is morally necessary" in order for a just end to be accomplished that these things come to pass shortly. This is the same word which Jesus used when he said it was necessary for him to go to Jerusalem and to die.[9] It was morally necessary in order for the end in view to be accomplished. In this passage in Revelation we find that it was morally necessary for the things to be fulfilled shortly in order for God's oppressed people to see his arm revealed and his comfort given in a time of seeming disaster.

The second Greek term we are interested in is the phrase ἐν τάχει which is translated "quickly" or "shortly." The futurists hold that this is only a term which means "certainty" rather than having any temporal idea connected. Paul hardly uses it this way when he says to Timothy "Be diligent to come to me quickly (ταχέως)."[10] We can almost hear him say, according to the futurists: "Timothy, I want you to come to me here in Rome. Bring the coat I left with Carpus. I am cold and need it, but there is no hurry—just so you get here in the next two or three thousand years! I need those Scripture scrolls I left there. Bring them so I can read them. There are some passages I want to brush up on in the next millennium or two. I want to see you. I don't know how long I can hold out, so come in the next few thousand years (ταχέως)—any time will be all right." *Mirabile dictu!* But this is no more absurd than to take the position that the phrase in Revelation 1:1 means "certainty of fulfillment" rather than a speedy fulfilment. Hear John saying to the beaten, broken, suffering, persecuted Christians of Asia Minor: "That's all right. Don't be disturbed. After a few thousand years the nations will

---

[9] Cf. Matthew 16:21.
[10] Cf. 2 Timothy 4:9.

32

gather together for a great battle in the valley of Megiddo, and when it is all over God will set up an earthly kingdom and reign with his saints, and all the followers of the Antichrist will be destroyed." Such a message would have had little meaning and less comfort to those in need. They needed a revelation from God which would say: "Christ is alive. He is in the midst of his people. He is going to see to it that his cause triumphs over those who are trying to stamp it out. And he is going to do it *now*. Therefore, be comforted and hold your own." There was a moral necessity that these things be fulfilled "quickly." The need was an urgent one, and the message was one to meet the urgency.

It is beyond the bounds of any reasonable interpretation to consider nothing of the book as yet fulfilled. Certainly the above words cannot be stretched to cover the last judgment which comes at the end of the book. But the last judgment occupies only a small part of this lengthy prophecy of God's dealing with his people.

> Approaching the shores of the United States by sea, one can say with perfect propriety: "We are getting close to America now," without forgetting or denying that the furthest limit of America is still three thousand miles away. So, if the prophecy deals with things that began to happen not long after it was written, this statement is true in its natural sense, even though the completion of the fulfillment is not attained for two millenniums more.[11]

Thus it appears that the time was at hand for the fulfilment of the prophecy as it was given to John. This interpretation and the futurist method stand at opposites.

(2) One of the strongest objections to the futurist method is that it leaves Revelation altogether out of relation to the needs of the churches to which it was addressed and which first received it. One of the basic principles of prophecy is that it takes its start with the generation to which it is addressed. Its first purpose is to meet an immediate need—to comfort, to instruct, to warn. To say this is not to say that prophecy stops with its own generation. The prophets of the Babylonian exile began with the immediate needs of the people at that time. From this beginning they stretched out to the time of

[11]Pieters, *op. cit.*, p. 61.

the coming of Christ and the establishment of his kingdom. Just so, Revelation begins with the people of its day and, having comforted them in their immediate need, points the way to the final consummation of the kingdom in God's own time. Its first purpose was to help those who first received it. Certainly no interpretation can be regarded as the true one if it leaves the book out of relation to the churches who first read and heard the message. To know that Revelation is the answer to the cry of the Christians of the Domitianic persecution is to know that it was never meant to be a forecast of Roman Catholic apostasy or a chronology for the Lord's return.

(3) Much of the symbolism of the book of Revelation is incompatible with the futurist method. When the futurist comes to the twelfth chapter, he has either to reverse his position and hold that the symbolism speaks of a past event or to hold that the symbolism points to some activity of the Israel of the end-time. The symbolism very naturally speaks of the birth of Christ and of the devil's attempt to destroy him, but the futurist denies this and makes the book a Jewish rather than a Christian work at its very center.

(4) A final objection, one which may be more subjective than objective, is that the futurist method is associated with a materialistic philosophy of the kingdom of God and a basis of triumph for the cause of righteousness which appears to be unscriptural throughout. Any system which turns from the purposes of grace and the cross of Christ to methods of victory of any other description becomes repulsive to the sincere Christian mind. Futurism does this very thing, whether it will admit it or not. This dispensationalism is Jewish theology, largely of the apocryphal literature, and not New Testament theology.

2. Strong Points of Futurism

This section should perhaps be prefaced by a question mark. A thorough study leads one to wonder if there are any strong points in favor of this method. Below are cited the claims made by the futurists in favor of their system.

(1) The claim is made that the futurist method just takes the Bible at its word, takes it literally without adding or subtracting

anything. This appears, at first glance, to be a noble aspiration. However, sincere study reveals that the Bible is written in different styles and with different methods of presenting its truth. It must be interpreted in a way consistent with the method of presentation. To interpret a parable literally or to interpret poetry as history is a false procedure. In a similar way it is false procedure to interpret symbol as fact. This results in a perversion of Scripture rather than loyalty to its true meaning.

(2) Futurists claim that their method is the only one which will keep alive an active hope in the return of the Lord. They claim that all the other methods dim this hope and turn the eyes of men to the earth rather than to the clouds in which Christ is to come. This is not a just claim. There are many devout and sincere Christians who hold to other methods of interpretation yet recognize and glory in all the New Testament truths relative to the glorious doctrine of the Lord's return. Besides this, to assume a false method of interpretation of a book just to stimulate interest in some doctrine, even a true doctrine, cannot be viewed as a worthy motive. There are many places in the New Testament where the second coming of Christ is taught far more clearly than in the symbolism of Revelation.

(3) Futurists hold that to take any view of Revelation other than the one which holds to a millennarian position precludes any evangelistic fervor or endeavor. This, too, is a false claim often made and too seldom questioned. Its false nature is readily observed when one observes the many who hold to an opposite interpretation. It is true that many of the most devout men of Christian history have been millennarian. But it is equally true that many of the most devout and evangelistic have been opposed to this interpretation. Some have been in the group called "postmillennialists" and some have been in the much older group known as "a-millennialists," both of which groups positively deny the millennarian view of this school of thought.

Such a review of "objections" and "strong points" leaves the futurist interpretation of the book of Revelation weighed in the balances of serious thought and found wanting—wanting strength to survive the odds which pile up against it like the pyramids of Egypt.

II. The Continuous-Historical Method

A second method of interpreting the book of Revelation is the continuous-historical. This has sometimes been called by each of these names separately, but the hyphenated term is a better description of the method.

This method looks upon Revelation as a forecast, in symbols, of the history of the church. It has been held by the non-Catholic scholars from a short time before the Reformation. Essentially the theory has been the same since that time; there have been wide differences in detail of interpretation. The system makes the book of Revelation prophesy in detail the apostasy of the Roman Catholic Church. A few of the great names in this school of thought are: Wycliffe, Luther, Bullinger, Brightman, Fox, E. B. Elliott, Albert Barnes, Guinness, Lord, and Carroll. The following is an outline giving in essence the position of Barnes:[12]

> First Seal: Fulfilled in the state of the Roman Empire, from the death of Domitian, A.D. 96 to the accession of Commodus, A.D. 180.
> Second Seal: From death of Commodus, A.D. 193 onward.
> Third Seal: From Caracalla, A.D. 211 onward.
> Fourth Seal: Decius to Gallienus, A.D. 243–268.
> Fifth Seal: Persecutions under Diocletian, A.D. 284–304.
> Sixth Seal: Invasion of barbarians, A.D. 365.
> Seventh Seal: Fulfilled in the trumpets:
> First Trumpet: Invasion by Goths, A.D. 395–410.
> Second Trumpet: Invasion by Genseric, A.D. 428–468.
> Third Trumpet: Invasion by Attila the Hun, A.D. 433–453.
> Fourth Trumpet: Final conquest of Western Empire by Odoacer, King of Heruli, A.D. 476–490.
> Fifth Trumpet: The Mohammedans.
> Sixth Trumpet: The Turks.
> Chapter 10: The great angel is the Reformation, the little book opened is the Bible restored to general reading

---

[12]Albert Barnes, *Notes on the Book of Revelation* (New York: Harper and Brothers Publishers, 1864).

           after its enslavement by the papacy and the Vulgate. The seven thunders heard but not recorded are the anathemas hurled against the Reformation by the Pope. They were not to be written because there was nothing in them worth reading!

Chapter 11: The measuring of the temple, the determining of what constituted the true church at the time of the Reformation. The two witnesses represent those who testified against the errors of Rome.

Seventh Trumpet: Final triumph of the true church.

           What follows chapter 11 is not a chronological continuation but a view of the church internally. This has to do exclusively with the Catholic Church. The woman in chapter 12 is the true church. Her fleeing into the desert represents the condition of the church while the papacy was in the ascendency. The wrath of Satan against the remnant of her seed represents the attempt of the papacy to cut off individuals when open and general persecution no longer raged.

The First Beast: The papal ecclesiastical power that sustained the papacy.

The Second Beast: The papal ecclesiastical power.

The Seven Vials: Seven blows at the power of the papacy, such as the French Revolution, seizure of Rome by the French, capture of the Pope himself, etc.

The Great Harlot: The papacy.

The Destruction of Babylon: The fall of the papacy.

This view of Barnes's interpretation gives a general idea concerning this whole method. Interpreters of this school go into great detail in the development of these ideas. They compare the symbols of Revelation with the course of history so successfully that someone has observed that a study of Gibbon's *Decline and Fall of the Roman Empire* along with Barnes's *Notes on Revelation* is sufficient proof of the doctrine of the inspiration of the Scriptures!

One is forced to admit that, whether this is the true method of interpretation or not, the expositors have fitted the book to history in many places in an admirable way. Occasional hits, however, cannot be regarded as adequate proof of the correctness of a view where there are so many objections to be raised. Guesswork may hit the truth sometimes, but it is perilous to follow it altogether.

1. Objections

(1) Revelation, understood from this viewpoint, is entirely out of touch with the situation of the Christians to whom it was originally given. We must come back to a principle previously stated: No interpretation can be regarded as the correct one if it would have been meaningless to those who first received the book. Nothing could have been more useless in comforting and helping the persecuted Christians of John's day than a treatise on the apostasy of a church system which was several hundred years off in its origin. They could not have understood it, and it would not have relieved their suffering if they had. We can hardly think that the capture of the Pope centuries later would help the feelings of the beaten Christians as their loved ones were led to the executioner's block or the burning stake. Revelation must be kept close to Asia Minor of the first century if its meaning is to be known.

(2) This method attaches an undue importance to the apostasy of the Roman Catholic Church. Romanism has truly been characterized by many evils, but the Reformation is not the only thing of importance which has happened since the time of Constantine. The Pope is not the only enemy to true religion, nor is it the chief purpose of Revelation to furnish us with arms for ecclesiastical warfare. This is essentially the position of Luther, Barnes, Elliott, and others who hold this view.

(3) The horizon of this method is too narrow. The events of this book are confined to the countries where Roman Catholicism has held sway. The book can have no meaning to countries which have not known the Catholic system. There is no universal message for all mankind in these pages. This manner of conceiving the situation may have been a convenient one for the men following the Reformation, but assuredly it is out of date by now.

(4) This method of interpretation stoops to details as absurd as those of the futurist school. For instance, Elliott[13] finds an interpretation of the half-hour's silence in heaven (8:1) in the seventy years that intervened between Constantine's victory over Licinius, A.D. 324, and Alaric's revolt and invasion of the empire in A.D. 395. He calculates that half an hour in heaven is the precise equivalent of seventy years in Roman history and that the lack of war on earth is spoken of as silence in heaven. Just why, not even Elliott ventures to explain.

Another example of this has been previously cited. There we noted that Barnes looked upon the unrecorded seven thunders as the anathemas hurled by the Pope at the Reformation, and they were not to be written because there was nothing in them worth recording. This is perhaps a classic example of non-Catholic humor but it can hardly be taken as serious exegesis. It takes an exceedingly elastic imagination to conceive what comfort the above interpretations could have brought to the suffering Christians of Asia Minor in A.D. 95.

(5) Another valid objection to this method of interpretation is that it leads to calculations of times and periods which have constantly been falsified by the events and which have done much harm in the kingdom. These calculations, as in the futurist school, are made on the year-day theory that a day in prophecy always means one thousand years. Thus, the beast which is to have power for forty-two months is really to have power for 1,260 years. This evil power will come to a close after this many years—but the papacy, regarded by most as the Beast, has lasted much longer than that. On a similar basis, Lord[14] holds that a day in prophecy is equal to one thousand years and estimates that the millennium will last 360,000 years. Despite the fact that scriptural basis for this view is meager, if at all, the idea has been widely held by expositors and is a favorite of scholars who hold even to opposite views of Revelation.

---

[13]E. B. Elliott, *Commentary on Revelation* (London: Seeley, Burnside, and Seeley, 1844), I, 292–297.

[14]D. N. Lord, *Exposition of Apocalypse* (New York: Harper and Brothers, 1847), p. 515.

The following passages of Scripture are usually used in support of the position:

> Numbers 14:34, which records that the Israelites had to spend a year in the desert for every day in the 40-day journey of the spies.
>
> Ezekiel 4:4–6, where the prophet is told to lie on his side for a certain number of days and is told that the days correspond to years.
>
> Daniel 9:25, which prophesies the seventy weeks. Practically all expositors agree that this deals with a period of 490 years. If the weeks are taken as periods of seven days each, then we do have a prophecy in which a day stands for a year.

Even if this is true, it does not follow that this is a general rule in prophecy. For instance:

> Isaiah 7:8 prophesied that Ephraim should be broken in 65 years—he did not mean days.
>
> Isaiah 16:14 prophesied that in three years the glory of Moab would be made a thing of contempt—he did not mean days.
>
> Isaiah 23:15 said that Tyre would be forgotten 70 years—he did not mean days.
>
> Jeremiah 29:10 said that Judah would be subject to Babylon 70 years—he did not mean days.
>
> Daniel 9:2 "understood by the books" that the 70 years of the captivity were almost accomplished—he did not understand days.
>
> Matthew 20:19 records that Jesus prophesied that he would be crucified and buried but would rise again on the third day—this was prophecy but it did not mean that his body would be in the grave three years.

Alford seems to be correct when he says, "I have never seen it proved, or even made probable, that we are to take a day for a year in apocalyptic prophecy."[15] This year-day calculation has aroused ex-

---

[15]Henry Alford, *The Greek Testament* (London: Rivingtons, Waterloo Place, 1862), Part II, 251.

pectation many times only to lead to disappointment. It was due to such a method that Miller predicted the end of the world to come in 1843, which prediction caused much excitement and led to the founding of the Seventh Day Adventist Church. Different authors have set various dates. These dates have passed, and the expositors have shifted their ground into the safer future. In reality there is no "safer future" for such a system.

2. Strong Points

This whole continuous-historical method, giving first importance to the apostasy of the Roman Catholic Church, has been shown by events of history to be a false view which leads to endless and profitless speculation. It breaks down under the sheer weight of its obvious fallacies. Apparently it has no strong points except that it avoids a literal interpretation of the book and it foresees the complete overthrow of evil.

III. THE PHILOSOPHY OF HISTORY METHOD

This method of interpretation divorces Revelation almost completely from its historical background. It looks upon the book as containing a discussion of the forces which underlie events but not a discussion of the events themselves. Revelation is viewed as an expression of those great principles of God's government whose operation may be observed in every age. It is a book setting out the principles on the basis of which God deals with all men in all ages. Symbols are understood to refer to forces or tendencies and may thus be fulfilled over and over as these forces or tendencies are repeated in history. For example, the wild beast arising out of the sea in Revelation 13 is interpreted as the secular powers antagonistic to the true church whenever and wherever that power arises. Likewise the second beast with horns like a lamb but a voice like a dragon represents corrupt religious power in league with corrupt secular power to bring injury to God's people.

John is considered by this school of thought to be the giver of truth concerning the most powerful influences which work underneath all human activity. Some of these influences work wonders for good in civilization. Others have their seat not only in hostile anti-Christian religions or in old Rome, but in powerful churches, reformed or unreformed, and not less in sects which have revolted from dogmas, and which do not permit their apostles to declaim against selfishness and greed. According to the proponents of this system of interpretation, there is no continuity in Revelation. The seals are not expected to be fulfilled and then the trumpets. The seals represent the entire course of history, and the trumpets cover the same territory only from a different aspect. The relation between the visions is not regarded as temporal but logical. They are compared to seven reels of pictures showing the same thing from different viewpoints and with dramatic climax.[16]

The principles here revealed are ageless and belong to all the days. John reveals the great principles which are always at work in the world. He points out the ultimate issues toward which human events and the cause of God are being guided by the risen Christ. The principles which controlled the history of John's time control the history of all times, and the things symbolized are just as applicable to one day as they were to John's day. This analysis of the philosophy of history method of interpretation leaves the objections (weak points) and strong points of the system obvious.

1. Objections

(1) The method removes the book too far from the situation for which it was originally written. This interpretation does not leave the work as far out of contact with the Christians who first received it as do the futurist and continuous-historical methods, but it makes their place too insignificant for a hearty reception. It recognizes that the principles involved were applicable to that early day but holds that they were no more so than they are to our day. But a close study of the needs of those first-century Christians reveals that they are so definitely met in this book that we cannot say its message is so universal that it had no special comfort and help for them.

(2) This method confines the book to too narrow a channel. It

[16]Richardson, *op. cit.*, p. 64.

holds that the symbols refer to forces or tendencies and that there are no specific prophecies of specific events in the book. This does not appear to be the case when we observe throughout the book definite evidences of the fulfilment of specific events. For example, it is a known fact that Imperial Rome fell through a combination of three agencies: natural calamity, internal decadence, and outside invasion. This fact is observed over and over in the symbolism of Revelation.

2. Strong Points

(1) This method does recognize that the book of Revelation had some meaning to those who first received it. The meaning is rather limited but it is present, and that is more than can be said of the two previously mentioned systems.

(2) The method also recognizes the hand of God in history. He has not left the world to its own devices but is still dealing with men on the basis of principles which are consistent with his character.

(3) This method recognizes that the goal toward which all history is moving is the complete triumph of the cause of God among the affairs of men. His purpose and his plan will not fail but will be victorious through the warrior who is called "King of kings" and who fights with the sword which proceedeth out of his mouth (19:11-21).

IV. THE PRETERIST METHOD

This method is practically the opposite of the futurist method. The futurists say that none of the book has yet been fulfilled. The preterists, in the strict meaning of the term, say that all the book was fulfilled in the days of the Roman Empire. The word "preter" is a prefix from the Latin *praeter,* meaning past or beyond. The derivative "preterist" in this usage means one who looks upon the fulfilment of Revelation as having taken place in the past. Pieters[17] finds two divisions in this school: a right wing and a left wing.

The right wing of the preterist school is represented in the work of Stuart, Beckwith, and Swete. They receive the book of Revelation

[17]Pieters, *op. cit.,* pp. 40-43.

as inspired literature. They hold that most of it was fulfilled in the days of the Roman Empire under Domitian. The final judgment and the perfected state of mankind yet await fulfilment. They look upon Revelation as a book for the day of persecution in Asia Minor but feel that it has only, at least to a great extent, a literary interest for people of our day.

The left wing in the preterist school has no respect for Revelation as inspired Scripture. They view the work as parallel with the other apocalyptic literature of the day and as valuable only as literature. According to the interpretation John knew nothing of the future by inspiration; therefore, they look for no fulfilment of the recorded events in the life of the church. This is the preterist school in the one hundred per cent meaning of the term.

1. Objections

It is difficult to state the objections to this method of interpretation without separating the two wings. To the sincere Christian who holds that Revelation is inspired Scripture and has a place in the canon of the New Testament because the Holy Spirit wanted it there, the left wing view can be only repulsive. It cannot be received by any who look upon John as God's spokesman concerning the affairs of men in John's day or any other. It is entirely rejected and has no strong points.

On the other hand, the right wing commends itself as having more good points than weak ones. The outstanding and perhaps the only objection to this method is that many of its advocates find no message in the book except a message for John's day. They do not see an application of the message of the book to church life in our own day. There are many of this group who by adopting some of the principles of the philosophy of history school find a universal application of the book.

2. Strong Points

Several strong points in favor of this method may be observed.

(1) It is true to the background of the work. No literature can be properly understood apart from background. We understand Eliza-

beth Barrett Browning's Portuguese sonnets better when we know the despair from which her love for Robert Browning rescued her. We understand Hawthorne's *Scarlet Letter* when we know the double-standard morals of the Colonial days. And we understand Revelation better when we know the background of Domitianic persecution. The preterist method recognizes this truth.

(2) The preterist method makes the book of Revelation meaningful for those who first received it. The primary purpose of the book was to "reveal" to the persecuted Christians the nearness of Christ and the certainty of a speedy victory of their cause over the imperial policies of Rome. The preterist method proceeds with this as its basic principle.

(3) This method also gives room for a universal application of the message of the book. Just as the risen Christ was victorious over all opposition in that ancient day, he will be victorious over the turbulent conditions in any day, including our own. The heathen may rage and the people may imagine empty things, but God is still on his throne and Christ still holds the keys to death and destiny. Surely this is a strong point for this interpretation.

(4) This system yields an interpretation which is consistent with scriptural teachings throughout the New Testament. One can follow this method and not have to believe that God's purpose in the cross of Christ will fail and that he will have to resort to the sword to bring in his kingdom. The same truths and principles which are observed in the teachings of Jesus and the preaching and writing of the apostles are observed in Revelation if one follows this method of interpretation.

V. THE HISTORICAL-BACKGROUND METHOD

It has been previously observed that this fifth method might be looked upon as a part of the preterist method. It seems desirable to discuss it as a separate division for two reasons. First, because the left wing group has left a very undesirable association attached to the entire preterist system. Second, because even some of the right wing group, with which this method has much in common, have held that Revelation has no message except to those who first received it. Therefore, it appears wise to treat the historical-background method as a separate method of interpretation rather than to view it as one division of another division of the preterist method. It deserves more recognition than that type of treatment would give to it. Perhaps the best manner of describing this method is to point out the principles of interpretation which it follows. None of the methods of interpretation previously discussed has a monopoly on the interpretation of Revelation. Each school has had in its number of advocates some who were devout and scholarly men. When we study the views and try to select one which appears correct, we are at a loss because there are obvious fallacies in each one. The principles listed here will perhaps suggest a method which combines a part of the right wing preterist method with a part of the philosophy of history interpretation.

1. This method keeps in mind that the writer wrote his message primarily for the encouragement and edification of the Christians of his own time. One who follows this method must, therefore, make a close study of the church of that day. He must, as far as possible, know the writer of the book, his condition when he wrote, and his relation to those who received the message. He must know the approximate date of the writing. He must acquaint himself with the moral, religious, social, and political conditions of the day when the book was written. He must know the mind of the people as they faced all the perplexities of a seemingly disastrous situation.

> An important landmark for the guidance of the interpreter is to be found in the purpose of the book and the historical surroundings of its origin. The Apocalypse is cast in the form of a letter to certain Christian societies, and it opens with detailed account of their conditions and circumstances. . . . The book starts with a well defined historical situation, to which reference is made again at the end, and the intermediate visions, which form the body of the work, cannot on any reasonable theory be dissociated from their historical setting.[18]

[18]H. B. Swete, *The Apocalypse of John* (2d ed.; London: Macmillan and Company, 1907), p. ccxiii.

The expositor continues to indicate that the book arises out of local and temporary circumstances, that it is the answer of the Holy Spirit to the fears of the Asian Christians under the perils toward the end of the first century, and that all that throws light on Asia Minor from A.D. 70–100 and upon Christianity there in that period is of first importance to the interpreter of Revelation.

> John was not writing about the twentieth century, nor any other century except that in which he lived. . . . To the struggling, persecuted churches which he addressed, the mere details of the future were a vanishing concern; what they needed was a revived confidence in the idea that Christianity was to have a future on earth. Dispensations and figures of distant ages could not have helped them in their desperate plight; they needed the light of Christian hope upon their own age.[19]

William Peter King adds his view of Revelation along with these others.

> The purpose of the book was to strengthen the courage and faith of the Christian by visualizing the downfall of the Roman Empire and the final victory of the Kingdom of God and the victorious Christ. The author writes from a situation that is apparently hopeless. . . . One is made to wonder how the Adventists persuaded themselves that a prediction of the rise and downfall of some modern pope or dictator could have been of any possible comfort and strength to the hard-pressed early Christians.[20]

Other authorities who hold to this view will be cited in the discussion of the historical background of the book. These are sufficient to indicate that the first step toward an understanding of this book is an understanding of its background.

2. A second principle of interpretation which must be kept in mind is that this book is written largely in symbolical language. The word "symbol" is from the Greek σύν, "with," plus the infinitive

---

[19]Dana, *op. cit.*, p. 86.

[20]William P. King, *Adventism* (Nashville: Abingdon-Cokesbury Press, 1941), pp. 100 ff.

βάλλειν, "to throw," hence "to throw together." A symbol is that which suggests something else by reason of relationship or association. It is a visible sign of something invisible, as an idea or a quality. In this book symbols are used to picture or represent abstract ideas which the writer desires to present to his readers.

> The book of Revelation (after the first three chapters) is a divine picture book, a book of spiritual cartoons, a pictorial presentation, through symbols of certain forces which underlie the historical development of the Christian Church and its unceasing conflict.[21]

For this reason the ordinary rules of interpretation cannot be followed. Usually the words of any passage of Scripture must be understood in their plain and natural sense, unless there is some reason to take them figuratively. The presumption is always in favor of the literal meaning; if one takes it otherwise, he must show the cause. This is not the case in Revelation. In this book, presented in pictorial form, one must assume that the symbols are to be taken figuratively unless there is good reason for regarding them as literal. There are few places where literal language is used in the midst of symbolical, but these stand out in bold relief as Greek words stand out in a context of English.

There is a double duty rather than a single one facing the interpreter of Revelation. When the Bible story of David and Goliath is read, one sees the boy, the giant, the armor, the sling and the victory. This is the entire story. But when one reads in the twelfth chapter of Revelation about a battle between Michael with his angels and the dragon with his angels, he must see not just the story but what it symbolizes. He must not take it as information concerning a heavenly battle in which Satan lost his position in heaven in prehistoric time, but he must see that the scene symbolizes some fact or truth in the spiritual life or experience of Christianity. The interpreter who starts out to understand Revelation, so far as possible, to be literal, starts in the wrong direction, and the further he proceeds in this direction the less he will understand the book.

---

[21]Pieters, *op. cit.*, p. 69.

The writer uses these symbols to communicate his thought to the initiated who will read the symbols but at the same time to conceal his ideas from those outside the Christian circle. At the present time this last may not appear to be of great importance, but the conditions of the day in which the work was written reveal that it was extremely important then. The meaning of the greater part of the symbolism of Revelation is quite clear to the modern reader who is willing to see it. There are some symbols which are not so easily understood and where there is much room for diversity of opinion. About these one can ill afford to be dogmatic. The wise thing to do is to seek earnestly to find the most probable meaning of the symbol to those who first received the book and consider that as the most likely interpretation.

The symbolism of this book is often weird and grotesque. Wild beasts with characteristics quite untrue to nature are used to represent heathen worldly powers. Why should an animal have seven heads, or ten horns, or the feet of a bear and the mouth of a lion? (13:1-2.) Surely there was never such a literal animal. All the combined efforts of P. T. Barnum and Robert Ripley could not have produced such a creature. The animal is so presented to symbolize a powerful and vicious antagonist met by the cause of righteousness in spiritual battle. No method of interpretation can get to the real message of Revelation unless it recognizes and follows this symbolism.

3. As a third important principle, one must keep in mind that Revelation uses Old Testament terminology with New Testament meaning. Old Testament expression and imagery thoroughly permeate the book of Revelation. Some expositors have fallen into the error of interpreting this language as it was used in the Old Testament. They have considered it as inevitable that if an expression means a thing in one part of the Bible it must of necessity mean the same thing every time it appears. This is a false premise which leads to countless errors. An expression or symbol means what the author intends it to mean in the place where he uses it. John uses some of the animals found in Daniel and much terminology from Ezekiel, but this does not mean that they are the same in interpreta-

tion; he has adapted them to suit his own message. Much of the dispensationalism that has cluttered the progress of interpretation has rested on the belief that Revelation foretells the "seventieth week" of Daniel just because some of the terminology is the same. The New Testament is primarily a Christian book, not a book of Judaism. Its message is its own whether the language is adapted from the Old Testament, the Apocryphal books, or is wholly original with John.

4. For the true meaning of Revelation, one must seek to grasp the visions or series of visions as a whole without pressing the details of the symbolism. It has been previously observed that many of the details are for the dramatic effect and not to add to the minute meaning of a passage. The details of a vision may have significance, but in most instances they are used only to fill out the scenery. This same principle applies in the interpretation of parables and often in the books of poetry. For instance, observe the Ninety-first Psalm:

> "Thou shalt not be afraid for the terror by night,
>   Nor for the arrow that flieth by day;
>   For the pestilence that walketh in darkness,
>   Nor for the destruction that wasteth at noonday."

Pieters says concerning this:

> Taken in connection with the whole purpose of the Psalm, as building up by concrete details the idea that the believer is always under the protecting care of God, this is fine, and true. Take any of the details by itself and it is not true. Believers fall in battle, and are ill with contagious diseases as well as others. The details are not so intended; they are for the cumulative effect to assure men that God cares for those who trust in Him.[22]

Similarly in Revelation the details are added to make a tremendous impression of the things discussed. In Revelation 6:12-17 we have an overwhelming impression of approaching doom and human terror. This is sufficient without asking the minute symbolism of each falling star, the removal of the heavens, and the moving of each moun-

---

[22]Pieters, *op. cit.*, p. 73.

tain. The safest policy is to find the central truth and let the details fit in the most natural way.

5. A fifth principle of interpretation is suggested by Pieters when he stresses the fact that Revelation is addressed chiefly to the imagination. The books of the Bible are directed to the different faculties of man; i.e., Romans to reason, psalms to emotions, etc. In a similar way Revelation is addressed to the imagination. As the expositor reads the book, he must seek to see in his mind's eye the various episodes intense with drama, just as if he were standing on Patmos with John and viewing them. He must yield himself to the majesty of the movement as Christ walks among his broken churches with healing for their hurt. Unless the reader can do this, he will miss the greatest messages of Revelation. The man who has not, or has and refuses to use, a fertile imagination, will do well to leave this book alone. This book was written to yield its message by creating an impression, and this impression makes itself realized as one yields himself to the drama that is enacted before him on the stage in Asia Minor A.D. 90–96. When the play is ended and the curtain falls after the reverent prayer of the writer, "Even so: Come, Lord Jesus," one is left with an overwhelming impression of majesty, reverence, and awe. He feels the assurance of victory in spite of seemingly insurmountable odds; he knows without doubt or reservation that, come what may, Christ is supreme and that no power can take from him the victory which is rightfully his.

CHAPTER III

The Historical Background of Revelation

The importance of the historical background in interpreting the book of Revelation has already been noted. It remains the duty of this work to indicate the nature of that background. The standard treatment of such a study deals with questions of authorship, date, place of writing, recipients and their condition, and the general conditions of the world out of which the work came. This method, with a few possible variations, will be followed in the section of the study at hand. Such a study may be very brief, or it may be voluminous, to suit the need of the work which is being done. The discussion will of necessity be rather full in this present study because so much in the interpretation of the book depends on accuracy at this point.

I. THE AUTHOR OF THE NEW TESTAMENT APOCALYPSE

The logical starting place in a study of the background of any literature appears to be the question of authorship. This is especially true in the case of Revelation because of the traditional position with reference to this matter. Some scholars have suggested the possibility of other men as authors of this book. Their arguments will be noted as the study proceeds, but the first treatment will be given to the traditional position.

Perhaps no violence is done to the message if we do not know definitely the identity of the author. Its place in the canon of the New Testament appears to be secure and its message is one of victory, whether from John the son of Zebedee, John the Seer, or some other John. A similar condition holds in this case as in the case of the Epistle to the Hebrews. Scholarship has been divided on the authorship of Hebrews through the years of its study, but its message pointing to Christ as the final revelation of God is still one of the pinnacles of redemptive truth. There is this difference between the two cases: Hebrews makes no claim as to authorship; Revelation claims to have been written by someone named John.[1] Either this is true or the work is a forgery.

It is a known fact that most of the apocalyptic literature was pseudonymous. This matter, with the reasons for it, has been discussed in a previous section of this book. Because of this truth many have held that the book of Revelation, along with all its kindred literature, was pseudonymous. It is profitable to review the position of Charles[2] at this point. He is recognized as the outstanding authority on apocalyptic literature, and he takes the position that Revelation is not pseudonymous.

In the post-Exilic period the idea of an inspired, adequate, infallible, and valid Law became a dogma of Judaism. When this condition became established, there was no longer room for a prophet or a religious teacher unless he was a mere exponent of the Law. Then, too, the formation of the Old Testament Canon with its three sections—Law, Prophets, and Hagiographa—encouraged the custom of pseudonymous writing. After this time no work of prophetic nature could obtain a hearing unless it bore the name of some ancient person worthy of a hearing. Therefore, when a man felt that he had a message to deliver, he issued the work in the form most likely to be received. When Revelation was written, this condition did not exist. The advent and advance of Christianity had thrust the Old Testament Canon into a subordinate place. The main consideration with reference to authority had to do with Jesus and what he said. The spirit of prophecy had come anew on the believers; belief in inspiration was kindled anew, and for several generations no exclusive

---

[1] Cf. Revelation 1:1, 4, 9; 22:8.

[2] Charles, "The International Critical Commentary," *The Revelation of St. John,* Vol. I, p. xxxviii f.

canon of Christian writings was recognized. There is no reason related to this ancient custom for supposing that Revelation was pseudonymous.

A second evidence that Revelation was not pseudonymous is seen in the fact that the writer claimed that the visions he used were his own and were for his immediate generation. The usual custom in apocalyptic was for the writer to claim that the visions belonged to some great person of the past and were for the generations of the future. The writer of Revelation claims to be the servant of Jesus Christ (1:1), a brother of the Christians of Asia Minor and a fellow sufferer in tribulation (1:9), an exile on Patmos for preaching the Word (1:9), and that he himself saw and heard the things recorded in this book (22:8).

> So far it is clear that the Apocalypse before us was written by a prophet (Revelation 22:9) who lived in Asia Minor, and that his actual name was John. This is just as assuredly the work of a John as 2 Thess. 2 and 1 Cor. 15 are apocalypses of St. Paul. . . . There is not a shred of evidence, not even the shadow of a probability, for the hypothesis that the Apocalypse is pseudonymous.[3]

Thus it appears that we are safe in holding that the book is not a forgery but was written by someone named John. Just which John this was will be discussed later. Before entering into that discussion, it seems the part of wisdom to review the things we know about the writer, whoever he was. This knowledge comes from a study of the text of the book and is summarized as follows:

John, to whom we owe the New Testament Apocalypse, was a Jewish Christian who had in all probability spent the greater part of his life in Galilee[4] before moving to Asia Minor and settling in Ephesus, the center of Greek civilization in that province. This conclusion comes from a study of his use of the Greek language. He

---

[3]Charles, *ibid.*, p. xxxix.

[4]This position that the writer had lived in Galilee is taken by authorities, not only because most of the apocalypses are reputed to have been written in Galilee but also because the writer appears to have been acquainted with these works.

takes unparalleled liberties with the syntax of the language and, to a certain extent, creates a Greek grammar of his own. The language which he had adopted did not furnish for him a normal and rigid medium of expression. It was in what has been characterized as a fluid condition, which yielded freely to the remodeling in syntactical usage and the unheard-of expressions used. The style of this writer is absolutely unique; he has set aside the usual rules of syntax and has defied the laws of the grammarians. This does not appear to be intentional. His one purpose is to drive home his message with all the power at his command. He does this, and in so doing is guilty of numerous breaches of Greek syntax. The reason for this appears to be that while he wrote in Greek, he thought in terms of Hebrew. Often he translated Hebrew idioms literally into Greek. He had a profound knowledge of the Old Testament and used its phraseology both consciously and unconsciously. This must be the reason for the unique syntax we find in the book.

We know another thing about the writer of this book. He exercised an unquestioned authority over the churches of Asia Minor. To seven of them he wrote his Apocalypse. The message was not confined to the seven; they were representative of all the churches. In the book he encourages the believers to resist even unto death the claims of the empire for state worship and he exhorts them to proclaim faithfully the victorious cause of God. This exhortation is directed to individuals and to churches. John lays down the only true basis for ethics and government—Christ the Supreme King. He claims this world as well as the next for God. In doing this he shows an unquestioned love for the churches. At the same time he "reproves, rebukes, and exhorts" as one whose authority will not be questioned.

This writer was a man of profound spiritual insight. He looks deeper into the mysteries of God's plans in some instances than perhaps any other writer of the New Testament. His eyes are lifted above the plains where the battle rages and are focused upon a throne. On this throne sits one characterized by sovereignty, holiness, righteousness, and grace. In his hand he holds a sealed book which contains the destiny of men. Only One is worthy to open this book. That One is the Lamb who conquered through his death and now lives forever. When the Lamb has opened all the seals and the records of God's dealings with men have been seen, the victory is apparent. God is still on his throne; it has not toppled before the combined efforts of the dragon and the two beasts. Not only is God still on his throne, his people are with him and securely provided for with a Perfect City and all the needs for nurturing eternal life (food and healing) evidenced. It is doubtful if any other writer of the New Testament has seen more really the certain victory of God's cause over all its enemies.

The writer of Revelation is a man who is very positive in his statements. The hostile Jews of Smyrna and Philadelphia are the "synagogue of Satan."[5] Domitian, and the empire itself in so far as it adopts his policies, is the "beast."[6] Rome is "Babylon,"[7] the mother of harlots and of the abominations of the earth. The tone of the book, when it lashes the persecutor, the idolator, the unclean, is almost warlike; the prophet's righteous wrath reaches a white heat. The conception of Christ in Revelation is infinitely majestic and august, but his predominant characteristic is unbounded power, showing itself in a just severity. As the Warrior he rules with a rod of iron;[8] as the Lamb he is terrible in his anger;[9] and as the King he treads the winepress of the wrath of God.[10] Only once or twice does the tenderness of the Lord's compassion make itself felt in this book. Those instances are, of course, where he is bringing comfort to his people rather than viewing with intense disfavor his enemies.

All the above information has to do with a general view of the author of Revelation. It looks at his basic characteristics and ideas without expressing any view as to the identity of the author. The subsequent treatment will consider possible authors with the evidences for and against them.

------

[5]Cf. Revelation 2:9 and 3:9.
[6]Cf. Revelation 13:1–18.
[7]Cf. Revelation 17:5.
[8]Cf. Revelation 19:15a.
[9]Cf. Revelation 6:16 f.
[10]Cf. Revelation 19:15b.

1. Evidences for and Against John, the Son of Zebedee

The traditional position with reference to this work is that it was written by John, the apostle and son of Zebedee. There has been much controversy throughout the course of Christian history at this point. Dionysius the Great, of Alexandria, held the opinion about A.D. 250 that John did not write the Apocalypse. He based this opinion on a study of the Greek style of the Fourth Gospel and of Revelation. His conclusion was that the same person could not have written both books. He believed that John wrote the Gospel; therefore, he did not believe that John wrote the Apocalypse. The opposite of this view is taken by Dana in a recent work. He recognizes that in the second century there was a "widely prevalent belief practically throughout the Christian world that John the Apostle, son of Zebedee, wrote the Fourth Gospel."[11] Concerning this he says:

> Such strong traditional evidence cannot be cast aside. It is difficult to explain its existence unless the Apostle John had some connection with the Fourth Gospel. Conservative criticism would probably persist in abiding by its verdict of apostolic authorship were it not for the fact that the external evidence for the authorship of Revelation is earlier and intrinsically stronger than that for the Gospel. The differences between the two books are too radical to admit a view of common authorship. Hence we feel constrained to assign the Apocalypse to the Apostle John and look elsewhere for the hand that wrote the Gospel.[12]

Thus it is observed that Dionysius of A.D. 250 and Dana of A.D. 1940 begin with the same premise but arrive at opposite conclusions. In between these views there has raged a battle all the years. The safest position appears to be for one to weigh the evidences and draw his own conclusions.

(1) Evidence for John, the son of Zebedee

a. External evidence.—One of the earliest of the church fathers whose work has come down to us was Justin Martyr. He was a mar-

[11]H. E. Dana, *The Ephesian Tradition* (Kansas City: Kansas City Seminary Press, 1940), p. 167.

[12]*Ibid.*, p. 167.

tyr under Aurelius about A.D. 166. His work, *Dialogue with Trypho the Jew,* is usually dated about A.D. 140–160. In it we find these words:

> . . . . there was a certain man with us, whose name was John, one of the Apostles of Christ, who prophesied, by a revelation that was made to him, that those who believed in our Christ would dwell a thousand years in Jerusalem; and that thereafter the general, and, in short, the eternal resurrection and judgment of all men would take place.[13]

The fact that Justin Martyr's home and principal field of service was in Asia Minor where the churches addressed in Revelation were located makes this statement a striking one.

The next direct witness to John the apostle as author of this book comes from Irenaeus, who died at Lyons, France about A.D. 190. This is regarded as one of the chief witnesses in John's favor. Irenaeus was born and educated in Asia, the territory of the seven churches. He was a pupil of Polycarp who was bishop of one of the seven churches, Smyrna. Irenaeus frequently mentioned Revelation in his many books. He appears to have been especially interested in the number 666, the number of the beast, which he considered to be identical with Antichrist.[14] Several times he says that the book was written by John the disciple of the Lord and identifies him with the John who lay upon the breast of Jesus at the Last Supper. He holds that John wrote the book in the time of Domitian the emperor.[15] His witness is a strong one since he was only one step removed from association with John. Only about seventy or eighty years elapsed between the writing of the book and the comments by Irenaeus. This period was one well within the memory of men who could have corrected the statements if they had been false. There is no reason for believing that Irenaeus and Polycarp would have been dishonest about the matter.

When we pass Irenaeus, we find no one else who had personal

---

[13]Justin Martyr, *Dialogue with Trypho the Jew, The Ante-Nicene Church Fathers* (New York: The Christian Literature Company, 1890), I, 240.

[14]Irenaeus, *Against Heresies,* chap. xxx, *The Ante-Nicene Church Fathers, op. cit.,* I, 558.

[15]*Ibid.,* I, 560.

knowledge or knew anyone who had personal knowledge as to the authorship of the book. We do find others who held to John as the author even though they did not have firsthand information. Some of these were Clement[16] of Alexandria (A.D. 223), Tertullian[17] of Carthage (A.D. 220), Origen[18] of Alexandria (A.D. 223), and Hippolytus[19] of Rome (A.D. 240). Eusebius quotes Origen as saying,

> What shall we say of him who reclined upon the breast of Jesus, I mean John? Who has left us one gospel, in which he confesses that he could write so many that the whole world could not contain them. He also wrote the Apocalypse, commanded as he was, to conceal, and not to write the voices of the seven thunders.[18]

Eusebius treats the Johannine authorship of the Apocalypse as a matter undetermined, but he does so in the face of all the above testimonies. Writers subsequent to his date constantly quoted the book as written by the apostle John. Some of these were: Basil the Great, Athanasius, Ambrose, Cyprian, Augustine, and Jerome. These were far from sharing whatever doubts may have been in the mind of the great church historian. This concurrence of testimony on the part of those who were in a position to determine a question of this kind, and in every way deserving of credit, can be set aside only by opposing evidence of the most conclusive sort. These witnesses represent a wide territory of Christendom. Justin Martyr worked in Asia Minor. Irenaeus worked in Asia Minor and then on to France. Tertullian was from Carthage. Clement and Origen were from Alexandria, the center of learning and information in the Eastern church. They represent all the chief centers of Christendom except Rome, and Hippolytus, after a few years, represented Rome in this opinion. Pieters[20] observes that the distribution of

---

[16]*The Ante-Nicene Fathers*, II, 504.

[17]*Ibid.*, III, 333.

[18]Eusebius Pamphilus, *Ecclesiastical History*, trans. C. F. Cruse (12th ed.; Philadelphia: J. B. Lippincott and Company, 1869), Book VI, chap. xx, p. 246.

[19]*The Ante-Nicene Fathers*, V, 211.

[20]Pieters, *op. cit.*, p. 15.

utterance in point of time falls something like this: 140–170–200–220–233–240. It is observed at once that the longest interval is thirty years of the end of the apostolic era. Such testimony, weighed in view of the fact that these were responsible men holding important places in the Christian work, stands with great conviction. If we accept a possible but disputed opinion of Papias regarding the book, the witness is pushed back to A.D. 125. Practically the unanimous opinion of second-century tradition held to the Johannine authorship. There were some objections raised in the third century,[21] but even there the testimony favoring the apostolic authorship is overwhelming. There are few books in the New Testament which have stronger support from ancient tradition.

b. Internal evidence.—Though there is much more ground for debate here than in the field of external evidence, there is much in favor of the apostle John from this viewpoint. Perhaps the first point of evidence here is the fact that the writer calls himself John. This he does in four places (1:1, 4, 9; 22:8). The manner in which the name is introduced implies that the name was well known and that the identity of the writer was sure to be recognized by those who first received the book. This was true of John. He had been in Asia Minor since the fall of Jerusalem in A.D. 70. He had worked in the churches there, especially Ephesus, and was well known to all of them. Another thing implied in the manner of introduction is that the writer bore such a relation to the churches of Asia Minor that he was a suitable medium for communication to them in that tone of authority and admonition which he employs. It is known that John spent his closing years with the churches in Asia Minor and that he held a position among them wholly consistent with the attitude that he assumes in this letter. In the third mention of his name (1:9), the words of the Lord to James and John (Mark 10:38–39) are recalled: "You do not know what you are asking for yourselves. Are you able to drink the cup which I am about to drink, or to be baptized with the baptism with which I am about to be baptized? . . . You shall drink the cup which I am about to drink, and you shall be baptized with the baptism with which I am about to be

---

[21]These will be treated in a subsequent part of the work.

baptized. . . ." Long ago James experienced the things which the Lord prophesied. Now John, too, is drinking the cup of suffering and being immersed in the persecution directed against God's own people. His very statement of fellowship in suffering is characteristic of the tender, sympathizing, and fraternal spirit which characterized John. There is also a marked similiarity between the writer's allusion to himself in Revelation 22:8 and a like allusion in John 21:24. Compare them. Revelation 22:8: "And I John saw these things, and heard them." John 21:24: "This is the disciple which testifieth of these things." The similarity is obvious. In every one of the four instances where the writer mentions his name, it may be safely claimed that the mention made of himself by the writer is in perfect consistence with the theory that he is none other than the apostle John. What manner of introduction some other John might have used is not known. Any conjecture would be an argument based on silence; and such an argument is never very satisfactory.

The characteristics of the writer as they have been observed previously may well fit John the apostle. As before observed, the writer was apparently a Jewish Christian who had lived the greater part of his life in Galilee before coming to Asia Minor. This was true of John. It was also observed that the writer thought in Hebrew but wrote in Greek. This, too, was probably true of John with his Jewish background and largely Gentile congregation. Another characteristic observed was the profound spiritual insight of the writer. This, too, was true of the John of the Gospels. He often grasped truths of deep import long before the other disciples understood them. The positive nature of the writer of Revelation was present in John the apostle. He is often called "gentle John." He became "gentle John" after the Lord's Spirit had possessed him for sixty or more years. His natural temperament was a quick and fiery one. It was a nature which led him to desire to call down fire from heaven to burn up a non-co-operating Samaritan village. It also caused him to stop one who was casting out evil spirits in the Master's name because the healer was not one of the immediate followers of Jesus. This nature led Jesus to nickname John and James "sons of thunder." The same nature is seen in the writer of Revelation as he denounces the enemies of Christ in scathing terms. The writer goes from the tenderest tones to the severest as he pursues his purpose. This is the combination of "gentle John" and "Brother Thunderstorm" with which we are familiar.

Other internal evidences are observed if one grants that the writer of Revelation is the same as the writer of the Fourth Gospel. This fact is denied by many competent critics, but the traditional position is likely to stand until proofs other than conjectures of a highly speculative nature are presented. On the whole there appear to be more difficulties in the way of rejecting the traditional position than there are in the way of accepting it. Taking the position that John the son of Zebedee wrote the Fourth Gospel, we find several similarities in the Apocalypse.

The Christology of the book is an important point of internal evidence. It is quite similar to that of the Fourth Gospel.[22] The expression in Revelation 1:1, "which God gave to him," Christ, is in perfect harmony with the general teaching of John's Gospel that the Son has everything which the Father has, and yet has nothing but what he has received of the Father. In the Apocalypse as in the Gospel, the Saviour depends on God the Father for his instructions. This is strikingly in harmony with the Gospel. The idea that the Son has only what the Father gave him is reflected in John 17:7-8; 5:19-20; 7:16. This relation is expressed in other terms in other places in the New Testament, but the resemblance is not so marked as it is here.

The use of the term λόγος to indicate a person and as the distinctive title of Christ is found only in the Johannine literature. It is in John 1:1, 14; 1 John 1:1, and in Revelation 19:13. In this last use the word is used as one of the titles of the conquering Christ as he goes forth to defeat the enemies of God.

John is the only one of the Gospel writers who tells of the spear which pierced the side of Jesus when he was crucified (John 19:34). It appears to be more than a matter of coincidence that the piercing is mentioned in Revelation 1:7: ". . . and every eye shall see him and those who pierced him. . . ." A close study of the two passages

---

[22]Dissimilarities will be discussed in the section on evidence against John.

reveals that the Greek word for "pierce" is the same verb in both instances. In Zechariah 12:10 we find a similar allusion. The translators of the Septuagint used a form of the Greek verb κατορχέομαι. Both the Gospel and the Apocalypse use a form of the verb ἐκκεντέω. The difference on the one hand and the identity on the other must be regarded as more than coincidence. It points to identity of authorship in the case of the two books.

In the Gospel of John, Jesus is pointed out as the "Lamb of God which taketh away the sin of the world" (John 1:29, 36). Neither of the other writers uses this title with reference to Jesus. Evidently it meant much to John because he was perhaps present when Jesus was pointed out and the descriptive term used. In Revelation Christ is called a Lamb twenty-two times.[28] It is pointed out by those who oppose John that a different word is used by John and the writer of Revelation. This is partly true. In John 1:29, 36 the word ἀμνός. is used. In Revelation the word ἀρνίον is always used. But it is interesting to note that John uses the word ἀρνίον in another connection (John 21:15), and he is the only New Testament writer besides the author of Revelation who does use it. This, too, appears to be more than coincident. Revelation's free use of the idea appears to be highly consistent with the marked and emphatic manner in which the idea is used twice in recording the testimony of John the Baptist concerning the Messiah in John's Gospel.

A striking statement is made in Revelation 1:1-2. "The revelation of Jesus Christ, which God gave to him, to show to his servants what things must come to pass shortly; and he showed it by signs through his angel to his servant John who has witnessed concerning the Word of God. . . ." The verb "he has witnessed" is in the aorist tense. It indicates that John has already borne witness regarding the Logos of God. Is this a claim by the writer that he is the writer of the Fourth Gospel? It sounds like it.

In spite of all the difficulties met in comparing the style and grammar of the two books, there is one outstanding likeness between the two: they are easy to read. The vocabulary and constructions used in both books are of such nature that the student of Greek can

[28]Counting the times it is repeated in a few verses, it is used twenty-eight times.

read them with much less effort and reference to lexicon and grammar than any other books of the New Testament except 1, 2, and 3 John which appear to be by the same hand. The contrast at this point with the writing of Paul, Peter, or Luke is remarkable. Many Greek teachers consider John's writings the best material for teaching students the language; they can get a longer lesson in less time and with less effort. On the other hand, some teachers regard the text as too easy for effective teaching of beginners. This structure marks the Johannine books as not only peculiar to the remainder of the New Testament but also very similar to one another.

(2) Evidence against John, son of Zebedee

Kiddle observes that,

> No subject of Biblical studies has provoked such elaborate and prolonged discussion among scholars as that of the five books of the New Testament which are traditionally ascribed to John. . . . And no discussion has been so bewildering, disappointing, and unprofitable.[24]

When the student tries to follow the innumerable lines of evidence, he is caught in a maze of conflicting arguments brought forward to support rival theories. Such a maze makes it extremely difficult for one to reach conclusions that are satisfactory. The evidences presented by those who oppose the traditional authorship of Revelation are complex and difficult to untangle.

a. External evidence against John.—The major witness against John from an external viewpoint is Dionysius of Alexandria (A.D. 265). He was the pupil of Origen but did not agree with his teacher on the authorship of the Apocalypse. He did this on the basis of grammatical and syntactical difficulties, which will be treated subsequently. Dionysius tells us that there had been others before him who had questioned the Johannine authorship of the book:

> Some, indeed, before us, have set aside, and have attempted to refute the whole book, criticising every chapter, and pronounc-

---

[24]Kiddle, *The Revelation of St. John,* in "The Moffatt New Testament Commentary," p. xxxiii.

ing it without sense and without reason. They say that it is a false title, for it is not of John. Nay, that it is not even a revelation, as it is covered with such a dense and thick veil of ignorance, that not one of the Apostles, and not one of the holy men, or those of the church could be its author.[25]

This indicates that Dionysius was not the first to deny the Johannine authorship. Others before him, though he does not name them, had held the same position. But in favor of John is this fact: The fact that some were denying the Johannine authorship is definite evidence that others *before* the denial had held to the Johannine authorship; hence, some started denying it.

While Dionysius agrees with the ones he mentions with regard to the identity of the author, he disagrees with them in some of their positions. This is made plain when he says:

> For my part I would not venture to set this book aside, as there are many brethren that value it much; but having formed a conception of its subject as exceeding my capacity, I consider it also containing a certain concealed and wonderful intimation in each particular. . . . I do not, therefore, deny that he was called John, and that this was the writing of one John. And I agree that it was the work of some holy and inspired man. But I would not easily agree that this was the apostle, the son of Zebedee, the brother of James, who is the author of the gospel, and the general epistle that bears his name.[26]

From this point Dionysius proceeds to enumerate his reasons, all of an internal nature, for rejecting the Johannine authorship. Note that he does not make an outright denial but states that he would not "easily agree" that the John who wrote the Apocalypse was the son of Zebedee.

The only other external testimony of note against John comes from Eusebius.[27] He does not make an outright denial. He recog-

---

[25] Quoted in Eusebius, *Church History*, p. 297.
[26] *Ibid.*, pp. 297 f.
[27] Eusebius, *Church History*, pp. 124 ff.

nizes that Dionysius had questioned the Johannine authorship. He admits the many who favor the Johannine authorship. Then he throws in a bone of contention by suggesting another possible writer—John the Elder who had been mentioned by Papias. As previously observed, the writers who followed Eusebius did not share his doubts at this point. They continued to refer to the Apocalypse as the work of John the son of Zebedee.

The Elder John, who has been introduced into the field of Johannine criticism, is a very shadowy figure at the most. It is not an impossible task to dispose of him altogether. Robertson does this in a convincing manner.[28]

This Elder John was first discovered in Papias by Eusebius. Before him Dionysius had held that John who wrote the Gospel was not the same John as the one who wrote the Apocalypse. Eusebius confirms this testimony, in his own thinking, by use of two tombs of John in Ephesus. This is only tradition and is denied by many competent scholars. Warfield, Plummer, Salmon, and Keim deny the existence of this second John of Ephesus. Bacon, McGiffert, and Schurer, who are known for their liberal positions on New Testament criticism, attribute the Fourth Gospel to this elder John. They are happy to find even a ghostly person to whom they may attribute the book so as to deny apostolic authorship. Lightfoot and Westcott are inclined to admit his existence though they deny his authorship of the Fourth Gospel. Dana admits the existence of the elder John and suggests that he is the most plausible author of the Fourth Gospel.[29] In view of all these conflicting opinions, it is well to review the testimony of Papias concerning John.

Eusebius quotes Papias as follows:

> If, then, any one should come, having followed personally the elders, I would question him concerning the words of the elders, what Andrew or what Peter said, or what Philip, or what Thomas or James, or what John or Matthew or any one of the

---

[28] The following argument is largely a condensation of: A. T. Robertson, *Epochs in the Life of the Apostle John* (New York: Fleming H. Revell Company, 1935), pp. 22–29.

[29] Dana, *The Ephesian Tradition*, p. 168.

disciples of the Lord said, and the things which Aristion and the elder John, disciples of the Lord, say.

Robertson holds that the mention of "John" twice in this sentence is the thing which led Eusebius astray in his interpretation. In the quotation Aristion and the elder John are pictured as still living at the time referred to by Papias. He uses "say" not "said" when speaking of their testimony. That language is easily understood if John was still living and the rest of the elders were dead. That fact, and it is a very possible one, explains why John's name was repeated: In his case it is not just a matter of what was reported concerning what he said; it was a matter of what he was still saying—John's own living witness to Papias. Papias calls John "the elder," it is true; but he also calls all the apostles named (Andrew, Peter, Philip, Thomas, James, John, Matthew) by the same term—"the elders." Aristion is merely called a disciple. In the New Testament John is called disciple, apostle, and elder just as Peter and the others are.[80] This view identifies the "elder John" with the "John" listed with the other elders. There is nothing in the words of Papias to demand two Johns; there is much to support only one John. Thus we would have not two Johns but two kinds of testimony from one John: what he was reported by others to have *said,* and what he personally still *says.*

Irenaeus (c. A.D. 140–202) lived much closer to Papias (c. A.D. 70–140) than did Eusebius (c. A.D. 270–340). In his witness concerning Papias, he identifies John the Elder, the disciple of the Lord, with the apostle John. Irenaeus studied Papias and quoted him frequently, but he never found two distinct Johns in Papias' work. He did not know Papias personally, but he knew Polycarp, who had known John the apostle. Three times he mentions that John was known by Polycarp. He states that he often heard Polycarp tell of what John had said and expressly holds that John, the disciple of the Lord, wrote the Fourth Gospel during his residence at Ephesus. This is direct historical tradition from one who knew only one John. It is very likely that Papias, properly interpreted, knew only one John.

---

[80] Cf. Luke 6:12; Matthew 10:1 f.; 1 Peter 5:1.

This seems far more plausible than the hypothesis held by some that there were two Johns, both personal disciples of Jesus, both made their way to Ephesus after the destruction of Jerusalem, both were so prominent in their work that men of their generation and the next could not tell them apart and got them hopelessly mixed.

Polycrates, bishop of Ephesus and contemporary of Irenaeus, confirms the residence of the apostle John in Asia and appears to identify him with the elder John. He wrote in a letter to the bishop of Rome that John who had leaned on the breast of the Lord later became a priest, being both witness and teacher, and that he was buried in Ephesus.[31]

George Hamartolus (George the Sinful) really confirms the residence of John in Ephesus and his identity as author of the New Testament books bearing his name.

Philip Sidetes cannot be trusted as a witness.

It appears, therefore, that the tradition of Irenaeus is correct and that it is the same as that of Papias when the latter is properly understood. The supposed tradition of Papias concerning two Johns turns out to rest on the most precarious, if not preposterous, foundation—if, indeed, it can be called a foundation at all. One is not surprised that sober, unbiased scholarship such as that of Lightfoot, Westcott, and Plummer have rejected its validity. With the scarcity of evidence before us we may permit the ghostly "John the Presbyter" to make his exit and allow the true John of Zebedee to proceed in his apparently rightful place.

Another matter which should be cited as external evidence against John is the theory that John died at an early date. New Testament scholarship is practically unanimous in the opinion that Revelation was written during the rule of Domitian about A.D. 95 or 96. If John died in the seventh decade of the first century as some contend, he is automatically eliminated. The evidence of this early martyrdom does not bear close examination and leave much certainty. It rests chiefly on a supposed testimony of Papias.

The first literary fragment which supports this position was discovered in the last part of the nineteenth century. It is a fragment

---

from a Georgius Hamartolus, an obscure monk of the ninth century. The following is his testimony:

> Then after Domitian, Nerva reigned one year, who, having recalled John from the Island, permitted him to live at Ephesus. Being at that time the only one of the twelve disciples surviving, after having compiled his Gospel he was honored with martyrdom. For Papias, bishop of Hierapolis, being a personal associate of the same, in the second book of his "Sayings of the Lord," says that he was slain by the Jews, fulfilling clearly with his brother the prediction of Christ concerning them and their own confession and undertaking for him. For when the Lord said to them, "Are ye able to drink of the cup of which I drink?" and they willingly consented and agreed: "My cup," he says, "Ye shall drink, and with the baptism with which I am baptized shall ye be baptized." And so it came to pass, for it was impossible for God to lie. And thus also the much learned Origen in his commentary on Matthew maintains—that is, that John met martyrdom, contending that he had learned this from the successors of the apostles. And then indeed also the well-informed Eusebius in his Church History says, "Thomas received by lot Parthia, but John Asia, among whom also he lived out and culminated his life in Ephesus.

Dana[32] points out the evident weaknesses of the testimony. Hamartolus was confused and contradictory in his statements. First, he did not understand history. He opened the fragment with a statement that John was recalled by Nerva from Patmos and, having compiled his gospel, was martyred. This is all quite possible, but the testimony does not stop. Hamartolus cites as proof of John's martyrdom the testimony of Papias that John was killed by the Jews linking his death to that of James, his brother. Such a connection would place his death several decades before the time of Nerva. To make it even more confusing, Hamartolus adds the testimony of Eusebius that John lived out his life and died in Ephesus. In a few words, it appears that the monk would have us believe that: (1) John was recalled from Patmos by Nerva in the late nineties; (2) he was mar-

---

*This paragraph is a condensation of H. E. Dana, *The Ephesian Tradition*, pp. 156–158.

tyred with his brother James before the fall of Jerusalem in 70—about A.D. 44; (3) he lived out his days and died in Ephesus near the turn of the century. Such a position is absurd. Hamartolus did not understand that he was suggesting such a contradiction. The thing he wishes to present is that John died at Ephesus at the hands of the Jews after the beginning of Nerva's reign. It is very doubtful if he understood that the supposed testimony of Papias was a contradiction to this view. Second, Hamartolus misinterpreted the testimony of Origen. Origen said,

> The sons of Zebedee did certainly drink the cup and were baptized with the baptism, since Herod killed James, the brother of John, with the sword, and the Emperor of the Romans, as tradition records, banished John to the Island of Patmos, for approving the word of truth with his testimony. John himself hands down in the Apocalypse . . . the circumstances of his martyrdom.

It is clear that Origen knew nothing of the supposed testimony of Papias concerning an early death of John. Hamartolus' tendency to misrepresent Origen makes one hesitate to accept his representation of Papias. Certainly we do not wish to impeach the testimony of Irenaeus concerning John's death at Ephesus at a late date in favor of such a witness as this one.

The second documentary evidence pointing to this supposed testimony of Papias was discovered about the same time as the first but is apparently a much earlier testimony. This fragment is believed to be from an abridgment of a *History of Christianity* by a certain Philip of Side, of the fifth century. The following is the text:

> Papias, bishop of Hierapolis, being a hearer of John the divine, wrote five treatises on "The Sayings of the Lord," in which, in making a list of the Apostles, after Peter and John, Philip and Thomas and Matthew, he included in the list of the disciples of the Lord Aristion and another John, whom he called the "Elder." So some think that to this John belong the two short or general epistles, which are published in the name of John, on the ground that the ancients only accept the first epistle.

Some also falsely ascribe to him the Apocalypse. And Papias also errs concerning the millennium and Irenaeus after him. In his second book Papias says that John the divine and James his brother were slain by the Jews. This said Papias told as reported by the daughters of Philip that Barnabas, who was also nicknamed Justus, being challenged by the unbelievers, having drunk a potion in the name of Christ, was preserved unharmed. Then he also tells about other wonders, especially that one about the mother of Manaim who was raised from the dead by Christ, that they lived until the time of Hadrian.

Dana[33] analyzes the fragment viewing its weaknesses. An important element of strength in the fragment is supposed to be that it was produced by a Philip of Side as early as the fifth century. But this is only a case of probability since the origin of the work is obscure. And even if it did come from Philip of Side, he is not regarded as very reliable authority. Robertson assures us ". . . he was a wild historian, who filled nearly a thousand tomes (his history comprised 36 books, each containing numerous tomes) with treatises on geometry, astronomy and geography, all under the name of history, and was unable to preserve any chronological sequence."[34] It is hardly desirable to lay aside Eusebius of Caesarea and rely instead on Philip of Side.

This work, like that of Hamartolus, involves a contradiction. It begins by saying that John lived until the time of Polycarp and Papias, yet he associates John's death with that of James on the supposition that they were contiguous in time as well as circumstances. He mixes two strains of tradition: one, that John died in Jerusalem at the same time as James, A.D. 44; another, that John died in Ephesus near the turn of the century, A.D. 98–100. Since the two are mutually contradictory, which is to be believed? Reason demands that we believe that one which has the stronger traditional support—that is, that John lived out his days to old age and died in

---

[33]The following paragraph is a condensation from Dana, *The Ephesian Tradition*, pp. 161 f.

[34]A. T. Robertson, *Epochs in the Life of the Apostle John* (New York: Fleming H. Revell Company, 1935), p. 28.

Ephesus. This must be our position until stronger confirmation is found for the supposed Papias testimony.

Such external evidence is not at all convincing when compared with the external evidence favoring John as the author of the book. The witness from an external viewpoint is clearly on the side of John from the standpoint of date of tradition, number of witnesses, and quality of testimony.

b. Internal evidence against John the son of Zebedee.—Apparently one of the first critics to doubt that John the son of Zebedee wrote the Apocalypse was Dionysius. His doubts were based on an internal study of the book in comparison with the Fourth Gospel which he attributed to John. Before beginning his discussion, he suggested that there were some before him who had denied the apostolic authorship of Revelation on doctrinal grounds. They had denied it because they interpreted it literally and found in it the teaching of an earthly reign of Christ, which doctrine they did not believe. There was a man named Cerinthus, a heretic, who held to a materialistic conception of the kingdom. He looked for an earthly reign of Christ and, according to Dionysius, "as he was a lover of the body, and altogether sensual in those things which he so eagerly craved, he dreamed that he would revel in the gratification of the sensual appetite, i.e., in eating and drinking, and marrying. . . ."[85] Because of his materialistic views some had attributed this book to him. Dionysius demonstrated that these people were wrong in placing a literal interpretation on the book of Revelation, which view had led them to think that Cerinthus wrote the book. He maintained that the book was a worthy one and should not be set aside. He then put forward his own reasons for rejecting John the son of Zebedee as the writer of the book.[86] His reasons were:

1. The Evangelist (writer of the Fourth Gospel) does not prefix his name or mention it anywhere else, either in the Gospel or in his Epistle. On the other hand the writer of the Apocalypse mentions his name four times.

---

[85]Quoted by Eusebius, *Church History*, p. 297.
[86]Cf. Eusebius, *Church History*, pp. 297 ff.

2. The writer of the Gospel claimed to be the disciple especially loved by Jesus. The writer of the Apocalypse makes no such claim.

3. There were two other Epistles attributed to John and both were anonymously written by "the Elder." But in the epistle included in the Apocalypse the writer boldly declares himself, "John to the seven churches of Asia, grace and peace to you" (Revelation 1:4).

4. The form and complexion of the composition of the book of Revelation is very different from that of the Fourth Gospel.

On the basis of the above objections, Dionysius suggested a diversity of authorship of the traditionally Johannine books, but he admitted that it was all in the realm of hypothesis. Other critics since his day have not been so free to admit that it is in the realm of hypothesis.

The first three of Dionysius' objections are rather easily met; the fourth calls for much lengthier explanation. The Fourth Gospel was rather general. There was to be nothing especially gained by a pronouncement of authorship. At the same time it was not the custom in Gospel writing for the writer so to identify himself. A comparison of the New Testament Gospels reveals the truth of these statements. Of course, there are many critics who deny the traditional authorship of Matthew as well as John; but Mark and Luke, recognized by practically all critics as being authentic as to traditional authorship, do not identify their author. The false gospels of later Christian times (Protevangelium of James, Gospel of Peter, the Gospel of Thomas, for instance,) assigned names of supposed authors, but this was not true in the gospel-writing period of the New Testament.

The first epistle of John is not much like an epistle. It has some of the personal elements of an epistle, but at the same time it is more of a doctrinal treatise which would not need an autograph as an epistle would. In some ways it resembles a doctrinal treatise even more than Hebrews, which is the great New Testament example of this type of work. The second and third epistles are personal. They stand at the opposite extreme from 1 John. It was not personal enough to demand an autograph; these are so personal that they do not need an autograph other than the affectionate term "Elder" gained through long years of service. The "Elect Cyria" of the second epistle and "Gaius" of the third epistle need no more than the term "Elder" to recognize the one writing them the very personal letters received.

With an apocalypse the case was different. One thing that made the book so valuable to those who received it was a knowledge that it came from this one who had worked with them for so long and who now suffered with them in their persecution. This would be far more effective than a letter of comfort from an unknown source and without definite information as to whether the writer knew their condition and could properly comfort them. The Apocalypse needed the name of its writer to make it effective. John's other works did not.

By far the most of the controversy relative to the authorship of Revelation has been centered around the matter of style and grammar employed by the writer. This was Dionysius' main objection and he has been followed by a long train of critics who compare the book with the Fourth Gospel to prove or to disprove that the two were written by the same hand.

In reading the Greek text of the Fourth Gospel, one finds it written in simple Greek, with few departures from the literary language of the time. On turning to the book of Revelation, a different situation is confronted. The Greek is simple, but one is immediately struck with ungrammatical constructions more numerous and more marked than in any other part of the New Testament. These cannot be considered here in detail. The ones most frequently noted are: the neglect of the ordinary rules of agreement and case structure such as a nominative as object of a verb or an accusative as subject of a sentence, and the repetition of the personal pronoun after the relative—this is after the manner of the Hebrew writers. To read the smooth grammar of the Fourth Gospel in conjunction with the uneven constructions of Revelation inclines one to believe that they were not written by the same hand. But this is not necessarily true. We could see how the same man wrote the two books if it could be demonstrated that he wrote Revelation about twenty-five or thirty years before he wrote the Gospel, and had learned more about Greek in the interim. This is the position taken by some who place Revelation during the Neronian persecution and the Gospel about A.D. 95. But the position is very insecure when we consider the preponderance of evidence favoring a late date for Revelation. Smith[37] tries to solve the difficulty by placing the Gospel about A.D. 78 and Revelation about A.D. 96, after the vigor of manhood had departed and the author lapsed into the language of youth; hence, the mistakes. This is not very satisfactory, especially when we consider that the Fourth Gospel must have been written about A.D. 95 or 96, the same as Revelation.

The most plausible explanation for the bad grammar of Revelation is found in the consideration of surroundings and mental condition. This appears to be about the best explanation: John wrote the Gospel while he was in Ephesus. He wrote with cool, deliberate intent to show that Jesus was the Christ. He had many competent Greek friends who could help him in his language difficulties or correct his errors when they were made. On the other hand, he was alone on the isle of Patmos when he wrote Revelation. There was no one to help him or correct his bad grammar. Besides this, he wrote under quite different circumstances, both physically and mentally. He was exiled from the people to whom he had preached for about twenty-five years. It was "the Lord's Day"—the day of Christian worship. John was looking across the sea which separated him from his "little children" who were being sorely persecuted and who needed him. He longed to comfort them but could not. While thus filled by the Spirit with a desire to help his people, he heard a triumphant (trumpet-like) voice speaking behind him. He turned to see the owner of the voice. He saw his Lord, whom he had last seen ascending to the Father from the Mount of Olives about sixty years ago. It was the same Lord, yet different. He was glorified and transcendent. With the voice of authority (a voice like the voice of many waters) he said to John: "Stop fearing. I am no ghost. They killed me but I am still alive. I hold the keys of Death and Destiny. I will give you a message which you may send to your churches—a

[37]Smith, *The American Commentary on the New Testament*, VII, Part III, ii.

message of comfort, assurance, victory. Write what you see and hear and send it to the broken churches of Asia." The voice ceased, the vision began, and John wrote. In the heat of excitement of writing, he forgot to be particular about case sequence and relative pronouns in their proper usage. He wrote just as he would have spoken had he been in the churches, speaking with no one to interrupt the progress of his message to correct an error in grammar. It is not likely that the Christians, when they received such a message, would have felt free to correct it in John's absence. Their reverence for it was too great; so it was passed on from one to another to let even its bad grammar speak an intense message of comfort, assurance, and certain victory to all who read it. This explanation is the most satisfactory one which I have found. It explains the peculiar syntax of the book whether it was written by the author of the Fourth Gospel or not.

There are other things which call for a different style in writing the book. It was natural that the gorgeous visions which passed visibly and rapidly before him, filling him with rapture, gave to John's style a form and coloring which would not appear when the writer was in a more calm and deliberate frame of mind. Too, there is new subject matter; subject matter which differs widely from anything else in the New Testament. It more nearly resembles portions of the Old Testament. While, therefore, we find many words and expressions in Revelation that remind us of John, it is not strange that we find much in the phraseology that is new, with Hebraisms originating in the fact that often the visions and imagery of the ancient Hebrew prophets are reproduced in his own.

The differences between the Gospel and Revelation have really been very much exaggerated. Even the most radical critics recognize that there are certain indisputable signs of connection between them. There are several characteristic Greek terms of frequent occurrence in both. Revelation contains such characteristic Johannine expressions as water of life, vine, shepherd, victory, light, darkness, and others. This abundance of internal evidence supports a strong traditional testimony to the effect that John wrote both books. "If, however, one must surrender the theory of common authorship, the balance of traditional evidence turns the Apocalypse to the Apostle."[38]

2. Evidence for and Against Other Suggested Authors

The work of Charles and others has indicated that Revelation was not written pseudonymously. This leaves us with the fact that the book was written by some person named John. John was, of course, a very common name at that time. But the manner in which this writer speaks of himself indicates that he was a John well known in Christian circles in the last decade of the first century A.D. Three Johns have been suggested as possible authors of the book—John the son of Zebedee, John Mark, and the elder John of Ephesus. John the son of Zebedee has been discussed. It remains that a few things be said about the other two.

(1) John Mark was first mentioned by Dionysius of Alexandria, but he promptly sets him aside on the score of his un-Asiatic career. He has been suggested by such critics as Hitzig, Weisse, Hausrath, and Beza. Their claims for him have proved worthless because of the lack of evidence that John Mark worked in Asia and because of the radical differences between Mark's Gospel and Revelation—differences much more marked and impossible to be reconciled than those between the Fourth Gospel and Revelation. Too, Mark is well substantiated in New Testament criticism as the author of the Second Gospel.

(2) John the Elder, or presbyter, has been the real rival of John of Zebedee for this position. It has been indicated previously that this shadowy John may be completely eliminated from the picture. It is difficult to get one's consent to believe that there were two men who were named John, were personal disciples of Jesus, went to Ephesus after Jerusalem was destroyed, and became so prominent in Christian affairs in Ephesus that men of their own generation could not tell them apart. But if we do not eliminate Elder John from existence by manipulation of Papias' testimony, we still have two great problems to face. First, we do not know what kind of writing the Elder John would have done if he had engaged in writing. All our evidence

[38]Dana, *New Testament Criticism*, p. 312.

78

must be from silence; and this type of evidence by itself can never be convincing. Second, we do know that there are many similarities between the content of this book and what we know of John the son of Zebedee.

Conclusion: Fairness seems to demand that we accept John the son of Zebedee as the author of this book. It is readily recognized that there are difficulties involved in this position. But when all evidences are weighed, there are far more difficulties in the way of rejecting than of accepting. So we accept the traditional position as being favorably supported by external and internal evidence, and recognize John the apostle as the author.

II. THE DATE OF REVELATION

All critics agree that Revelation was written during a period of severe persecution in the first century. Early tradition assigned the book to Domitian's reign and persecution. The persecution under Nero has been held by many as being the time of writing. Some have suggested the reign of Vespasian as the background. Modern opinion is swinging back to the Domitianic persecution for reasons that will be cited later. It is necessary to discuss all these periods in order to determine the most likely time of writing.

1. The Neronian date has been held by many critics throughout the history of the New Testament criticism.

(1) The evidences for this date are of an internal nature. Some hold that chapter eleven indicates that the Temple at Jerusalem was still standing; therefore, the book had to be written before A.D. 70.

The book was written during persecution, and it is a well-known fact that Nero persecuted the Christians.

Weigall[20] makes out a case for the Neronian date, or shortly afterward in the reign of Galba, on the basis that Nero is the one pictured in this book as the beast whose number is 666.

(2) There are many objections to the Neronian date. In the first place, one cannot safely hold that chapter eleven indicates that the

---

[20]Arthur Weigall, *Nero* (New York: G. P. Putnam's Sons, 1930), pp. 3 f. and 394 f.

Temple was still standing. The book is written in such symbolical terms that we cannot be positive that the Temple was still standing, especially when the preponderance of evidence points to a later date.

Many evidences forbid that the book was written during the Neronian persecution. Revelation clearly indicates that the Christians were being persecuted because they refused to worship the emperor. There was no such demand during the time of Nero. He persecuted Christians to divert from himself to others the blame for burning the city of Rome. Popular suspicion held that he himself was the author of the great fire which had just destroyed a large part of the city; as the culprit, he brought forward the Christians, who were hated by the populace, and inflicted upon them the most excruciating tortures. They were ferreted out in great numbers for this crime, but no mention is made of persecution for refusal to worship the emperor. The Neronian persecution was confined to Rome; it never reached the other parts of the empire. Exile is never mentioned as a form of punishment during the Neronian period; it was far too mild for the pagan city.

The internal condition of the churches forbids an early date. Some of these churches had been organized only a few years when the Neronian persecution came. It is impossible that such rapid growth and development had taken place.

Weigall's case for the Neronian date is insecure. For one thing, he adopts it out of prejudice against the traditional attitudes held by historians concerning Nero. He attempts to prove that if historians had not been prejudiced by uninformed Christians, Nero would never have been looked upon as the terrible tyrant which history pictures him to be. Weigall overlooks many important things to carry his point. Too, he is guilty of overstatement when he says that scholarship is pretty well unanimous, that the number 666 is a cryptograph for "Neron Kaisar" (Greek) reduced to "Nron Ksr" (Hebrew) reduced to the numbers 50, 200, 6, 50, 100, 60, and 200 which add up to 666. Scholarship is far from unanimous on this. Those who hold this opinion appear to be in the minority.

Finally, as an objection to the Neronian date, we find that while there are no real witnesses in the early church who hold to this date, there are many who hold to the Domitianic date. These will be discussed subsequently.

2. The reign of Vespasian (69–79) has been suggested as the time of writing of this book. This date has only one point of evidence and that is of an internal nature. In Revelation 17:9–11 we find: "Here is the mind that hath wisdom. The seven heads are seven mountains, on which the woman sitteth: and they are seven kings; the five are fallen, the one is, the other is not yet come; and when he cometh, he must continue a little while. And the beast that was, and is not, is also an eighth, and is of the seven; and he goeth into perdition."

This is evidently a discussion of the emperors of the Roman Empire. Our big problem is, Are the numbers literal, and if so, with which emperor do they start? Usually the numbers in Revelation are symbolical, but here they appear to be literal and to serve as the author's interpretation of his own symbol. In popular apprehension the first Roman emperor was Julius Caesar; in strict constitutional law, the first who held the empire as an established form of government was Augustus. The series of "kings" might legitimately begin with either of these but not with one later. Apparently John begins with Augustus and gives the following sequence: "Five are fallen" = Augustus, Tiberius, Caligula, Claudius, and Nero; "one is" = Vespasian; "one who is to come for a little while" = Titus, who ruled for only two years; "the beast who was and is not is also an eighth and is of the seven" = Domitian, who was pictured as the reincarnation of Nero; his was a revival of the same type of work as that of Nero but was much more intense and widespread. This plan omits Galba, Otho, and Vitellius, but they ruled for a brief time each and were never recognized as emperors by the provinces. Thus the one who was pictured as reigning ("the one who is") was Vespasian, A.D. 69–79. After him Titus was to reign two years; after him, the flood of persecution—Nero reincarnated, so to speak, in Domitian with full satanic power to bring everything evil upon the Christians and the State. This appears to settle the question and date the book during the rule of Vespasian. But all the other evidence is opposed to this position. Vespasian did not persecute the

Christians, and every bit of evidence, external and internal, points away from him. Verse ten points to Vespasian, but verse eleven points to an unnamed eighth who was one of the seven already mentioned. Two solutions are suggested: First, the writer of both verses, writing in the Domitian period, throws himself back into the Vespasian age, representing history under the form of apocalyptic prophecy so as to deceive the Romans as to the real time of writing. Second, verse eleven (Domitian recalling and playing the part of Nero) represents a later addition, inserted to bring the work up to date. Due to the fact already cited that all the evidence points to the writing of the work in the Domitianic period, it appears that the first of the two solutions is the proper one. In either case the final standpoint is Domitianic, and this is consistent with the general evidence of the rest of the book.[40]

Weigall[41] begins with Augustus and follows with Tiberius, Caligula, Claudius, and Nero as the five who had fallen. He continues in direct succession with Galba as "the one who is" and Otho as the "one who is not yet come." "The eighth" he makes to be Nero again in view of the Nero redivivus myth. Two fallacies are noted. Historically, Weigall is wrong because Galba was never recognized by the provinces as the emperor. He is also wrong in taking the position that John believed the Nero redivivus myth. He did not believe it. He adapts it to his usage to illustrate the evil of Domitian.

Tertullian was so sure that the book was written during the reign of Domitian that he begins with Domitian as the "one who is" and reasons forward and backward. He commits several historical blunders in doing so. His system makes Galba the *first* Roman emperor—that is unforgivable! His system also makes Trajan the reincarnation of wicked Nero. That is unhistorical, to say the least, since Trajan was, according to the unanimous tradition of antiquity, the best of the Roman emperors. Tertullian's theory is worthless except as it reflects the belief of the day that the book was written under Domitian.

---

[40]The theory here outlined is followed by Swete, Beckwith, Hengstenberg, *American Commentary*, Dana, Pieters, and *Expositor's Greek Testament*.

[41]Weigall, *op. cit.*, p. 395.

3. The Domitian period is the date most generally accepted by New Testament criticism for the writing of Revelation. This is the traditional date going back to a time near the writing of the book. Irenaeus V. 30.3 says that the book was written at the end of the rule of Domitian. Origen says that John wrote the book while exiled on Patmos, no doubt holding the tradition of the Domitianic exile though he does not name the emperor. Victorious says John wrote what he saw while on the isle of Patmos at the order of Domitian. This same position was held by Hippolytus, Clement of Alexandria, Hegesippus, and Jerome. This indicates the belief of the early church that the book was written during the Domitianic persecution.

The general situation presupposed by the book is consistent with this early tradition. The condition of the Asian churches is that of a period considerably later than the death of Nero. Their inner life has undergone many changes since Paul's ministry in Ephesus and even since the writing of the epistles to the Ephesians, the Colossians, and the two epistles to Timothy at Ephesus. Deterioration has set in at Ephesus, and at Sardis and Laodicea faith is dying or dead. The Nicolaitan party, of which there is no certain trace in Paul's epistles, is now widely distributed and firmly rooted. Of course, these evils can grow rapidly, especially in a pagan environment, but it is hardly to be expected that they could grow so fast in a period of four or five years. They would have to do this for the book to represent true conditions and fall into the Neronian period. The character of the heresies described in chapters two and three presupposes an acquaintance with incipient gnosticism which requires a later period than A.D. 70 for its development.

The persecution of the Christians which is reflected in the book fits the Domitianic period alone. There were several periods of persecution of a sort. Caligula (c. 41), the "mad emperor," carried on some religious persecution; Claudius (c. 52) drove the Christians from Rome because of their conflict with the Jews; Nero (c. 64-68) carried on intense persecution in Rome for reasons already cited; very little persecution was carried on by Vespasian (c. 69-79); Domitian (c. 81-96) is the emperor who has gone down in history as the one who bathed the empire in the blood of the Christians.

His persecution was for the purpose of enforcing emperor worship. Strange as the ascription of divinity to an emperor may seem to our thought, the religious conceptions of the ancient Gentile world presented no obstacle to such apotheosis. Polytheism, with its gradation of rank among the divinities, made easy the deification of men whose office, power, or achievements so far surpassed the ordinary as to appear superhuman. Julius Caesar boldly claimed divine honor and placed his statue among those of the gods in the temples. Augustus forbade the offering of divine honors to himself in Rome; yet he accepted the title "Augustus," hitherto the epithet of the gods, and in the provinces he sanctioned temples to himself in conjunction with the goddess Roma. The cult thus established continued through the following reigns, varying somewhat in the emphasis laid upon it according to the disposition of the respective emperors, but gradually becoming an essential factor in the imperial religious system.

It is in the reign of Domitian that we reach an insistence upon emperor worship more threatening and more vehement than before. This emperor, who, because of his infamous career, failed to receive the honor of apotheosis from the Senate at his death, was strenuous in claiming divinity in his life; to his subordinates he became *"deus et dominus."* According to Suetonius, he began his letters, "Our Lord and God commands that it should be done so and so," and formally decreed that no one should address him otherwise, either in writing or by word of mouth. He had images of himself erected throughout the empire to make this worship more convenient. According to Cassius, when Nerva became emperor, one of his first acts was to have the very numerous gold and silver images of Domitian melted and turned to better usage. According to Pliny, Domitian regarded any slight to his gladiators or resistance to his officers as an act of impiety toward his divinity. Pliny continues his discussion by stating that Domitian raised himself above all the other gods and chose for his statues the most hallowed sites in the temple and caused entire hosts of victims to be sacrificed for refusal to worship him.

Hence, it is self-evident that, under Domitian, Christianity had to enter a struggle of life or death with the imperial power, which always claimed, even in the hands of the most discreet possessors, more than Christians could yield. A sharp collision was inevitable. The forms of punishment were many. Some were put to death, some were exiled, some were tortured into a confession of the divinity of the emperor, some had their property confiscated, some received combinations of these measures. All this is very plainly reflected in the book of Revelation. The major portion of this punishment fell on Asia Minor because that was the main stronghold of Christianity after A.D. 70. It is natural that since the majority of the Christians were there, the majority of the resistance to emperor worship would be there, and hence the brunt of the punishment would fall upon Asia Minor. This is reflected not only in the book of Revelation but also in other works concerning that period. Revelation was God's word of cheer to the Christians under these conditions.

The Nero redivivus myth is another evidence for the Domitian period. This myth, which will be discussed in detail later, held that Nero did not actually die from his self-inflicted wounds but escaped to the East, where he was appreciated by the Parthians, and that he was gathering an army to come back and take possession of Rome. This myth took several years to develop; so it could not fit the Neronian period but could be well enough established by the Domitian period to be successfully used for the purpose of illustration by John in Revelation.

It is clear, then, that for all that respects the conflict of the world power with the kingdom of Christ, we obtain an excellent historical starting point when we understand Revelation to have been composed under Domitian, while such is entirely wanting on any other hypothesis. Thus the death of Domitian (c. 96) is our *"terminus ad quem"*; a *"terminus a quo"* is supplied by the date of his accession (c. 81) but the superior limit may with great probability be pushed forward to about A.D. 94–96 since Domitian's jealous insistence on his claims to divine honors and his encouragement of the delators (spies) belong to the later years of his reign. We feel safe in this position since we have such strong external and internal evidence supporting it.

III. The Recipients of Revelation

The text of Revelation indicates that the book is addressed to "the seven churches that are in Asia . . . unto Ephesus, and unto Smyrna, and unto Pergamum, and unto Thyatira, and unto Sardis, and unto Philadelphia, and unto Laodicea" (1:4, 11). This gives a key to the identity of the recipients, but we are not to suppose that the book was restricted to these churches. The use of the number "7," which is the symbolical number for completeness, indicates that the book was for all the churches of Asia Minor. The seven were selected because they were representative of all the churches of Asia Minor. The conditions reflected in these churches were to be found in the other churches as well. The seven were to serve as messengers to make this Revelation known to all their sister churches. All the seven cities stood on the great circular road that bound together the most populous, wealthy, and influential part of the province, the west-central region. They were the best points on the circuit to serve as centers of communication with seven districts: Pergamum for the north, Thyatira for an inland district on the northeast and east, Sardis for the wide middle valley of the Hermus, Philadelphia for upper Lydia, Laodicea for the Lycus valley, Ephesus for the lower Maeander valleys and coasts, and Smyrna for the North Ionian coasts. Planted at these seven centers, Revelation would spread through the neighborhoods, and from thence to the rest of the province. The route prescribed provided for the circulation of the book through all the churches of the province and beyond it.

Speaking generally, then, the book of Revelation was directed to the Christians of Asia Minor. Its first message was for them. Its message is universal. The same message of victory and triumph is to characterize Christians in every age until "the kingdom of the world is become the kingdom of our God and of his Christ."

The condition of the Christians who first received Revelation was very critical. Christianity had remained for several decades unnoticed by the Roman Government. It had been regarded as a part of the Jewish religion, which was a legalized religion of Rome.

When it became known that Christianity was not just a new patch on the old garment of Judaism, the Christians found themselves in difficulty with the government as well as with their fellow men. There are several reasons[42] for the antagonism directed against the Christians.

(1) Christianity was an illegal religion—*religio illicita.* The Roman Government tolerated the religions of conquered provinces. They gave to the conquered people the right to place an image of their deity in the Hall of the Gods if they so desired. So long as the religion did not try to proselyte, it was thus legal. But the Christian religion could not thus be bound down. Its very purpose is that of making Christians of other people. For this reason it was outlawed.

(2) Christianity aspired to universality. With the Romans the State was the main thing; with the Christians the kingdom of God throughout the whole earth was the main thing. Christians had no sympathy with the idea that religion was to be promoted only as an aid to the State. Their position set them up as dangerous rivals of the best interest of the State.

(3) Christianity was an exclusive religion. Its adherents refused to mingle freely with heathen social life and customs. It was necessary for them to refuse intercourse with the pagan world because of the idolatrous practices in which the Romans engaged. Their refusal to go to idol temples and their refusal to have idols in their homes caused them to be looked upon as enemies to the gods. Nothing was too bad to be believed of such people.

(4) They were accused of all manner of evils. They were known to hold secret services at night, and they were observed to be very fond of one another. The Romans put these facts together and decided that these meetings were for the gratification of lust on a large scale. When they heard Christians speak of "eating flesh and drinking blood" (references to the Lord's

---

These reasons are condensed from Allen, *op. cit.,* pp. 59–63, and A. H. Newman, *A Manual of Church History* (Philadelphia: The American Baptist Publication Society, 1899), I, 148–150.

Supper), they accused them of cannibalism—eating the bodies and drinking the blood of the offspring of their orgies. Most of the persecution which the Christians received grew out of this popular hatred and misunderstanding.

(5) The Christians refused to go to war.[43] There were two reasons for this according to Tertullian. First, a part of the oath and initiation of the soldiers included service to the idols of the State and the wearing of idolatrous insignia on their uniforms. Second, Christ had taken their sword from them and had given them the ways of peace. But whatever their reason, the populace hated them and accused them of being traitors.

(6) Christians were recruited chiefly from the poor and the outcast. This caused Christianity to be looked down upon by those who regarded themselves as the "respectable."

(7) Christians shared with the Jews the contempt which the Romans held for this people; because of their refusal to compromise, they were regarded as worse than the Jews.

(8) Christians were looked upon as wild fanatics because of their enthusiasm. They shocked the sensibilities of the passive philosophers of the day.

(9) Christianity came in conflict with the temporal interest of many of the Romans—priests, makers, and venders of sacrificial animals.

(10) Christians refused to worship the emperor. If they had been content to worship the emperor as the chief deity of the empire, they would have been tolerated. But they could not say that the Kurios Caesar was superior to their Kurios Christ. Therefore, persecution and martyrdom became their lot. Domitian tried to annihilate altogether this recalcitrant and traitorous faith. Because of their attitude toward the Roman gods, the Christians were blamed with all the calamities which befell the empire. If there was no rain, the Christians were blamed for offending the deities. If there was a flood on the Tiber, the Christians were blamed. A famine, an earthquake, military reversals—all were blamed on the Christians.

[43]*Ante-Nicene Church Fathers,* III, pp. 98 f.

The verdict of the imperial government was that this seditious religious group must be destroyed in order to safeguard the permanence and integrity of the empire. This policy of the government to exterminate Christianity was by itself a sufficient menace to have brought despair to the hearts of the baffled churches, but this was not all. While this danger threatened without, another fierce monster stalked within in the form of pernicious heresy. The heresy of Judaism combined with that of Gnosticism which expressed itself practically in Antinomianism to produce bewilderment, controversy, and dissension to destroy fellowship and threaten to destroy the permanence of Christianity. For the deepest appreciation and clearest understanding of Revelation we must keep this in mind. When people were being killed, exiled, and robbed of all their property for refusal to renounce their religion, when evils were threatening to strike a death blow within the church, is there any hope for the future? Revelation is God's answer to this question.

The relation of John to these Christians is such as to qualify him as the medium for this Revelation. He went to Ephesus after the destruction of Jerusalem in A.D. 70 or shortly before during the Jewish rebellion about A.D. 65–70. He was the leading Christian in Asia Minor for the next twenty-five years. He knew their condition. Large numbers of them were no doubt converted under his ministry. They had shared in the joyous experiences which had come. Now they were sharing the affliction and tribulation which had come upon all Christians. John was exiled when he received the vision and when he wrote the book. With tender regard for the churches and agony of heart over their condition, he was gazing in their direction with such questions in his mind as: What will be the outcome? Will Christianity fail? Has God lost his power? Why does God not intervene? when the transcendent Christ appeared to "unveil" the future events for him. "In such a frame of mind one is able to catch the note of sobbing sympathy, yet triumphant faith which pervades this entire book."[44]

—————

[44]Dana, *Epistles and Apocalypse of John*, p. 94.

IV. THE CONDITIONS IN THE ROMAN EMPIRE[45]

Since Revelation pictures the Roman State in conflict with the Christian church, it is well to get a clear picture of this great enemy to the church. During the last part of the first century A.D., the period in which Revelation was written, Rome was near the zenith of her greatness. Her boundaries extended from the British Isles to the African desert, and from the Atlantic Ocean to the Euphrates. The city of Rome is pictured in Revelation 17:1 as a harlot sitting "upon many waters"; these waters are identified in Revelation 17:15 as "peoples, multitudes, and nations, and tongues." The people over whom Rome ruled were many. To the people of that day it seemed that Rome was the whole world.

The empire was bound together by large and well-trained armies. The distant frontiers were characterized by garrisons of experienced soldiers schooled in the discipline of Roman army life. The fear of the Roman legions had spread far; they seemed invincible. They were the ones who made possible the city of wealth and luxury which was the capital of the world.

Rome was built on two things: conquest and commerce. The great system of highways made possible the wide commerce of the day. A view of this is reflected in Revelation 18:11-14 where over thirty different articles of trade are mentioned in the weeping of the merchants over the destruction of the city. These articles represented trade relations with Spain, the Red Sea, Tyre, North Africa, Central Africa, India, East Asia, Arabia, Egypt, Gaul, and the Danube lands. Most of the trade thus carried on consisted of articles of luxury or slaves, things which only the rich could buy. What a picture we have here of the vast wealth of the city of Rome! The palaces of the rich were dazzling in their beauty. Men rivaled one with another in extravagances. Caligula spent $500,000 on one

---

[45]This section is largely from Allen, *op. cit.*, pp. 27-53, E. G. Hardy, *Christianity and the Roman Government* (New York: The Macmillan Company, 1925), pp. 68-77, and W. M. Ramsay, *The Church in the Roman Empire* (New York: G. P. Putnam's Sons, 1912), pp. 274-290.

banquet. A patriot gave a dinner in Nero's honor and spent $160,-
000 for roses alone. The main banquet hall in Nero's famous Golden
House was circular and revolved day and night in imitation of the
heavenly bodies. Slaves were everywhere to assist their masters and
help to show off their lord's riches. Many of them were far more
cultured and educated than the men who owned them.

The women were not to be outdone by the men. Fashionable
women of Rome had a different slave to apply each separate shade
of color used on cheeks, lips, or eyebrows. The jewels which they
wore were so costly that Seneca, Nero's teacher and friend, cynically
remarked that some of the wealthy ladies wore two or three estates
suspended from their ears! Caligula's wife wore a set of emeralds
valued at two million dollars.

In contrast with such wealth and extravagance there was much
dire poverty. There was no work for hire; the slaves did that kind
of work. The idle poor swarmed to the capital to be fed by the
enormous dole system and to be amused by the many interesting
things of the city life.

Such conditions were conducive to bad morals. The picture of the
moral conditions of the Roman life can hardly be painted in colors
too dark. The teachers of the day were inconsistent; they taught
purity and lived immorally. Seneca taught contempt for material
wealth, yet amassed over twelve million dollars in a few years. He
preached purity of morals but was openly accused of adultery and
worse and made no attempt to deny it. The pupils were like their
teachers in their living. The moral depravity of the day is so well
reflected in the first chapter of Romans that we do not like to read
it publicly. According to their own testimonies the Romans cast
away everything that was good and honorable. Crimes were multiplied; vice made no attempt to hide; a monstrous contest of lust and
wickedness was carried on. Marriage came to be a commercial
transaction easily effected and as easily dissolved. Seneca said there
were women who counted their years not by the number of consuls
but by the number of their husbands. Marriage was held in such
contempt that laws against celibacy had to be passed. Children were
a burden, and they were left to the slaves for rearing or were sold as

slaves themselves. Naturally the Christians looked with abhorrence upon such conditions. They saw their religion about to be crushed by such a system and wondered about the outcome of it. Revelation was badly needed to assure them of victory.

Rome was not only the center of government and wealth, it was the headquarters of religion as well. The religion of the day was a mixture of fear, superstition, and ceremony. The majority of the people believed in the existence of gods, but their confidence was shaken when their gods failed to help them. Form and ceremony had occupied a large part of the religion of the day. For many years the failure of their religion in a practical way had led to a breakdown in the old religions. Christianity had found this condition to be fertile soil and had realized great harvests from the sowing of the seed. But in the background of the Roman law was the fact that the emperor was considered divine. Some of the emperors capitalized on this; others did not. At the period of the empire in which we are interested there was being fostered a new emphasis on this old idea. Domitian delighted in being looked upon as divine and in being so worshiped. To the Christian such homage was idolatry and an utter denial of faith in Christ. To the Romans the refusal to worship the emperor was a sign of disloyalty to the State and an act of treason. Emperor worship was forced upon the Christians as a test of their loyalty to the State. At first Christians were called upon to perform the ceremonies of loyal service and worship to the emperor—the placing of a pinch of incense upon the altar. To refuse was disloyalty; to agree was to prove that one was not a Christian. There were many who saw in this meaningless act no harm done to their Christian faith and performed it so as to escape punishment. These were practically ostracized by their fellow Christians for denying the faith. As the demand for emperor worship grew, Christians were outlawed as a body as soon as their adherence to the sect became known. Detailed methods were worked out to enforce the State religion and to punish the Christians.

There was appointed an official body known as the *"praefectus urbi"* for the enforcing of worship in each town. These were responsible for punishing people in the various cities over a province.

The group with the greatest authority was the *concilia*[46] composed of deputies sent from the various towns or divisions of a province. Their duty was to build images of the emperor, altars for his worship, and in every way sponsor the state religion and make it effective. They forced the people to worship the emperor, identified all who did, and punished in various ways all who refused. Many Christians were beheaded, some were exiled, and others had all their property confiscated and were reduced to poverty. All this is perhaps reflected in Revelation 13:5. The purpose of Revelation is in the background of all that has been said as to the Christians, their condition, and their need. It is to show that so great a power as Rome was doomed to overthrow, that in the end the kingdom of God would triumph and Christ would reign supreme. It is to present a ringing call to maintain loyalty to the faith at all costs, even in the face of martyrdom.

This message is peculiarly relevant today—the call to choose the eternal rather than the temporal; to resist temptation, to refuse to compromise with pagan secularism, to place the claim of conscience above all demands against it; to cherish the confidence of ultimate victory for the kingdom of God, not only in the reign of Domitian but also in every other chaotic period of world history, including the twentieth century.

---

[46]Hardy, *op. cit.*, p. 72.

PART TWO

INTERPRETATION

Introduction

Revelation is a series of apocalyptic images given to John by the Holy Spirit to set forth Christ as eternally victorious over all world conditions and thus to encourage the Christians of John's day and every succeeding day until the return of our Lord. It is a message of warning to the church to keep itself pure and free from worldly entanglements. It is a message of warning to the enemies of the church that the church through Christ will eventually triumph and that all who oppose it will find themselves broken by the righteous power of God. The book is a message of comfort for those who sorrow; it reveals freedom from sorrow and pain in God's own time. It is a message of hope for those who are discouraged; it tells them to lift up heads and hearts since God has not abdicated his throne in favor of anyone or any power. It is a book peculiarly adapted to any age of great trouble and perplexity.

The structure of the book is a most interesting study. One's approach to the book determines his treatment of the structure. Some interpreters have divided the book into two general sections—chapters 1-11 and chapters 12-22. Some have held that chapters 12-22 constitute a second book and present the message of the "little book" of 10:1-11. Its message is the one which John is told to deliver to other peoples, nations, tongues, and kings. Whether or not the book should be divided at this point remains a moot question. There is a change in the tempo of the work here. The action is much more rapid as it begins in chapter 12 to build in intensity until the climax of victory is reached in the closing chapters.

Some interpreters have felt that the book should be divided into seven parts, exclusive of preface and conclusion. They find the complete number "7" appearing even in the structure of the book. For instance, Moulton[1] presents in sevenfold approach The Throne, The Seals, The Trumpets, The Triumph, The Bowls, The Word of God, The New Jerusalem, with prologue and epilogue. In similar fashion Dana[2] presents, with prologue and epilogue, seven episodes built around the symbols and suggesting Majesty, Judgment, Warning, Conflict, Retribution, Consummation, Destiny. He further divides each of the first six episodes into seven parts and divides the last episode into two parts—the wicked and the redeemed.

From the very beginning of the book the action is dominated by the Christ, who is presented as the Lamb that had been slain but still lived. For this reason the present work is so divided as to present this Christ as central. It is through the *redeeming* Lamb that victory comes to the people of God—"Worthy is the Lamb."

Preface, 1:1–8

The opening words of the book state that this is "the revelation of Jesus Christ." The thought of the writer is that this is a revelation which belongs to Christ and which is revealed by him to the readers. He is the Revealer as well as the One who is revealed in the book. In the book he is unveiled and disclosed to human view. John, then, did not look upon this as the "Revelation of John" as our common versions indicate. In other Jewish apocalypses the revelation is ascribed to some great man of Israel: Abraham, Ezra, Moses, Enoch, Baruch, etc. John ascribes this revelation directly to the Christ who reveals it; John is only the scribe. The message is that of the *risen* Lord, and John wants that clearly understood by the churches. Only this understanding can help them to receive the message of hope and comfort here afforded them. This is a message which God gave to Christ to show or demonstrate to his servants.

This is an uncovering of "the things which it is necessary to come to pass shortly." The nature of the kingdom of God is such that it

[1] R. G. Moulton, *The Modern Reader's Bible* (New York: The Macmillan Company, 1920), pp. 378–388.

[2] H. E. Dana, *The Epistles and Apocalypse of John*, pp. 95–98.

cannot suffer defeat. When John was on Patmos, it appeared that it was going to suffer defeat unless God intervened quickly. This is a message to say that God is coming to the rescue of his people shortly. The Greek construction has been discussed in connection with the futurist method[8] of interpreting this book. A brief restatement of the matter is sufficient here. The verb translated "it is necessary" or "must" is an impersonal verb which indicates that a moral necessity is involved; the nature of the case is such that the things revealed here *must* come to pass shortly. The aorist tense of the infinitive "to come to pass" adds to the truth that immediate action is necessary. The prepositional phrase translated "shortly" means just what it says—shortly, quickly, hastily. Two or three thousand years will be too late. The things revealed here must happen shortly, or the cause will be lost—Domitian will stamp out Christianity completely. Any attempt to make this phrase mean no more than "certainty" fails to meet the situation which is confronted by the churches. They were in need of assurance of help in the immediate present—not in some millennium of the distant and uncertain future.

The revelation was "signified" by Christ through his angel to his servant John. The word translated "signified" means to show by signs. Thus we are introduced to the nature of the book. It is a revelation (unveiling) of God's message through signs (symbols). This must be kept in mind and followed if the truth of the book is to be known. Its message comes not through literal understanding of its words but through the interpretation of the symbols. It is a divine picture book.

The human agent for giving this book to the churches is John. He will further identify himself as the contemporary of his readers in verse 9. For the present he identifies himself as the John who has previously borne witness to the Word of God. This is a typical Johannine conception of the incarnate Christ (John 1:1-18).

Blessings are pronounced upon those who rightly receive this message. The word "blessed" is one which denotes the blessed condition of a person because of the inner spiritual life of the person involved. It is parallel with the word used in the first Psalm to de-

⁸Cf. p. 32.

scribe the godly man. It is the same word used by Jesus in the Beatitudes of Matthew 5. This is the first of a series of beatitudes in Revelation:

1:3 —"Blessed is he that readeth and those that hear."

14:13—"Blessed are the dead who die in the Lord."

16:15—"Blessed is he that watcheth and keepeth his garments."

19:9 —"Blessed are they that are bidden to the marriage supper."

20:6 —"Blessed and holy is he that hath a part in the first resurrection."

22:7 —"Blessed is he that keepeth the words of the prophecy of this book."

22:14—"Blessed are they that wash their robes."

These magnificent beatitudes open with the receiving of the revelation of Christ and close with the washing of the robes and the entrance into the Holy City. The qualitative idea is present in all of them. In this first one the reference is to the manner of making known the revelation to the churches by public reading. Blessings are pronounced upon the reader, the hearers who hear with understanding (this is the significance of the grammatical construction) and those keeping the things written in the book. John had before his eyes the churches of Asia. There can be no question but that the book was, first of all, for the Christians at the close of the first century.

The closing statement of the third verse, "for the time is at hand," is a restatement of the truth that the message is an unveiling of events which are to take place shortly. This does not mean that every detail of the book is to see an immediate fulfilment. The interval of time between the beginning of relief for the Christians and the final consummation was not revealed to John; neither he nor the other Christians needed to see that. They needed the assurance of immediate relief and final complete victory. That is exactly what was given to them.

The salutation of verse 4 is typical of letter writing of the day. The writer identifies himself and addresses himself to the seven churches of Asia. His reasons for doing this have already been discussed.[*]

Cf. p. 86.

Now, with his audience of distressed Christians before him, he sends grace and peace from God. These words, "grace and peace," are customary words of salutation. They appear in most of the epistles of the New Testament. They appear in this order because there can be no peace in man's heart until grace has done its work. Grace is the redemptive, unmerited work of God in man's heart; peace is the resultant and abiding condition following that work. Grace and peace are here pronounced as coming from "the one who is and the one who was and the one who is coming." This was a typical Jewish conception of God. It is a good reproduction of the Hebrew word for Jehovah—"the eternally existing one." Incidentally, the use of the nominative ὁ after the preposition ἀπό introduces us to the unusual Greek constructions found in Revelation. Ordinarily we expect to find the ablative τοῦ after this preposition. This wish of grace and peace is also pictured as coming from "the seven spirits" which were before the throne of God. This is likely an apocalyptic method of referring to the Holy Spirit since seven is the number for perfection. The Third Person of the Trinity is not left out. The wish is also extended from "Jesus Christ the faithful witness, the firstborn from the dead and the ruler of the kings of the earth." It is interesting to note, against the background of emperor worship, the statement that Jesus is the ruler of the kings of the earth. Temporal kings or emperors claim divine power and authority; here is one equal with God, one who is ruler even of the kings. Eternal glory and dominion are ascribed to "the one who loves us." The proof of his continuing love (present tense) is seen in the fact that he has loosed us (aorist tense) from our sins by his blood. This can be nothing less than a reference to the sacrificial death of Christ on the cross—the historical manifestation of the eternal love and redemptive character of God. With it there is the assurance of the eternal lordship of Christ instead of a brief temporal lordship like that of Domitian who was trying so hard to annihilate Christianity.

Christ is pictured as returning as he went away (v. 7). "He comes with the clouds" points to the Christian hope of the fulfilment of the angelic promise of Acts 1:11. "Every eye shall see him" assures us that his coming will be a self-evident matter and that all men will recognize it and its significance. Even those responsible for his death will recognize the grave importance of his return. This linking of the three persons of the Trinity together with the assertion in verse 8 of God and his power serves to give the strongest divine authority to the message which John is about to deliver. It is a message which comes from the eternal and omnipotent God.

CHAPTER IV

The Lamb

(Revelation 1:9-20)

The paragraph beginning with verse 9 and extending through verse 20 is a presentation of the Christ, the *redeeming* Lamb, who dominates the action of this book. Perhaps nothing could have served to quicken the hopes of the distressed Christians better than this vision of the exalted and triumphant Christ. It served the same purpose for John personally.

John was on the isle of Patmos, in exile there for his loyalty to the Word of God and his testimony concerning Jesus Christ. This means that he was under sentence of the empire for failure to yield to the demands for emperor worship. Early Christian tradition confirms this position. He was thus a partaker with the Asian Christians of the tribulation which was upon them, the kingdom of God, and the patience which comes from Jesus Christ. All three of these were presented as present realities with John and his readers— not something to be experienced later.

John was "in the Spirit." This doubtless refers to the nature of his experience. He was in the midst of great trouble and tribulation, but still he was in communion with God's Spirit and under his power and direction. The word used here for tribulation is a word which pictures the grinding of wheat in the mill or the crushing of grapes in the wine press. It is outside pressure which appears at first sight to crush and ruin, but it proves to make the grain (as flour) and the grapes (as wine) to be of greater service. So it was with John and his friends; the persecution appeared to be crushing and ruining, but in reality it was only preparing them for more effective service. How frequently in Christian experience have God's people found trouble working in this way! This is one of the most beautiful truths of the New Testament.

This experience of John was on "the Lord's day"—the day of worship for Christian people, Sunday. Thus on the day of worship when John's heart longed for those Christians who had depended upon him so long for spiritual comfort and guidance, and while he pondered upon his condition and theirs and the outcome of it all, he heard a voice saying in essence, "You cannot be with those people but you can send them a message; it is a message which I will give to you."

John describes the voice as a great trumpet-like voice. Thus the note of triumph is sounded even before John identifies the speaker. He turned to see the speaker and beheld the living Christ whom he had last seen more than sixty years before ascending from the Mount of Olives to the Father who had sent him. The Lord had appeared at other difficult times in John's experience. He appeared in the upper room on the evening of the resurrection. When the disciples were returning from a night of fishing—empty-handed, fishless-netted, heavy-hearted—he appeared on the shore with cooked fish and bread to show that he could still provide for his followers even as in the days of his flesh when he had multiplied fish and bread for their need. Now again when John is facing such tragic discouragement, Jesus appears with a message of hope. This time he is different in appearance.

Hearing the trumpet-like voice, John turned to behold the transcendent and triumphant Christ. He was clothed with a long flowing garment and a golden girdle—the clothing of a priest and a king. His hair was "white as white wool . . . white as snow"—symbolical of his holiness. His eyes were as piercing as "a flame of fire"—symbolical of penetrating vision which meant omniscience. His feet were like "refined brass"—symbolical of strength; brass was the strongest metal known in John's day. His voice was the "voice of many waters"—symbolical of his authority over peoples and nations. (Compare the usage in other parts of the book.) His face had the

brilliance of the "sun shining in full strength," i.e., at noonday—
symbolical of his majesty. In his strong hand he held "seven stars"
—symbolical of the destiny of the churches as it lay in the pastors.
Out of his mouth went a "sharp two-edged sword"—symbolical of
keen and accurate judgment upon the deeds of men.[1] He stood
in the midst of "seven golden candlesticks"—symbolical of the
churches.[2]

Certainly we are not to suppose that this is the literal appearance
of Christ today—such would be a grotesque appearance. It is
through the significance of the symbolism that we see the full meaning of the vision and the glorious assurance vouchsafed to John and
his fellow sufferers. Here is the meaning of the vision: A living,
holy, majestic, omniscient, authoritative, powerful Christ stands in
the midst of the churches, holds their destiny in his hand and says:
"Stop fearing. I was dead. I am alive forever. More than that, I
hold in my hand the keys to death and the grave. You should not
fear to go to any place to which I hold the key. You may be persecuted to death but I am still your king." The grammatical construction forbids the continuance of an act already in progress. They
were afraid almost to the point of despair. They are told to stop
fearing. Then they are given the reason. Christ is alive; he is in
control of the entire situation.

This glorified, triumphant Christ dominates the movement of the
entire book of Revelation. There may be in the minds of some of
the self-styled "masters of prophecy" today doubts as to the outcome
of the struggle between good and evil. There was never any doubt
in the mind of the One who gave this revelation to John. Christ, the
redeeming Lamb, is the victor in every sense of the word. This truth
headlines the story of the struggle, and we know the outcome, even
though there are times in the progress of the account when the evil
forces seem to have the advantage.

---

[1] Some interpret this to mean his ability to protect his own.

[2] This symbolism is condensed from Beckwith, Dana, Hengstenberg, Richardson,
Smith, and many others *in loco.*

CHAPTER V

The Lamb and the Churches

(Revelation 2:1 to 3:22)

This study is presented from the point of view that these were actually seven churches in Asia Minor. It stays by the principle announced that the book must be interpreted in a way that would have been meaningful and helpful to those Christians who first received the message. Hence, it rejects the frequently confronted approach that the seven churches represent seven stages in the development of apostasy of the church. Such a view would have been futile for the purpose of the book and in direct conflict with the teaching of Jesus. In holding the view that these were seven actual churches, we are not implying that there were only seven churches in Asia Minor at that time. There were many churches in that territory, which had come to be the strongest point of Christian activity in the Roman Empire. But these seven were representative churches and they were strategically located for spreading this message to every part of Asia Minor. The number "7" suggests the idea of completeness; hence, the message of this book is for all the churches of Asia Minor. The conditions discussed in these letters were the conditions which characterized many of the churches. One of the marvelous things about the book is the impression that conditions in churches of every age, including the twentieth century, are illustrated by the conditions of these churches. The message is one of universal application. Wherever the conditions exist, the corrective procedure indicated will find application. The letters are best understood when presented against the historical background of the cities of the day. The conditions in the cities are reflected in the churches.[1] Such is the approach of this study.

There are some important matters of a general nature which must be observed as the letters to the seven churches are studied. Note that in each instance the letter is addressed to the "angel" of the church. Many suggestions have been made as to the meaning of the term. Various interpreters have held that it means the spirit or destiny of the church, some messenger which the church had sent to visit John on Patmos, or the "guardian angel" of the church. The most probable view is that it refers to the elder, the leading pastor, of the church. New Testament records, as well as others, indicate that the churches sometimes had several pastors charged with differing responsibilities in the life of the body. "The angel of the church," then, is the leading pastor. The responsibility of presenting the message of this book to the church is his. He led the "candlestick" as it sent out the light of Christ to a dark world.

There is a definite pattern followed in each of the letters. The identification of the sender (Christ) is in each letter a part of the description of the glorified Christ of the first chapter. He claims intimate knowledge of each church. He commends the church for whatever it has of a commendable nature. He issues his complaint against the church or his counsel to the church. This is followed by a promise to the faithful. This content and order will vary with the letters, but it is the predominant pattern all the way through.

Ephesus: Loyal but Lacking, 2:1–7

At the time of writing of this book, Ephesus was a great and opulent city of Ionia. All kinds of people lived there—the wealthy and the learned, as well as the poor and the illiterate. The general condition of life was that of a wealthy, cultured, corrupt city. Just why Ephesus was selected as the first of the seven is not revealed. It could have been that it was because Ephesus was the natural starting place on the continent for a circular message from the isle

---

[1] In the bibliography of this book will be found sources of invaluable aid at this point: Dana, Hardy, Ramsay, Morgan, and others.

of Patmos. If one grants that the book was written by John the son of Zebedee, he will find a likely suggestion in the tradition that John had been the chief leader of the Christian forces around Ephesus for a quarter of a century. The history of the founding and early operation of this church is recorded in Acts 18–20. The church had been in operation about forty or forty-five years when this message was sent.

IDENTIFICATION, 2:1

The Lord introduces himself to the Ephesian church as the one who holds in his right hand the seven stars, and the one who walks in the midst of the seven golden candlesticks. This positionizes him so that there can be no question about what follows as to his knowledge of the church—he is there and knows what is going on. He is caring for it, holding in his strong right hand its destiny as it is wrapped up in the pastor. He observes its every virtue and flaw and speaks a message to reveal them.

COMMENDATION, 2:2–3, 6

It is interesting to observe in these letters that where there is anything to be commended in the church, the Lord mentions it first. There are many things for which the church at Ephesus can be commended.

1. Loyalty in practice.—"I know thy works, and thy toil, and thy patience." "Works" probably has reference to actual service which is being rendered. This was an active and aggressive congregation. "Toil" lies deeper than works. The word translated toil has reference to the effort that produces work at the cost of pain. They were working at the price of great difficulty. In the word is the echo of men who beat upon their breasts with cries of anguish as they push forward toward a desired end. This was a working church. "Patience" reveals the attitude of persistence in the toil that produces work. It is not, in the New Testament, the passive word of current usage; there is no folding of the hands in waiting in this word; it

literally means "to remain under." It means staying when the burden is heavy; it means holding one's own in the face of every difficulty. The three words together give a strong impression of loyalty in practice. They are all the more meaningful as they come from the lips of the transcendent Christ.

2. Loyalty in doctrine.—"Thou canst not bear evil men" indicates that the gnostic teachers had gained little ground at Ephesus. They had come claiming to be genuine apostles, missionaries, but the church had tested them, found them false, and rejected them. The Ephesians have borne much in their loyalty to the name of Christ. They have not grown weary in the midst of difficulties caused by persecution and the inroads of false doctrine. To the unstable Galatians, Paul had once said, "Stop getting tired of doing good" (Gal. 6:9). But these Ephesians have great reserve strength and need no such warning.

The work of the Nicolaitans has met in Ephesus an emotion which can be described only as hate—righteous wrath against all iniquity. This attitude of the Ephesians regarding the Nicolaitans is shared by the living Christ. He, too, exercises a constant displeasure against evil of every kind. The exact identity of the Nicolaitans has not been made. From their relationship to those who held the doctrines of Balaam (2:14-15) their evil appears to have been the promotion of some form of antinomianism. Whatever the false teaching, it was hated in common by the Christ and the Christians at Ephesus.

This entire commendation leaves one inclined to question if there could be anything wrong in such a church. It carried on its services in the face of difficulties; it rejected false teachers; it hated sin; it did not grow weary in the Lord's work. That is what one would expect from a church which had been blessed by the services of great leaders: Paul, Apollos, Priscilla and Aquila, Timothy, John the beloved disciple. But the Lord looks with a piercing eye of flame and discovers a great flaw.

COMPLAINT, 2:4

"This I have against thee—thou hast left thy first love." This brief statement covers the whole field. A student stated it aptly, if lightly, when he turned in a lesson assignment with this Scripture and the subject, "The Honeymoon Is Over!" The church had departed from that fervor and love which had characterized their first experience as Christians. They were carrying on the active program of an aggressive church, but they had departed from the right motive for worship. When love for Christ as a motive for worship is absent, service means little.

COUNSEL, 2:5, 7a

The counsel which Christ offers the church at Ephesus may well be stated in three words—remember, repent, return. Remember your early joy and zest in your love for Christ and his work. Remember the driving force of that love. Repent of the condition of service without love which you have allowed to creep into your life. It is a deadly enemy to effective work in the Lord's kingdom. Return to that original state of service out of a heart of love. Christ warns that if they do not return to that first state, they are forfeiting their right to exist as a church. He threatens to remove the candlestick out of its place. The candlestick is the church (1:20), and it has no right to exist if it is not going to carry out the purpose which Christ has for it. Strong warning to any church!

The first part of verse 7 serves as a transition from warning to promise. "He that hath an ear, let him hear what the Spirit saith unto the churches." Those with spiritual perception are warned to listen. This is not just the message of a man. The eternal God is speaking his warning against the deadly peril of spiritual apathy.

PROMISE, 2:7b

"To him who overcomes I will give to eat of the tree of life which is in the garden of God." The concept of overcoming is one of the outstanding ideas of the book of Revelation. It means to be victorious over the circumstances in which one finds himself. In its context in this book it appears to mean living a life of service to God out of a heart of love. To one who is living such a life the Lord promises fruit from the garden of God. In symbol he is saying, "I will give spiritual food and sustenance to the one who is loyal to me." God never fails his people in their time of need. He is able to provide all their needs, but he expects victorious living on their part.

Smyrna: Suffering Saints, 2:8–11

Smyrna had been for many years a prosperous city. It had passed into obscurity at one time but was rebuilt by Alexander the Great and Antigonus. It became a noted and wealthy city almost at once and maintained that condition long past the New Testament period. We have no account of the planting of the church there. Perhaps it took place when Paul in Ephesus divided his disciples so that all Asia came to know the gospel. History tells of the persecution there and of the ministry and martyrdom of Polycarp. His martyrdom was in the second century, but he may have been pastor at Smyrna when this letter was written. It is interesting to observe that only good is spoken of this church.

Identification, 2:8

The Lord identifies himself as "the first and the last, who was dead and lived again." Thus he tells them that he has been through what they are suffering. He is well qualified to comfort them and bring them assurance from firsthand knowledge.

Commendation and Comfort, 2:9–10a

Christ weaves together a pattern of commendation and comfort. The commendation is partly one from the silence; he finds no complaint to bring against them. He knows their "tribulation." This is the word previously discussed which pictures outside pressure which

threatens to ruin. He knows their "poverty." This is no doubt a reflection of the confiscation of property used by Domitian as a means of
persecution. These Christians at Smyrna have lost all their material
possessions, yet Christ who sees and knows all says, "but you are
rich." Wealth, true wealth, is enrichment of character, not possession
of gold. This is indeed a rich church. He knows "the blasphemy of
them that sꞏ, they are Jews." This is perhaps a reference to the Jews
who had escaped persecution and confiscation of property by compromise. Theirs was a legal religion and, by offering up prayers for
the emperor, they escaped the fate of the Christians. Now they mock
and speak evil of the Christians, who have lost all out of loyalty to
their religion. Christ says that these are not really Jews; they are "of
the synagogue of Satan"; they are the devil's people.

It is interesting to note in verse 10 that the Lord does not promise to take away their difficulties. He warns them of the coming of an additional deluge of suffering and temptation to renounce
their religion. They will be tempted by extreme outside pressure
for ten days—a number symbolizing extreme, complete tribulation.
He does not offer to take away the difficulties, because the overcoming of difficulties is the means of building character.

PROMISE, 2:10a, 11b

His promise is twofold: "Be faithful even if it means death and I
will give thee the crown of life. . . . He that overcometh shall not
be hurt of the second death." Christ tells them not to fear death,
because eternal life awaits them. He will give to them the crown of
life—a reward for a race won. They shall not be hurt by the "second
death," which symbolizes eternal punishment. The unbeliever dies
and finds another "death" awaiting him; the believer dies and finds
eternal life. Here as always the promise is to the overcoming life.

WARNING, 2:11a

Here, as in the other letters, the warning is against the peril of
spiritual apathy: "He that hath an ear, let him hear what the Spirit
saith unto the churches."

Pergamum: Hell's Headquarters, 2:12–17

History records that Pergamum was an illustrious city of Mysia, given over almost entirely to wealth and fashion. The city was the headquarters for emperor worship.[2] It was the chief city of the province, and here was located the "concilia" which had in charge the matters of state religion and incense offering before the image of the emperor. The city had always been loyal to Rome, so it was only natural that they would be unrelenting in their persecution of the Christians. We have no account of the planting of this church.

IDENTIFICATION, 2:12

The Lord identifies himself as the one who has "the sharp two-edged sword." This may have a twofold symbolism. It may picture his ability to protect them even in the midst of persecution and where martyrs are falling. It may also symbolize the power of discerning judgment. The fitness of this is in the fact that this church was harboring error. He comes with the sword of his mouth, keen and accurate judgment on the deeds of men, to deal with the false teachers.

COMMENDATION, 2:13

Christ commends the church for fidelity under extreme difficulty. They dwell "where Satan's throne is." In 29 B.C. there had been erected an altar in Pergamum for the worship of Augustus. The city had been retained as the center of state religion, and thus it is spoken of as the place where Satan's throne was located. The reference to the death of Antipas is no doubt a reference to a well-known martyrdom at the altar for incense worship. Many other martyrs were falling. This one was outstanding enough to call forth

---

[2]W. M. Ramsay, *The Letters to the Seven Churches* (London: Hodder and Stoughton, 1904), pp. 292 f.

the notice of the Lord. It has been suggested, due to the term "my faithful witness," that Antipas may have been pastor of the Christian congregation at Pergamum. This is interesting but uncertain.

The Christians have held fast the *name* of Christ. His name stands for his personality. The name Κύριος Καίσαρος (Lord Caesar) over against the name Κύριος Χριστός (Lord Christ) was the big test of the day. To acknowledge the Lord Caesar was to escape persecution. To hold fast the Lord Christ meant persecution but loyalty. For doing the latter the Christians were commended. They were also commended for not denying the faith of Christ. His faith perhaps has reference to the entire scope of their religion, their belief in his atoning work and supremacy. For loyalty at this point, even when it meant great danger, the Lord commends them.

COMPLAINT, 2:14–15

Not all the church membership was so loyal as the group commended. Heresy had come in. There were some in the group who held the "teachings of Balaam." In Numbers 23–24, we find that Balaam was willing to make material gain at the cost of spiritual loss. He led the way to idol worship and impure living for Israel. There are some people at Pergamum who are doing the same. They are willing to make spiritual compromise in order to further their material safety; they advise idol (emperor) worship as a means of safety; they teach evil living as a means of being friends to the Romans and escaping persecution. Their story is told in the phrase, wrong creed—wrong conduct. This has often been true in church history. At Pergamum the combination of heretical teachings of the Balaamites and heretical living of the Nicolaitans had caused a bad condition. It was one which could not be tolerated by the Lord and he warns the true church people against their tolerance.

WARNING, 2:16, 17a

The church is warned to repent of its attitude of leniency and toleration of the sin present. If they do not take action to eliminate the evil, the Lord is determined that he will personally "make war against them" with the sword of his mouth. Just what action he will take is not indicated, but he leaves no doubt as to his ability to handle the situation that has developed. "He that hath an ear, let him hear. . . ."

Promise, 2:17b

The promise to the overcoming life is twofold. "I will give the hidden manna." As the needs of Israel in the wilderness were divinely provided, so will the Lord provide for the needs of his faithful ones. He will give them "hidden manna"—spiritual sustenance which the world cannot understand.

"I will give him a white stone, and upon the stone a new name written." What is the symbolism of this statement? Pergamum engaged in the mining of white stone and the use of it as a commercial product. The use of a piece of this stone with a name on it was varied. Perhaps to one of the four following ones[3] the Lord had reference:

(1) The white stone was given to a man who had been tried and justly acquitted. He carried it as a sign that he was free of the charge of crime which had been placed against him.

(2) The white stone was given to a man who was freed from slavery and made a citizen of the province. He carried the stone as an indication of his citizenship.

(3) The white stone was given to the winner of a race or contest as an indication that he had overcome opposition.

(4) The white stone was given to a warrior returning from battle with victory over the enemy.

The application of either or all of these usages is evident. Perhaps it is the "preacher" spirit in Morgan that leads him to accept all four. The promise may have had reference to one of these; it may have been something else understood by the Christians at Pergamum. It was a sacred promise to them, one calculated to increase their efforts at loyalty.

---

[3]Morgan, *op. cit.*, pp. 72 f. thinks it may be a combination of all four!

Thyatira: Wait for the Star, 2:18–29

We have no direct account of the origin of the church in this small city of Asia Minor. It may have been by one of Paul's disciples from Ephesus, by Lydia, a native of Thyatira, who was converted at Philippi, or by some unknown Christian representative. Although this was a small city, it was an important trading point. It was in easy connection with Pergamum; one of the chief Roman highways ran through it, and it was visited by many people. The same heresy as at Pergamum is also at Thyatira, but it appears to be worse. The city teemed with pagan people, and such heresy found fruitful soil.

IDENTIFICATION, 2:18

Christ identifies himself to the church as "the Son of God, who hath his eyes like a flame of fire, and his feet are like unto burnished brass." He is thus infallible (as God's Son), omniscient (piercing eyes like flames), and strong (feet as brass refined in service); therefore, the church must hear him. He has perfect understanding of the conditions in the church and is, hence, qualified to speak judgment.

COMMENDATION, 2:19

He acknowledges their virtues as a means of commending them. He knows their works, their services rendered to God; their love which is the basis of their works and which was absent at Ephesus; their faith, fidelity to their religion; their ministry, which pictures love in action, ministry to those in need; their patience, ability to hold their own, peace under pressure. In addition to this he commends them for progress made in their work—"thy last works are more than the first." Apparently, then, this is a good church. They are carrying on with the regular work of the Lord faithfully and with patience and manifest love. They are "growing in grace" as they make progress. If the letter closed there, the church would be considered ideal. But the letter does not close there. Evils are present which must be condemned.

COMPLAINT AND JUDGMENT, 2:20-23

The complaint is that the church is harboring one guilty of heresy and spreading the heresy—"thou sufferest the woman Jezebel." The church, true church, is not guilty of the heresy, but they condone it on the part of others. Many views have been presented as to the woman Jezebel and her sin. Some have held that she was the pastor's wife[4] because the word γυνή from which this form comes may mean wife; it often does in the New Testament. There is no other basis for the theory, and it is rather unsatisfactory. Some have held that this is merely an allegorical way of presenting the heresy. It appears that the best suggestion is that there was a corrupt woman in the church teaching and claiming some special mystic revelation from God. Verse 24 appears to suggest this. The woman may have been named Jezebel, but it is more likely that this name was assigned to her because of her character. She is misleading Christians and seducing them to fornication, either actual fornication growing out of the gnostic teachings or spiritual fornication of breaking one's vows with God. This reflection of an Old Testament idea, especially found in Hosea, appears to be the true case. She will not be permitted to continue in her evil. She is going to meet destruction, and her followers with her, in the very sin in which she is engaged (2:22-23). This is coming about as a proof that God still has charge of affairs and still judges men according to their works (2:23).

PROMISE, 2:24-29

The Lord promises to those who overcome that he will not put upon them any more spiritual obligations than they already have, no additional duties through special gnostic revelations (2:24). They are to be loyal in what he has already given (2:25). He promises

[4] Carroll, *op. cit.*, vol. on Revelation, p. 72.

that those who overcome will receive authority over the nations. They will find themselves completely vindicated as Christians before men who are now persecuting them. The picture of their ruling with rods of iron is symbolical of the certainty of their vindication and triumph with Christ. He further promises to give to the overcoming one the morning star—his guidance and leadership in the dark hour of troubles and trials. One who has frequently observed the brilliant beauty of the morning star in the dark hour which precedes the dawn will understand the beauty of this promise. He may often walk in darkness and in many perplexities, but the morning star will be given to guide him; he must refuse to follow the false leadership of gnosticism and *wait for the star*.

Sardis: Dead or Alive? 3:1–6

For many years Sardis was the outstanding Greek city of Asia Minor. It had little influence in the Roman period but lived in the pride of its past history. Dana[5] calls it a typical example of brokendown aristocracy. The city was arrogant and self-sufficient and in need of warning from God. The term "awaken or decline" might well be used to describe the city and church—usually the attitude of a city is reflected in its churches.

IDENTIFICATION, 3:1a

The sender is identified as "he that hath the seven Spirits of God, and the seven stars." He has fulness of power and wisdom. He has, too, the destiny of the church in his hands. They do well to heed his warning.

COMPLAINT, 3:1B

There is a marked change in the Lord's manner of speaking to this church. Heretofore he has commended and then complained. At Sardis there is so little commendable and so much to complain

[5]Dana, *The Epistles and Apocalypse of John*, p. 108.

about that he reverses the order. "I know thy works, that thou hast a name that thou livest, and thou art dead." Thus in a few words he voices a tremendous complaint. In this church there was plenty of outward activity but no inner spirituality. No doubt the organization was perfected and running smoothly. An outsider looking on would see the ideal church so far as outward manifestation went, but there was no life, no real life, in the church. Someone has said that "there are few things better organized than graveyards, but there is little life there!" So it was at Sardis; they had a reputation that they lived, but the One with perfect knowledge said they were dead.

ADMONITION, 3:2

The church is admonished to get busy and "establish the things that remain, which were ready to die." There were left in the church at Sardis a few things that were alive; they were on the verge of death but could be rescued by prompt action. The forms were all right, but they needed to be filled with power and devotion. A Christian cannot prosper on ritual alone. Christ states that he has found no work of the church perfect in the sight of God. They were good starters but poor finishers, like the Galatians who ran well for a while and then stopped. The church at Sardis had a name before men for doing good work, but Christ judges it not by what men see but by what God sees, and indicates that they have not really finished one thing which they started.

WARNING, 3:3

The church is warned of disaster unless it remembers the real content of religion as it had first received it and unless it returns to those first principles and practices them. If it fails to do this, he will come upon it in judgment and destruction. This warning to "watch" had a definite meaning for Sardis. The city was built upon a hill, surrounded on three sides by precipitous cliffs. It was thus easily defended against an enemy. But carelessness had caused it to fall twice.[6] When Croesus was king and was besieged by Cyrus, he and his soldiers slept, thinking they were safe, only to have the city captured by the adventurous soldiers of the enemy. At another time the city under Achneus fell before Antiochus the Great under similar circumstances. The Lord uses that to warn the church. "Remember your history. If you do not watch, the same fate will come to you." In the New Testament "watching" is not just a matter of keeping the eyes open; it is a matter of keeping busy, active for the Lord in his service.

Commendation, 3:4a

There are a few in Sardis who are worthy of commendation. They "did not defile their garments"; they took no part in the pagan worship and worldliness of the day. They had been true to their God all the way.

Promise, 3:4b, 5

To this faithful group the promise is made that they shall walk with the Lord in white; they are worthy of fellowship with him because of their purity and loyalty. The one who overcomes will "be arrayed in white garments." Sardis was proud of its business in colored cloths,[7] worn by the worldly, reveling people. Those who have overcome will be given white robes symbolical of their purity. The overcoming one will not have his name blotted from the book of life but confessed by Christ before God and the angels. Because of his refusal to yield to the demands of emperor worship, he may have his name blotted out of the record book of men as he is added to the list of martyrs. But his name is still in the Lamb's book of life and he is secure. Perfect security and honor are his. The New Testament teaches the security of the believer with the emphasis that the fact that one overcomes, holds out faithful, is an indication

---

[6]Ramsay, *Letters to the Seven Churches*, pp. 359 ff.

[7]David Smith, *The Disciple's Commentary* (New York: Ray Long and Richard R. Smith, Inc., 1932), V, 611.

that he was genuinely redeemed to begin with; this is the emphasis of this passage.

Philadelphia: The Church with an Open Door, 3:7–13

This city dates back to about 159 B.C. It won its name from Attalus II, whose loyalty to his brother Eumenes won him the epithet Philadelphus, "brother-lover." It was founded as a center for the spreading of the Greek language, culture, and manner. From its beginning it was a missionary city for the promotion of loyalty to Hellenism throughout the land. In this letter we find a promise of opportunity for missionary enterprise of another nature.

IDENTIFICATION, 3:7

The Lord identifies himself as being in character, "holy and true"; in official position, as the one who "hath the key of David"; and in administration, as the one who "openeth and none shall shut, and that shutteth and none openeth." His character of holiness and truth is his right to kingship. Because he is king, he exercises his kingly office and administers the affairs of his kingdom.

COMMENDATION, 3:8

Only good is spoken about this church; there is no condemnation to offer. The Lord knows her work and is setting before her an open door which none can shut. He is giving her the open right-of-way to full spiritual enjoyment and opportunity for service. No one can stop her work if she will take advantage of this open door to service. This is the meaning of the "open door" in New Testament usage.[8] Christ knows that the church is weak—"thou hast little power"—yet she has been faithful. She has kept the faith and not denied his name even though weak. His name "Jesus" meant Saviour; his name "Christ" meant God's anointed one. To the implications of this name the church was faithful. This is in contrast to some of the

---

[8] Cf. Acts 14:27; 1 Corinthians 16:9.

churches which were strong from every viewpoint yet had not been faithful. With an open door of service they go forward even though they are weak.

PROMISE, 3:9–10, 12

Because of their loyalty under weakness and difficulty, the Lord promises complete vindication for them. He will make the persecuting Jews who are doing Satan's work to realize that these despised Christians are the ones whom he really loves (v. 9). Because they have been faithful, he promises his sustaining grace in the tribulation that is about to engulf the world; it will not overcome them (v. 10). A *warning* (v. 11) is inserted here before the last part of the promise. It is a warning to hold fast what they have—his name, his word, his patience, his promise to return, his opportunity for service —lest someone by causing them to give up these things rob them of their reward. Sardis had been threatened by his coming; Philadelphia, because she had been faithful and had nothing to fear, was encouraged by his coming. The last part of the promise is voiced in verse 12. Several things are promised. "I will make him a pillar in the temple of my God." Because one has been faithful, Christ will make him an important part of the sanctuary—symbolized as a pillar which keeps the temple from falling. Philadelphia was true and experienced the fulfilment of this promise. Christianity, though perhaps not in its purest form, survives in the city today. The historian Gibbon[9] says that among the churches of Asia, Philadelphia remained erect, a column in a scene of ruins, a pleasing example that the paths of honor and safety may sometimes be the same. The statement by Gibbon should be qualified; the paths of honor and safety are always the same ultimately.

"I will write upon him the name of my God, and the name of the city of my God, . . . and mine own new name." There is to be perfect security for the overcoming one. The name of God is branded upon him; the name of the city of God is there as a mark of his

---

[9]Edward Gibbon, *The Decline and Fall of the Roman Empire* (Chicago: Thompson and Thomas Publishers, n.d.), IV, 381.

place of habitation; the name of the triumphant Christ is upon him. Many of the pagan religions used brands or marks to identify their adherents. Later in this book we find the State religion of Rome using the custom. Jesus here symbolizes the relation of his followers to himself by speaking of his new name branded upon them. There is no more glorious promise given to any of the seven churches than this one given to Philadelphia.

Laodicea: The Church with a Closed Door, 3:14-22

This was a city characterized by exceeding riches. It had needed no help from the Roman treasury when it was partially destroyed by an earthquake about A.D. 60. It was the main commercial city of the region. Three Roman roads met there making it a city of great prominence. Such a city easily fell prey to lethargy and self-satisfied complacency. This spirit of the town had made itself felt in the church.

IDENTIFICATION, 3:14

Christ identifies himself to this church as "the Amen, the faithful and true witness, the beginning of the creation of God." All this evidences a declaration of his essential glory. To Laodicea, an example of abject failure, he addresses himself as One incapable of failure. The word "Amen" came from Hebrew to Greek to English untranslated. In its original meaning it carried the idea of nursing or building up. The derived use which has come down to us is that of something which is established, positive. Here it indicates the stability of Jesus who writes to this weak church. He is the faithful and true witness because of his stability. When he was here, he said, "I am the truth" (John 14:6). He is the truth about God, and in life and deed he bore true witness concerning God. He is the beginning of the creation of God—not that he was the first thing which God created but that he is the original agent in God's creative work. This is a similar statement to that of Paul in Colossians 1:15-18—"who is the image of the invisible God, the firstborn of all creation, for in him were all things created . . . all things have been created by him . . . and in him all things hold together."

COMPLAINT AND COUNSEL, 3:15-18

Christ's complaint has to do with the spiritual lethargy of the church. It was neither cold—complete and utter indifference; nor was it hot—characterized by fervent heat or zeal. It was lukewarm, tepid. Travelers coming across country to near-by Hierapolis found beautiful springs of water. Weary and thirsty, they stopped, expecting to quench their thirst. But the water turned out to be tepid mineral water; perhaps nothing is more distasteful. The Lord said that he felt that way about a tepid church; it was distasteful to him; he would "spew it out" of his mouth. It is easier to deal with a frozen church than one that is tepid. A church with no enthusiasm, no urgency, no compassion, was repugnant to him.

Counsel and complaint are woven together in verses 17 and 18. The commercial background of the city is here reflected. There were three chief businesses in the city.[10] The Lord uses all three to illustrate the attitude of the church.

1. This was a banking center for the region. Great riches were gathered into this city. They were proud, arrogant, and self-sufficient because of their riches. They said, "We have gold; we need nothing anyone can give." That was their feeling and witness. The faithful and true witness says, "You do not realize that you are wretched, and miserable and poor." They had material wealth but they were spiritually poverty-stricken; they had no enrichment of character and were too lukewarm to miss it. The Lord counsels them to come and receive from him the true spiritual riches that they may indeed be rich. A man can own all the money in the world and still be a pauper, or he can have none of the world's goods and still be rich. It depends on what one counts as riches.

2. The second ranking business in Laodicea was the black wool markets. They produced a black glossy wool which was

---

[10]Smith, *op. cit.*, V, 671, quoting Strabo.

made into fine garments in demand everywhere. Christ says: "In spite of this you are naked. You need to come and obtain from me a robe, a covering, that will really hide your exposed condition before God." Their robes of haughty self-sufficiency did not cover them up before God as well as they did before men. What they called clothing left them naked before God.

3. The third business was the preparing of an ointment used as a balm for the eyes; there was a medicine center there. Travelers over the sand with the sun and wind beating in their eyes found this balm a welcome relief. "You are blind and do not know it. Come to me and I will give you spiritual eye salve that you may really see." He possesses all that the church so sorely lacks. He is ready to bestow it if they desire it—true wealth, true raiment, true vision. He will not force it upon them if they do not want it.

Warning, 3:19

He will not force these true riches upon them but because he loves them, he will reprove and chasten them. He does love them. Even his complaint is voiced in tones of pity and compassion. It is his way to chasten those whom he loves. This is well brought out in Hebrews 12:5 ff. Everyone who is a child of God is punished when he rebels and sins. Therefore, he warns them to turn from their lethargy, to be zealous, to be filled with zeal rather than a lukewarm condition.

Promise, 3:20-21

The church at Laodicea had everything in it except Christ. He was on the outside seeking entrance. If anyone would respond to his knocking, he was ready to come in and start fellowship with the church. He could begin with even one individual whose heart was responsive and desired him.

To the one who overcomes the spirit of lethargy and becomes zealous for God, he promises glory and fellowship. They will sit down together even as he and the Father, once he has overcome the obstacles in his way. Neither hope nor imagination can go beyond the possibilities offered in this promise. Perhaps he makes this great promise because of the extreme difficulty of overcoming the lukewarm condition in the church; no greater incentive for overcoming could have been offered.

The glorified Christ, standing in the midst of his churches, seeing with piercing eyes of flame, brings his commendation, complaint, warning, and promise. The message delivered first to the churches of Asia Minor is universal. Its truth applies wherever similar conditions are found today; and it is difficult to find churches where at least some of these conditions are not found. The warning against spiritual apathy still stands, "He that hath an ear, let him hear what the Spirit saith to the churches."

CHAPTER VI

The Lamb and the Sealed Book

(Revelation 4:1 to 5:14)

Here begins the main part of the Apocalypse. Up to this point the materials presented have been preparatory. John is about to witness the "Drama of Redemption."[1] The way is prepared by the vision of the living, victorious Christ in chapter 1. The audience for whose benefit the drama is produced is presented with its vices and virtues in chapters 2–3. Now it is time to draw the curtain and reveal the stage set for the drama. From here forward, in rapid sequence, will be presented scenes to assure the persecuted Christians that the cause of Christ is not a lost cause. Hard and bitter is to be the struggle, but when the final curtain falls at the end of the play (22:21), complete assurance of victory is demonstrated.

Chapter 4 prepares the way for all that follows. It is assisted by chapter 5 in presenting the sovereignty of God vindicated by the work of Christ. Chapter 4 says, in the language of John 14, "Believe in God"; chapter 5, with Christ as the leading figure, says, "Believe also in me."[2] Then in chapters 6–18 we find pictured the wrath of God against the enemies of his cause. In chapters 19–22 the final complete victory of God and the eternal destiny of men are set forth. In such presentation it is clear that this vision (chaps. 4–5) prepares the way for the entire message. Two ideas stand out in this vision.

---

[1] Dana's approach, *The Epistles and Apocalypse of John*, p. 112.
[2] Cf. Richardson, *op. cit.*, p. 67.

The Reigning God, 4:1–11

The "after these things" refers to the preliminary matters of chapters 1–3. It is a device for presenting the visions in their sequence. With this statement John begins his record of the visions showing God's rescue of his people from the peril of Domitian's persecution. A vision of the triumphant Christ was necessary before the following visions would have any meaning. Likewise it was necessary to show the condition of the churches in order that the real meaning of what follows could be known. This indicates that the book was meant to bring needed courage to the people who first received it, not just to reveal events at the consummation of the age several hundreds or thousands of years from John's time.

John's first object of vision is a door standing open in heaven. By means of this door he is able to see what is going on in heaven. He is invited by the first voice (1:10, the voice of Christ) to come to a place of advantage from which he will be able to see things from God's viewpoint. From John's point of view on Patmos there is a dark picture meeting the eye. But when he is able to see things from God's point of view, the coloring is changed radically. From that point of view he can see the eternal throne of God, which does not shake before the threats of Domitian and men of such character. From the heavenly angle there is no doubt about the outcome of the struggle in which the Christians are engaged. Immediately the spiritual experience was intensified, and John saw the first guarantee of victory—God on his throne. The Christians needed assurance; here it is: God has not abdicated in favor of Domitian or any other. In the very center of the vision is the sovereign God on his throne.

The name of God is not called until verse 8, but there is no doubt about the identity of the one described. He has the appearance of a "jasper stone and a sardius." Perhaps the pure white of the jasper stone symbolizes the holiness of God, and the blood red of the sardius stone symbolizes his righteousness.

About the throne of this holy and righteous God is a rainbow "like an emerald to look upon." This is a symbol of hope or mercy. Green as the "living" color is the predominant characteristic of this rainbow. In Genesis 9:12–17 the rainbow was given as a symbol of hope in the midst of judgment. Here, too, it appears to represent living hope in the midst of judgment; it is hope based on the faithfulness of a covenant-making God. The awe-inspiring splendor of God is thus reinforced by this assuring token of hope and mercy. The punitive righteousness of God will deal with those trying to destroy his cause, but his grace and mercy are ever present for his people.

Twenty-four thrones (4:4) were placed about the main throne, and on these were twenty-four elders. Various opinions have been given as to the identity of these twenty-four. Carroll[3] looks upon them as representing the eternal priesthood of God's people. Dana[4] views them as symbolical of the victorious destiny of the martyred saints of Asia Minor. Others[5] think they represent the twelve patriarchs of Israel and the twelve apostles of the New Testament as they bind together the redeemed of the two periods in a common destiny of triumph and glory with God. This appears to be the best interpretation. The number is the duplicated number "12" which symbolized organized religion. This whole picture symbolizes comfort for the persecuted Christians. They were faced with death. What of that? After death they would find themselves perfectly safe in the presence of God, arrayed in white garments symbolical of their freedom from spiritual fornication of idol worship and with crowns of gold symbolical of their victory over the enemy. The Lord had twice cheered the twelve (Matthew 19:28; Luke 22:30) with the assurance that they would reign with him; now it is symbolized for all the faithful.

The manifestations of divine wrath are the next symbols (4:5a). From the throne of God came "lightnings and voices and thunder" showing God's displeasure at the enemies of the cross. In Exodus 19:16 a similar expression is found concerning God's presence and speaking. These terror-striking signs of his presence and power are given to show the latent powers of his omnipotence as they threaten

---

[3]Carroll, *op. cit.*, vol. on Revelation, p. 111.

[4]Dana, *Ibid.*, p. 114.

[5]Hengstenberg, Richardson, Allen, Pieters, D. Smith, and J. Smith, *in loco*.

vengeance to those who are the enemies of the ones symbolized in the four and twenty elders. God has not left his people to the mercy of their foes.

The seven lamps of fire interpreted as the seven Spirits of God comprise another symbol (4:5b). Lamps give light; "7" is the perfect number. Seven Spirits picture God in his perfect spiritual essence. Therefore, we must have symbolized here as a token of God's sovereignty the perfect operation of the Holy Spirit in his work of illumination and revelation to man of the things of God.

The crystal sea (4:6a) before the throne made the throne unapproachable. This symbolizes the transcendence of God. The sea separated John from his churches. The sea of crystal separated the transcendent God from the people. In Revelation 21:1 we will find that "the sea is no more" and men are in direct fellowship with God. Thus were the persecuted Christians separated from God, but this was not always to be.

The four living creatures (4:6–8) form the next symbol of God's sovereignty. They are in the midst of the throne and round about the throne. They are full of eyes before and behind, round about and within. They have different appearances: one like a lion, one like a calf, one like a man, and one like an eagle. Each one has six wings. Day and night without ceasing they speak terms of adoration to God. There are two major interpretations of the symbolism of the four "living creatures"—not "beast, brute" as in Revelation 13:1; this is a different word. One is that they represent attributes of God to show his eternal vigilance on behalf of his people.[6] By this theory the lion represents bravery, the young bull represents strength, the man represents intelligence, and the eagle represents swiftness or speed. Together they symbolize the eternal watchfulness of God; he has not forgotten his people and is swift and strong to avenge them. This is an appealing view but for the fact that in verse 8 the four living creatures are pictured as adoring God and in 5:8 they are pictured as falling down to worship him. This seems a little out of the line of duty of attributes. The other view[7] is that they

---

[6]Dana, *Ibid.*, p. 115.

[7]D. Smith, J. Smith, Hengstenberg, Richardson, and others, *in loco.*

represent the fourfold division of animal life so that all God's creatures are worshiping him. The lion represents wild animal life, the
calf represents domestic animal life, the man represents human life,
and the eagle represents bird life. All are represented as constantly
watchful to adore and worship God. The whole creation—man,
beast, and bird—is pictured as glorified with him as part of his sovereignty. Each has six wings, and if this has any connection with
the six-winged seraphim of Isaiah 6:2, we understand that with one
pair they showed reverence, with another, humility, and with the
third swift obedience to God's command. They are "in the midst
of and round about the throne." The suggestion of Smith[8] in the
American Commentary seems the most logical. The animals are
around the throne so that one is at the middle point, "in the midst,"
of each side of the throne. Their eyes "before and behind" make it
possible for one to see them surrounding the throne, no matter what
viewpoint he takes. Thus are they ever watchful to render praise
and adoration to God. The whole picture is such as to produce encouragement to the obedient, terror to the disobedient. This in
reality is what the sovereignty of God does.

This vision of God on his throne is concluded by a song of praise
(4:9–11). The praise is twofold. First, the four living creatures speak
of glory, and honor, and thanks unto the sovereign eternal God.
Thus all creatures are symbolized as adoring the eternal God, not
the temporal Domitian. Second, the twenty-four elders representing
redeemed humanity fall before the throne of God, take off their
crowns, cast them before his throne, and praise him for his great
creative power. He alone is morally worthy to receive glory and
honor and dominion because all things are his by creation. This
"Song of Creation" is directed as praise to God; in chapter 5 a
"Song of Re-creation (Redemption)" will be directed as praise to
Christ (5:9–10).

By way of summary we find in this chapter, which begins the
visions, the truth of a sovereign God. He is eternal; he is Creator;
he protects his people; he visits punishment upon the disobedient.
He is on his throne. The enemies of the cross may rage against him,

---

[8]Smith, *op. cit.*, p. 80.

but he is unmoved. The invincible sovereign God as the center of activity is the point of emphasis in this chapter. Such were the initial encouragements given to the beaten Christians of Asia Minor in the first century and to all Christians in every century. Suffering was only temporary since God was their defender.

The Redeeming Lamb, 5:1–14

In chapter 4 is seen the power of God as Creator; in chapter 5 is seen the love of God as Redeemer. The Christian believes in God the Creator who is all-wise and all-powerful; he also believes in God who loves and proves his love by redeeming man from sin. This is the view presented here.

The One on the throne holds in his strong right hand a book written on the inside and on the outside and sealed with seven seals. This was a roll of papyrus, the customary writing material. The fact that it was covered on both sides with writing indicates that it was filled with meaning and importance; so many were his judgments that he was pressed for space! The book was "close sealed" with seven seals. The perfect passive participle, together with the perfect number "7," indicates just how securely the book was sealed. The book has been variously characterized. One has called it the book of Justice.[9] Another calls it the book of God's Eternal Counsels, his foreordained purposes.[10] Another thinks it to be a prototype of the book in Ezekiel 2:9–10 and hence a book of lamentations, mournings, and woe.[11] Still another considers it the book of Destiny.[12] This idea and the idea of justice are closely related. The book appears to hold the destiny of men faced by the visitations of God's just wrath upon their sins. The fact that the book was securely sealed indicates the impossibility of anyone's explaining the destiny of man. Here it is in God's hand. The Christians feel their hearts leap within them at the sight of it when they think on the unfolding

---

[9]Dana, *Ibid.*, p. 116.
[10]D. Smith, *The Disciple's Commentary*, p. 624.
[11]Hengstenberg, *op. cit.*, p. 277.
[12]Richardson, *op. cit.*, p. 71.

and reading of it. But it is perfectly sealed and closed to their eyes. Here are God's providential dealings with the world, but they cannot be seen; the outcome of the struggle is yet unknown. Here is the future of Christianity in its struggle with emperor worship, but it is sealed up and cannot be seen. No wonder John "started weeping much"—the imperfect of the verb "to weep audibly" as a disappointed or hurt child, is used—when he heard no one respond to the invitation, "Who is morally worthy to open the book?" There was no one found thus worthy. It appeared that the mystery would still be unsolved, and John, thinking of the distressed condition of the churches and longing to know the outcome, fell to the loud weeping of disappointment and pain which was more than physical. But John was bidden to "stop weeping" because there was one worthy to open the book and reveal God's purpose for men.

This indicates that the book was the introductory means of bringing forward the central figure of this chapter, the triumphant Christ. The description of the Lamb and the work ascribed to him leave no doubt that the figure here portrayed is the *redeeming* Christ. One of the elders tells John that the "Lion of the tribe of Judah" has "overcome," and this has made him worthy to open the book. John stopped weeping and looked to see a Lion, but beheld instead a Lamb, a "little lamb"—used only in this book and in John 21:15. Just as figures change forms rapidly in dreams, they changed in John's vision. A Lion quickly becomes a Lamb. No doubt there is significance in this symbolism. The Lion represents absolute strength and bravery; the Lamb, a religious symbol, represents absolute goodness. The characteristics of the Lamb are significant. It stood as "one slain." The word indicates the wounds received in cutting the throat of the young lamb sacrificed on the altar. Christ is here pictured in his atoning sacrifice. He had been slain but is now alive forevermore. He has "seven horns." Horns in apocalyptic literature are symbolical of power. The Lamb has "7" horns, the perfect number. He is perfectly equipped for putting down opposition to his kingdom. He has "seven eyes, which are the seven Spirits of God, sent forth into all the earth." This, no doubt, represents ceaseless and perfect vigilance on behalf of his people;

the perfect spiritual essence of God is thus engaged on behalf of man.[13]

There is expressed in the next action a vividness which is difficult to bring out in the English. The Lamb "came," the aorist tense picturing the whole action in one flash, and "taketh the book." This last verb is εἴληφεν, the perfect of λαμβάνω—"to reach out and take." Beckwith[14] calls this the "aoristic perfect." Dana,[15] more to the point, calls it the "dramatic perfect." It shows an unhesitant attitude and a spirit of strong determination on the part of the Lamb as "the first thing you know he has taken the book right out of the hand of him who sat on the throne." Only Christ can open the book and carry forward God's judgments on wicked men. The destiny of men is in the nail-pierced hands of the Lamb who was slain.

This action called forth great joy on the part of all those around the throne. No doubt it brought joy to the persecuted Christians when their Lion-Lamb Saviour became their champion. At any rate we find recorded the reaction of those around the throne and beyond. The Lamb was worshiped by the four living creatures who had worshiped God in the last scene. The Lamb was also worshiped by the twenty-four elders. With harps of praise and offering the prayers of the saints whom they represent, they fall before him and sing the Song of Redemption. The song which they sing is new; not new in point of time, νέος, but new as to kind, καινήν. This is a unique song; there is nothing else like it—man redeemed by death of God in the flesh. In the song (5:9-10) praise is attributed to Christ because he is worthy to open the seals—worthy is the Lamb! He is worthy because of his redemptive work. This redemptive work is described by four qualitative terms:

1. It is *for God,* primarily—"thou didst purchase unto God." This same idea is reflected in Ephesians 1:1-14. The redemption of man is first of all for God's benefit.

2. It is *through Christ's blood*—"thou wast slain . . . thou didst

---

[13]Beckwith, *op. cit.,* p. 510.

[14]*Ibid.,* p. 511.

[15]*Ibid.,* p. 118.

purchase with thy blood." This can have reference only to the sacrificial death of Christ on the cross.

3. It is *unlimited*—"men of every tribe, and tongue, and people, and nation." The grace of God through Christ is not limited to any nation; it is for all nations.

4. It *makes the redeemed a kingdom*—"and madest them to be unto our God a kingdom and priests; and they reign upon the earth." As men partake of the redemptive work of Christ, they become parts of God's kingdom; they become priests to serve him here in this world.

For such redemptive work the elders praise the Lamb. A multitude of angels join in to sing the worthiness of the Lamb. Natural creation joins in to sing "blessings, and honor, and glory, and power, and dominion" unto the One who sits upon the throne and unto the Lamb.

John's first vision closed with this thrilling scene of the triumphant saints and an adoring universe offering praise and homage to the triumphant Christ. Such a scene was calculated to bring new courage and new hope to the hearts of John's first readers, the persecuted Christians of Asia; it brings the same cheer to Christian hearts in any age. Believing in the power of God (chap. 4) and the redeeming love of God (chap. 5), there is no enemy or force of evil which Christians need to fear. They can enter the conflict or endure the evil knowing that God is still on his throne; he has not laid aside his scepter; he has not abandoned his throne to any other. He is mightier than all the forces arrayed against his people. Faith in him gives man the proper evaluation of life, of its issues and their outcome.

CHAPTER VII

The Lamb Opens the Seals

(Revelation 6:1 to 11:19)

The main action of the book of Revelation begins with this vision. The remainder of Revelation is in reality an explanation of the seals of the little book of destiny. Back of all history is God in Christ; in this book we see the hand of Christ opening the sealed book of God's dealings with men. The seal was a sign of ownership. Only an official representative could open one's seal. Here Christ is God's official representative, and he is qualified to open the seals.

First Seal, White Horse: Conquest, 6:1-2

The Lamb opened the first seal. One of the four living creatures said in a thunder-like voice, "Come." There is a variation on this reading in the ancient manuscripts. Codex Sinaiticus has a double imperative, "Come and see," as though addressed to John. Codex Alexandrinus, which is considered the text which shows the least evidence of alteration, has the single imperative, "Come" as a signal for the horseman to ride across the stage of activity. It makes little difference which is correct; the latter seems to fit the circumstances better.

When the voice said "Come," a man on a white horse rode across the stage. This is pantomime. There are no lines and no action other than the riding of the horse across the path of vision. From the color of the horse and the description of the rider, we must identify him. There are two main views as to his identity. Some[1] have held that

[1]Richardson, *op. cit.*, pp. 79 ff. gives the clearest treatment of this theory.

the man on the white horse represents Christ, or perhaps the cause of Christ, the progress of the gospel. The color of the horse would suggest heavenly purity; the crown suggests royalty; the bow represents his means of overcoming his enemies; he goes forth to a continued victorious march for God. The progressive advance of the cause of Christ will continue until every foe is vanquished. The victorious rider on the white horse represents the victorious course of the gospel. This is a theory with much appeal, but there appear to be too many things against it. From all appearances the white horse marches the same way as the others; this would not be true if they were opposed to one another in vital conflict. Too, it is rather crude to picture Christ as the Lamb drawing back the curtains, changing quickly to the garb of a Persian soldier and riding a horse across the stage.

The better theory[2] seems to be the one based on the historical reflections in the picture. This first horseman represents conquest, militarism, armed strength with lust to subdue some new foe. The white color of the horse represents victory. A white horse was always ridden by a conqueror in a triumphal march. This horse symbolized, along with the others, one of the forces which was to bring about the downfall of the Roman Empire. The Christians were to see in it a token of victory. The horseman is not a Roman but a Parthian cavalryman—the most dreaded enemy that Rome had. The Roman warriors did not use a bow; however, it was the favorite weapon of the Parthians. Roman rulers never wore a crown. When the Tarquins were driven out about 500 B.C., a precedent was set against monarchial rule. There was a traditional hatred for the crown which suggested it; many rulers had been killed because they longed to be king. In contrast to this, coins of Persia have been found showing a horseman with bow in hand and a crown on his head. Thus is pictured to the Christians that victory is coming. Mighty Rome is not always to stand. Outside conquest will be a part of the method of her destruction. God held in his hand the means of deliverance for his people.

---

[2]Cf. Allen, Dana, D. Smith, *Expositor's Greek Testament*, Ramsay, Charles, and others.

Second Seal, Red Horse: War, 6:3-4

When the Lamb opened the second seal, John heard the second living creature say, "Come." At his summons a man on a red horse rode across the stage. This is more pageantry. The man speaks no lines. He rides, and lets the color of his horse identify him. His horse is red, and to him is given "to take peace from the earth" and cause men to slay one another. He carries a great sword which, added to all the other details, identifies him as War. War was the bloody means of carrying out conquest, so it was natural that the red horse should follow the white one.

Third Seal, Black Horse: Famine, 6:5-6

The third seal is opened, the third living creature speaks his summons, and a man on a black horse rides silently across the stage. The man on the horse carries a balance in his hand. A voice off stage, from the midst of the four living creatures, said, "A measure of wheat for a shilling, and three measures of barley for a shilling; and the oil and the wine hurt thou not." All this identifies the third horseman as Famine. In wartimes food became scarce and was weighed out to families. The prices on the necessities of life were high; wheat sold for $6.40 a bushel, barley for $2.00 a bushel. A measure, χοῖνιξ, of wheat was the usual ration for a day for a working man. In wartime it was to cost twelve times its normal price. At the same time a day's labor would not command more than an eighth of the ordinary twenty-four measures of the coarser barley. Foodstuffs were scanty, with hunger stalking the land. Oil and wine, which were luxuries and not necessities of life, would flow freely to cause even more exasperation as men saw them in abundance but watched the slow trickle of grain into the hands of the famished.[8] Famine always follows in the wake of war.

Fourth Seal, Pale Horse: Pestilence, 6:7-8

At the opening of the fourth seal and the bid of the fourth living creature, a very gruesome sight took place. In the pageant unfolded

[8]Moffatt, *Expositor's Greek Testament*, V, 390.

before John's eyes, a pale, livid horse rode across the stage. His name was Death, and Hades, the Region of the Dead, followed behind him to gather up his prey. To them was given authority over a fourth part of the earth to kill with every conceivable means. Here we see the dread effects of pestilence which always follows war and famine. It had swept Asia Minor many times and could easily destroy more than conquest, war, hunger, and evil beasts put together. It was a ready instrument of retribution in the hands of divine justice. This judgment is only partial; it touches only a "fourth part" of the earth, but it gives the needed impression of horror as we see a horse the livid color of a corpse, ridden by Death with the Grave running along greedily gathering up fallen bodies.[4]

All the above—military conquest, war, famine, pestilence—are forces which God can use to destroy the oppressors of his people. His Christians are to take courage. Their cause is not lost by any means.

Fifth Seal, Martyred Saints: Persecution, 6:9-11

When the Lamb opens the fifth seal, the symbolism changes. Up to this point we have observed the means of judgment; we now see before us the reason for judgment. Underneath the altar John sees the "souls of them that had been slain for the word of God, and for the testimony which they held." These can be no other than the martyrs of the Domitianic persecution. John names one of them, Antipas, in this book (2:13). Historians record the death of many others. Here, symbolically, they cry out that their blood be avenged. Critics have said that this is a non-Christian attitude and have wanted to reject Revelation from the New Testament canon. They overlook the fact that wrath against sin is an essential part of the righteousness of God. This paragraph reflects the moral necessity for judgment. God could not be a righteous God and allow such evil to go unavenged. The chief reason for God's judgment on the Roman Empire was their persecution of God's people. The only non-Christian attitude reflected is the impatience of the mar-

---

[4]D. Smith, *The Disciple's Commentary*, V, 629 and Moffatt, *Expositor's Greek Testament*, V, 390.

tyrs, and that appears to be a non-Christian attitude which touches almost everyone. The martyred saints know that judgment is coming, and they do not understand why God waits so long.

Each one of them was given a white robe, symbolical of their victory and purity, and they were told to be patient. The time was not ripe for God's retribution; there were others in the churches who were to suffer, but in the end certain victory would be realized; judgment was on its way.

Sixth Seal, Earthquake: Judgment, 6:12–17

When the sixth seal was opened, John saw a great earthquake, with all its attendant horrors. The sun was turned to darkness; the moon was blood-red; stars fell like figs before a great wind; the heavens rolled up like a scroll of paper; mountains and islands disappeared. People of every class and condition hid themselves in caves and cried for the mountains to fall upon them and hide them from the wrath of the One on the throne and of the Lamb; "because," they said, "the great day of their wrath is come; and who is able to stand?" The swift agony of being crushed to death was preferable to being left face to face with an angry God.

There are two views about this symbolism. One group[5] holds that this does not represent the final judgment but only a temporal judgment by natural calamity. As a representative case of natural calamity, the earthquake was used. They were frequent in Asia Minor, and the people would understand it. The combination of earthquake and volcanic eruption had destroyed Herculaneum and Pompeii about A.D. 79. Sardis and Philadelphia had been almost completely destroyed by earthquake at one time. Such natural calamity pictured in a very graphic way the visitation of divine wrath, God's judgment on those who were oppressing his people.

Those who hold to this view point to the evident fact that final judgment does not appear until Revelation 20:11–15. They object to making this the final judgment because:

(1) That view ignores the Old Testament usage of this idea. It is used in connection with national temporal affairs in Joel 2:10;

---

[5]Dana, Pieters, *American Commentary*, Charles, Hengstenberg, *in loco.*

Jeremiah 4:23-24, 28; Isaiah 13:9-10. *But* we are not to forget, as these men seem to, that one of the main features of Revelation is the use of Old Testament language with New Testament meaning; this fact weakens this objection.

(2) The view that this is the final judgment overlooks the fact that this is a vision and given in symbol and takes this literally. This is a half-truth. The futurists are guilty of this, but there are many others who hold that this symbolizes final judgment but do not make it literal.

(3) The view that this is the final judgment introduces the final judgment at the wrong place in the scheme of things. This is true if the recapitulation theory is wrong. But if these visions are pictures of the same things, each complete within itself but growing in intensity, then this has the final judgment in the right place.

Another group[6] holds that this *is* symbolical of the final judgment. They hold to the recapitulation theory stated above, and this is the natural sequence. They do not hold to a literal fulfilment of these things. The events pictured here were matters drawn from the things familiar to the Christians of that day to show the complete and final overthrow of the enemies of the Christian cause. Proponents of this theory point to the statement, "For *the* great day of their wrath is come; and who is able to stand?" as an indication that this is the last judgment. Pieters[7] and Charles[8] answer this with what appears to be a truthful statement that that was the consciousness of the terror-stricken sinners, not John. They thought it was the end of things; John put no interpretation on it.

There is such good argument on both sides of this question that it is difficult to choose one and reject the other. My sympathy is with the views which look upon these visions as each complete within itself and covering the field of activity. Therefore, I should hold to the view that this symbolizes final judgment and be con-

---

[6]Richardson, Moffatt, Kuyper, *in loco.*

[7]Pieters, *op. cit.*, p. 126.

[8]Charles, *The Revelation of St. John,* Vol. I, "The International Critical Commentary," p. 183. See also Swete, *op. cit.*, p. 93.

sistent. I am very strongly moved to be inconsistent because of a strong feeling that this does not represent final judgment but that it represents natural calamity as an instrument of judgment in the temporal affairs of men. Moffatt[9] may have a means of escape in his suggestion that this does symbolize the beginning of final judgment, but John introduces an *entre-acte* which puts off final judgment and makes this give the inhabitants of Asia Minor only a foretaste of the destruction that is coming. Under any condition this part of the pageant symbolizes God's destructive power against those who reject him and his plan of salvation. As these forces—conquest, war, famine, pestilence, natural calamity—rage, "Who shall be able to stand?" This question is answered in chapter 7.

Provisions for the Redeemed, 7:1–17

The last series of symbols pictured the destruction of the enemies of Christ. The next series will carry a similar idea. The question which would naturally arise is, What becomes of Christ's saints while this destructive work is in progress? Do they escape or are they subject to this destructive force? For this reason the parenthesis is introduced to show that God has provided for their protection. The forces of destruction are symbolized as being held in restraint until the saints are sealed for eternal glory and protection.

In this vision John saw four angels standing one at each of the four corners of the earth. They are holding back the four winds which symbolize divine retribution.[10] As John looks, he sees another angel come out of the light of the rising sun, the direction from which light comes to a dark world. This angel carries the seal, branding iron of the living God, and cries with a great voice, one that could be heard everywhere, to the four angels to hold back the divine retribution until he has placed God's possessive and protective seal upon the foreheads of God's true people. John does not see the

---

[9]Moffatt, *op. cit.*, p. 394.

[10]God's judgment pictured as wind is a prominent idea in the Old Testament. Cf. Jeremiah 4:11–12; 18:17; 49:32, 36; Ezekiel 5:2; 12:14; Psalm 106:27; Job 38:24; Isaiah 41:16.

sealing take place, but he hears the announcement of the number "a hundred and forty-four thousand, sealed out of every tribe of the children of Israel." He also hears that the one hundred and forty-four thousand was made up of twelve thousand from each of the twelve tribes of Israel. All scholars appear to recognize that this sealing is a symbol of protection. The language is similar to that in Ezekiel 9:1 ff. where a mark is placed upon the forehead of God's people, and the agents of destruction are forbidden to touch every person who is thus marked. Here in Revelation those sealed bear the mark of God; Oriental sealing instruments usually bore the name of the owner. They are protected so that the destructive winds do not harm them. Up to this point the scholars agree. When an attempt is made to identify the two groups mentioned in this chapter, there is wide disagreement. Revelation is written in symbolical language, and it is never becoming to be dogmatic when dealing with symbols. It is best to review the different opinions, the evidences, and draw whatever conclusions appear to be best supported.

First, there is a theory that the one hundred forty-four thousand represent Jewish Christians, and the great host which no man could number represent Gentile Christians. At first glance this seems a natural choice. Dana[11] refers to the first group as the remnant of Israel and the second as the redeemed of the nations. Of course, "12" is the symbolical number for organized religion. It is the perfect number for this idea. One hundred and forty-four thousand is a great multiple of twelve and is meant to convey the idea of an immense throng. Therefore, this sealing of twelve thousand from each of the twelve tribes of Israel symbolizes an immense throng of Jewish Christians who are sealed for protection. The great throng (7:9-17) is a symbol of the great numbers of Gentiles who are saved. John does not leave them without hope. They are joyous in triumphant anticipation of God's protection. This view is substantially the same as the one taken by Stuart.[12] Bengel also holds this position. There are others who hold to this view but adopt the futurist view, which

---

[11]Dana, *The Epistles and Apocalypse of John*, p. 123.
[12]Stuart, *op. cit.*, II, 171 ff.

really puts them out of the comparison at this point.[13] It is quite surprising to find Dana in the company of Bengel and Stuart at this point which turns from a symbolical interpretation to a rather bold literal one.

The second theory is that the symbolism here used does not divide the redeemed into Jews and Gentiles. This is held by Pieters, Moffatt, Kiddle, D. Smith, J. Smith, Richardson, Charles, Swete, Beckwith, Milligan, and Hengstenberg. These men represent the very best in the study of Revelation for the last one hundred years. Here in condensed form are some of the statements:

Pieters: The first group represents the true believers on earth while they are still subject to the storms of divine judgment that break over the world; while the second group symbolizes the believers who are already in heaven. . . . The two groups, then, are, respectively, The Church Militant and The Church Triumphant.[14]

Richardson: The church universal, all Christians, are sealed and their safety assured. Not one member of the true church is lost. Again the saints of both the Old and New Testaments are indicated by the multiple twelve. There is no distinction here between the Jew and the Gentile.[15]

D. Smith: A vision of God's care for his people amid their earthly tribulations. . . . These were the true Israel, "the Israel of God" (Gal. 6:16); . . . . A vision of the heavenly triumph of the martyred host. . . .[16]

Swete: The Israel of the first vision is coextensive with the whole church. . . . The two visions depict the same body, under widely different conditions.[17]

Beckwith: Who . . . are the 144,000 that are to be sealed? The answer which, in spite of some difficulty raised, is most conformable to the conceptions of the New Testament in general, as well as those of the Apocalyptist—the one that does least violence to the universal-

---

[13]Larkin, *op. cit.,* p. 65 is a good example of this group.

[14]Pieters, *op. cit.,* p. 129.

[15]Richardson, *op. cit.,* p. 88.

[16]D. Smith, *The Disciple's Commentary,* V, 632 f.

[17]Swete, *op. cit.,* p. 99.

istic spirit of the book—is that they are the whole body of the church.
. . . The redeemed here are those that come out of every nation
and tribe . . . Jew and Gentile alike.[18]

Charles: It is not believers descended from the literal Israel . . .
but from the spiritual Israel that are here referred to. . . . These
(the second group) are they who had been sealed in the vision just
recounted, and had already by martyrdom won the martyr's privilege of immediate blessedness and perfection. . . .[19]

Hengstenberg: To understand by these (144,000) simply the
Jewish Christians, is the greatest arbitrariness. . . . Those who
were before assured of preservation amid the judgments that are
decreed against the world are here presented the innumerable host
of 7:9 before us in that heavenly glory which awaited them.[20]

Milligan: The first impression produced by the vision of the
sealed is undoubtedly that it refers to Jewish Christians, and to
them alone. Many considerations, however, lead to the wider conclusion that, under a Jewish figure, they include all the followers of
Christ, or the universal church.[21]

All these are affirmative statements to positionize the writers.
From a more or less negative viewpoint there are many reasons
suggested against the view that the two groups represent Jewish and
Gentile Christians, respectively. Some of these reasons deserve notice.

    1. A distinction between Jewish and Gentile Christians is not
drawn elsewhere in Revelation. To the eyes of John, the church
is one. There is in it neither Jew nor Greek, barbarian nor
Scythian, bond nor free. There is not a single word to suggest
that the body of believers is divided into two parts. The epistles
to the seven churches unquestionably suggest a representation
of that body of Christians whose fortunes are afterward described. In these epistles Christ walks in the midst of every part
of it, and promises are made, not in one form to one member

---

[18]Beckwith, *op. cit.*, pp. 535 and 539.

[19]Charles, *The Revelation of St. John*, Vol. II, "The International Critical Commentary," pp. 206 and 209.

[20]Hengstenberg, *op. cit.*, I, 363 and 371.

[21]William Milligan, *The Book of Revelation* (New York: A. C. Armstrong and
Son, 1889), pp. 116 f.

and in another form to another, but always in precisely the same terms, to "him that overcometh." It would be out of keeping were we here, where a similar topic of preservation is on hand, to introduce a line of cleavage between Jewish and Gentile Christians.

2. It is the custom of the author to heighten and spiritualize Jewish names. The Temple, the Tabernacle, the Altar, Mount Zion, Jerusalem are to him the embodiments of ideas deeper than those literally conveyed by them. Analogy suggests that this is the most natural usage of the word Israel in this instance.

3. Some of the expressions of the passage are inconsistent with the limitation of the sealed to any special class of Christians. Why, for example, should the holding back of the winds be universal? Would it not have been enough to restrain the winds that blew on Jewish Christians and not the winds of the whole earth? Then, too, the designation "servants" seems to include the whole number, and not some only, of God's children.

4. If the second group represents the Gentile Christians, nothing is said of their being sealed for protection; and they evidently would need it as much as the Jewish Christians.

5. The seal of protection is placed on their foreheads, and in Revelation 22:4 all believers are marked in a similar way.

6. The number 144,000 is found again in chapter 14. It can hardly be doubted that the same persons are included in it on both occasions; in chapter 14 it is clear that the whole number of the redeemed is symbolized.

7. Revelation is a book of contrasts. In many of the passages of this book (13:16-17; 14:9; 16:2; 19:20; 22:4) we find all Satan's people branded on their foreheads. This seems to be an antithesis to the passage here discussed. Therefore, all God's people are sealed.

8. It is undeniable that the second vision—the great host before the throne and before the lamb—unfolds a higher stage of privilege and glory than the first. It will thus follow on the supposition now combated that at the very instant when John is said to be rejecting the Gentiles from the sealing and giving them a

position inferior to the Jew, treating them as simply an "appendix" to the Jews, he speaks of them as the inheritors of a far greater privilege and glory. The apostle could hardly be so inconsistent with himself as this.

The conclusion from this preponderance of evidence is plain. The vision of the sealing does not apply to Jewish Christians alone but to all Christians. When the judgments of God are abroad in the world, all the servants of the Lord are sealed for protection. The two visions must represent the same group under different circumstances. These circumstances must now be discussed.

An attentive examination of the structural principles marking the Johannine writings will show that they are distinguished by a tendency to set forth the same object in two different lights, the latter of which is climactic to the former. The writer is not satisfied with a single utterance of what he desires to impress upon his readers; he uses repetition. Often in Revelation, after he has presented a matter, he brings it again before his readers, works upon it, enlarges it, deepens it, sets it forth with stronger and more vivid coloring. The second expression is the center of a circle of wider circumference, and it is uttered in a more forceful manner. This appears to be what we have in the passage under discussion.

The 144,000 of the first consolatory vision represent not Jewish Christians only but the whole body of believers. The sealing symbolizes their God-given protection under the judgments that are to fall upon the world. The number "12," a sacred number of religious significance, is first multiplied by itself and then by a thousand, the number used to signify completeness. The resultant 144,000 is used to represent absolute completeness; not one member of the true body of believers is lost.[22] The unnecessary naming of each several tribe, with the repeated number 12,000, emphasizes in the strongest possible way the inclusion of every member of God's people. John has a truth of the highest importance to explain, and, with the artistry of a skilful storyteller, he explains it in such a way that his readers are kept in suspense about the culminating horror to be launched upon the world at the breaking of the seventh seal.

---

[22] Cf. John 17:12.

They must learn something which affects them more closely than the spectacular portents of chapter 6. Conquest, war, famine, and pestilence have been seen as threatening. Four angels hold back the four winds, which are alternative symbols with the four horsemen, from their grim mission. They are held back until God's people may be sealed safely from the threatening destruction. Before the crisis, good and evil must be discriminated; the righteous are immune from this destruction which hunts down the wicked. The seal is God's mark of protection and ownership; it identifies them with his worship; it places them beyond harm. Thus this first group represents the true believers on earth where the storms of divine judgment break over the world. They are not taken out of the world, but they are sealed. They are kept in the hollow of God's hand; for them all things work together to a good end.

"After these things," the sealing of the protected saints on the earth, John saw a vision of greater joy and encouragement. He saw a great host beyond the ability of man to number. They were "out of every nation, and from all tribes, and peoples, and tongues." They were before the throne and before the Lamb dividing their praise between the God "who sitteth on the throne" and "the Lamb." They were dressed in white robes and held palm branches in their hands.

This group is not sealed for protection because it has passed beyond the need of protection. They are already out of the world and in the presence of God. They have been victorious in trial. This is symbolized in the white robes they wear. They are joyous. This is symbolized in the use of the palm branches. Palm branches were used on many occasions in that day, all of which were occasions of rejoicing. Roman conquerors wore garlands of palm leaves.[23] Greek athletes found a palm branch awaiting the winner at the end of the course.[24] However, the usage here probably has nothing to do with either of these occasions. In all likelihood its use is a reflection of the use of palms in the Feast of Tabernacles.[25] They were carried

---

[23]Charles, *The Revelation of St. John,* Vol. I, "International Critical Commentary," p. 211.

[24]Moffatt, *op. cit.,* p. 398.

[25]Swete, Dana, Hengstenberg, Richardson, Beckwith, and Milligan, *in loco.*

at the Feast of Tabernacles and used in constructing the shelters required for that occasion on housetops and streets. The Feast of Tabernacles was pre-eminently a feast of joy—joy at deliverance and preservation and assurance for the future. So here they are used in the same way. The song is one of praise which attributes salvation—deliverance—to God on the throne and to the Lamb. Thus do they recognize the source of their victory; the angels around the throne join in the praise of God for what he has done.

One of the elders, seeing John's interest and perplexity, asked him, "Who are these that are arrayed in white robes, whence do they come?" John confesses his own ignorance at that point, but he also expresses his belief that the elder can enlighten him. He is then told, "These are they that are coming out of the great tribulation, and they have washed their robes and made them white in the blood of the Lamb." For this reason, their victorious emergence from the distress upon the world, they are before the throne of God, not down on earth, and they serve him continuously; moreover, he gives them perfect fellowship and protection and fulfils all their needs. The *redeeming* Lamb has become their *providing* Shepherd; he shall guide them to fountains of water of life, and God shall remove all grief from them.

Altogether this presents a glowing picture of the saints after they have been through the distress threatened in the first part of the chapter. It is glorious to see them as they are coming (present participle) through the distress victoriously and joyously to render their praise to God and Christ as the source of delivery. The great thing is not just to emerge from trial but to emerge from it with unstained faith and conscience.[26] This is possible only through the power of Christ's sacrifice for us. The strength of redemption was behind their victory over persecution. This is the reason they claim no credit for victory but attribute it all to God and the Lamb.

Review the relation in which the two divisions of the chapter stand. The persons referred to are the same; their positions in the two divisions differ. In one they are sealed and safe as judgment rains down upon the earth. They are under God's protection and are

[26]Moffatt, *op. cit.,* p. 399.

delivered not from it but through it. In the second division they are seen after they have come through the difficulties. They possess peace, joy, victory. Every want is supplied; every sorrow healed; every tear wiped away. They were sealed on earth; they wear victorious robes and carry joyous palm branches as they worship around the throne of God in heaven. The two visions together give the most complete picture of the security of God's people before the judgments pictured in chapters 6 and 8. "Who is able to stand?" Here is the answer.

Seventh Seal, Incense: Victory, 8:1–5

Here as in other sections of Revelation the last subdivision of the vision is transitional. It prepares the way for what is coming in the next vision. The transitional section is divided into two parts: the silence in heaven (vv. 1–2), and the incense of victory (vv. 3–5).

The silence in heaven (8:1–2) has been interpreted from two points of view. One view looks upon the half-an-hour space of silence as being symbolical of delayed judgment;[27] judgment is coming but it is delayed; it will come in God's own time. This idea of delayed judgment was brought out in the restraining of the winds (7:1–3), and it may be the significance here. The second view is that the silence in heaven is for dramatic effect.[28] Already John has seen the *instruments* of judgment, the *demand* for judgment, *terror* of the wicked at approaching judgment, and *provision* for God's people during judgment. What is next? Even the hosts of heaven are silent, waiting anxiously to see what comes. They see, as does John, seven angels each with a trumpet in hand. The seal, as used in the last vision, was to hide things; trumpets were used to summon armies, give orders to charge—they were to announce things. What will they announce? This is the question in the minds of the heavenly hosts as they wait with silent expectation. This is a dramatic touch of no prophetic or doctrinal significance within itself; it is a period of trembling suspense, a silence of reverence, expectancy, and prayer

---

[27]Milligan, *op. cit.*, p. 135.

[28]Pieters, Richardson, Dana, Beckwith, D. Smith, Moffatt, Swete, and Kiddle, *in loco.*

in which the heavenly hosts wait in breathless silence for the pageant to continue. It is not at all improbable that both ideas are here symbolized—dramatic expectation as judgment is delayed.

The incense of victory (8:3–5) seems to be easier of explanation. An angel came to the altar with much incense. The incense was added to the prayers of all the saints. A censer was filled with the fire, which was a mixture of incense and prayers, and the fire was cast upon the earth. The incense of victory was thus scattered upon the living coals of Christian intercession. As a result the whole earth was pictured as being in turmoil in the grip of divine judgment. From what follows through the rest of the book, it appears that the thing symbolized here is the fact that the conquering Christ is coming to visit God's retribution on the oppressors of his people. The thing which brings this about is the combination of the prayers of "all the saints." The thunder, lightning, and earthquake which follow are premonitory of a great visitation of destruction. The whole scene in verses 3–5 is a prelude to the seven trumpets which now begin to sound.

John's practical purpose in this passage can be easily overlooked. The symbolism of this vision can be more readily visualized than in many of his other visions; therefore, there is a tendency to concentrate attention on the pictorial details. The results of such an approach have often been unfortunate. For example, the plagues have been subjected to a close scrutiny as though John were giving a scientific treatise on the last things. Commentators have claimed to discover inconsistencies and contradictions. They point out that in 8:7 John declares that all the green grass was burned up, and yet in 9:4 the locusts are told not to harm the grass. They overlook that John means in 8:7 that all green grass on the third part of the earth injured by the fire and hail was destroyed. John was not concerned in these details except as they added to the general picture which he was presenting. What the whole picture signified is the thing which he desired to present to the Christians.

The revelation which John imparts was occasioned by a severe oppression of the Christians through the heathen world power, Rome. Accordingly we expect such a revelation as will bring destruction to this hostile power but triumph to the Christians. In this light the introductory vision of the angel with the incense (8:3-5) was interpreted. The fundamental thought was that God would hear the fervent prayers of his struggling and afflicted people and cause his judgments to go forth against their enemies. Hence, in the "trumpet vision" only such things can be suitable here as are salutary to the Christians and destructive to the great oppressing world power. This is what is naturally expected and what is found when the trumpets are interpreted from the historical point of view. The trumpets are warnings of judgment; they are calls to repentance. When the trumpets sound, the forces of vengeance will begin to fall upon Rome.

The first four trumpets are represented as bringing woes upon nature[29] or partial destruction of the world.[30] They represent woes upon nature in its fourfold aspect. This is the classification of nature as it was known to men in that day: land, sea, fresh waters, heavenly bodies. Part of the symbolism is taken from the plagues of Egypt; part is from historical events of John's own day. This should not be looked upon as a prediction of literal events which are to take place and destroy one third of everything. It is simply a picture of God's warning judgments sent upon wicked men.[31] This is not final judgment; only one third of everything touched is destroyed. It is partial judgment to warn wicked men. A "third" was a conventional way of expressing a "large part." These terrible afflictions were not to be universal; if they were universal, no flesh could be saved, and they were sent for the very purpose of giving those who escape them warnings of so forcible a character that no vestige of excuse for refusal to repent would be left. No opportunity of inducing men to repentance was to be neglected. See again Revelation 9:20-21.

(1) *The sounding of the first trumpet* resulted in woes upon the land (8:7). There was observed a terrific storm of blazing brimstone mingled with hail and blood raining down out of the skies. As a

---

[29] Dana, *The Epistles and Apocalypse of John*, p. 124.
[30] Kiddle, *op. cit.*, p. 148.
[31] Cf. Revelation 9:21.

result a third part of the earth was scorched and swept by forest fires.

(2) *The sounding of the second trumpet* was followed by a volcanic eruption which cast a large blazing mountain into the sea. A third part of the fish died, and a third of the ships on the sea were destroyed.

(3) *The sounding of the third trumpet* sent a huge star burning like a torch to crash on a third part of the fresh waters: rivers and springs. This caused a third part of the water to be turned to bitter poison so that many, drinking the water, died.

(4) *When the fourth trumpet sounded,* a third part of sun, moon, and stars were turned to darkness, leaving a third of the day dark as night and a third of the night still gloomier.

All these are pictures of natural calamity as an agent of destruction against Rome, the enemy of the Christian people. One of the main things that led to the breaking down of the Roman Empire was a series of natural calamities causing disaster over the empire: earthquake, volcanic eruption, floods, etc. Many such things had happened within the memory of John and his readers. God used such environmental phenomena to present his revelation of destruction to their enemies. A few years before this writing Mount Vesuvius had erupted (August, A.D. 79) pouring forth a fiery flood which engulfed Herculaneum and Pompeii and many other small villages with a horror long remembered by all in that country. The younger Pliny, writing to Tacitus, told some of the horrors of the event which took the life of his distinguished uncle, Pliny the naturalist. Ashes from the burning mountain fell on ships far out in the sea and upon the distant shores of Egypt and Syria. Pliny relates that there was first an earthquake followed by the eruption which sent an avalanche of fire down the mountainside into the sea. Many who eluded the streams of lava were suffocated by the sulphurous fumes which reached far away. The sky was darkened so that Pliny said, "It was now day elsewhere, but there night blacker and thicker than all nights."

At another time the island volcano Santorin had erupted, giving the suggestion of a burning mountain. Fugitives told how fiery blasts destroyed vegetation, how sulphurous vapors killed the fish in the sea, and how the waters were turned red like blood. Such things were in the consciousness of John's readers. Doubtless God gives his revelation through things they would understand. Thus is he saying to them, "I have the means of destroying your enemies." And by just such things he called those enemies to repent and turn from their evil.

In each of the three series of symbols (seals, trumpets, bowls) the writer's plan is to divide them into four, two, and one, leaving the one to act as a transitional agent. Here it is noted that the first four trumpets pronounce woes upon nature; the next two pronounce woes upon mankind. John heard an eagle, a bird of prey, crying as it flew through the air that the next trumpets would bring woes upon man. The last ones had caused destruction upon nature, but "the worst is yet to come." In common superstition the eagle was a bird of ill omen and was a suitable harbinger of the woes to follow. This announcement came with dramatic effect as the readers, the storm past, looked upon the charred waste before them.

(5) *The sounding of the fifth trumpet* brought the scourge of locusts (9:1-12). A huge star becomes personified and, having fallen, exposes a yawning abyss. At first there come out great clouds of smoke which darken the sun. Gradually the smoke gives way to locusts, or what first appeared to be smoke turns out to be locusts. Locusts were a common pest in that day, but these are uncommon locusts. There follows a dramatic description of the locusts. They had stingers like scorpions; they were armored like battle horses; they had men's faces, women's hair, and lions' teeth; the sound of their wings made a noise like many chariots. They were told not to hurt the grass, common food for locusts, but to spend five months, length of life of a locust plague, in tormenting men until they desire to die rather than live. They were to hurt only the enemies to God's cause; they were to injure no one who was marked as God's man. They have a king who has the very appropriate name "Destruction."

It must be understood that this is symbolical language. It must also be understood that this is pageantry, and the details are used

to make the play more impressivè. One is not to become so interested in the details of appearance that he misses the actor's "lines."
Many attempts have been made to determine the exact meaning of
each detail in this picture. Such efforts have been unprofitable.
What is symbolized by these locusts from *within* the earth and led
by one named "Destruction," a name often associated with the
devil? Some scholars make them parallel with the horsemen of the
next paragraph. But the distinction between the two remaining
woes announced in 8:13 seems to forbid this. Some scholars think
it unimportant and pass it up without an interpretation. The best interpretation in the light of the historical background seems to be that
of Hengstenberg[82] and Dana.[83] They view this vision as symbolizing
the hellish spirit which penetrates the earth (Hengstenberg) or the
forces of decay which God has in his hand for retribution upon
defiant Rome (Dana). It symbolizes the hellish rottenness, the
internal decadence in the Roman Empire. One thing which brought
about Rome's downfall was a series of corrupt rulers and leaders.
Such a spirit of internal rottenness is pictured here as coming from
within the empire (out of the earth) to work toward her destruction.
Such a condition injured Rome, but it could really do no hurt to
God's persecuted Christians because they were not really a part
of wicked Rome. God has now indicated two instruments which he
can use to cut down the oppressors of his people: natural calamity
and internal decadence. A third instrument follows in the next
vision.

(6) *The sounding of the sixth trumpet* brings the second woe
upon men (9:13-21). The sixth angel sounded his trumpet, and then
a voice came from the altar telling him to loose the four angels that
were bound at the great river Euphrates. The four angels were
loosed and led a great cavalry host bent on destruction. These had
been especially prepared for this work. The symbolism of this vision
is packed with dramatic details. The army of horsemen measured
200,000,000, or twice ten thousand times ten thousand, a number
designating a great host, a complete number. In regular formation

---

[82]Hengstenberg, *op. cit.*, I, pp. 429 ff.
[83]Dana, *The Epistles and Apocalypse of John*, pp. 126 ff.

this would make a troop of cavalry one mile wide and eighty-five miles long! The men wore breastplates of fire. The horses had heads like lions; fire, smoke, and blazing brimstone came from their mouths. Instead of regular horse tails the horses had snakes for tails so that they could bite and bring hurt to man. A third part of mankind was killed by this cavalry.

Again, the details are added for the purpose of making the vision more dramatic; within themselves the details have no prophetic or doctrinal significance. The whole picture presents the Parthian cavalry[34] from the land of the Euphrates. This group was Rome's most dreaded enemy and a constant threat to her eastern boundary. As before noted, they were never completely conquered by Rome. The description given in this passage is such as to terrorize any opponent. Feature a horse with a lion's head, with fire, smoke, and blazing sulphur coming from his mouth, with a poisonous snake in place of a tail! The combined efforts of P. T. Barnum and Robert Ripley could not produce such an animal! Now multiply that by 200,000,000 and get the picture of the army marching on Rome. This whole picture is given to symbolize external invasion which would serve as an instrument in God's hand to punish the oppressors of his people.

This completes the *three instruments.* Running like a thread through the entire work by Gibbon, *The Decline and Fall of the Roman Empire,* is the truth that three great things combined to overthrow the Roman Empire. They were partly working in John's day. The three were natural calamity, internal rottenness, and external invasion. All these are symbolized in Revelation as instruments ready for God's use to rescue his people. Natural calamity (flood, earthquake, volcanic eruption), internal rottennness (a long line of corrupt rulers), and external invasion (from new and old enemies) combined to overthrow what appeared to be so invincible.

Verses 20 and 21 indicate that such judgments as the above were judgments on the world power, not on the Christians. The Christians might suffer from them but not in judgment. They may be a part of their trial as they mix with the world during their

---

[34]D. Smith, Dana, J. Smith, Kiddle, Moffatt, Swete, Charles, and Stuart, *in loco.*

earthly pilgrimage, but trial is not judgment. The vision is given as a means of reassurance to the Christians to help them see that Rome will never triumph over Christianity. The judgments were to be sent as punitive measures on the wicked oppressors and as a call to repentance. This is indicated when we see in these verses that the rest of the men, those not injured by the plagues, refused to repent and turn from their evil: idols, murders, sorceries, thefts, and fornications. Still after the sixfold judgment they continue in their evil ways. Nothing would make them repent. Nothing is left for them except the still heavier judgments of God.

Announcement of Retribution, 10:1 to 11:13

At this point the regular progress of the trumpet judgments is interrupted, in precisely the same manner as between the sixth and seventh seals, by two consolatory visions. The first is contained in chapter 10, the second in 11:1–13. At 11:14 the series of the trumpets is resumed, reaching from that point to the end of the chapter. This is the longest of the interludes regularly placed between the sixth and seventh symbols of a series. It contains the announcement of swift retribution presented in four pictures.

The angel and the seven thunders (10:1–7) comprise the first part of the interlude. John sees a strong angel radiantly clad coming down out of heaven. He is a messenger of divine vindication. There seems to be little support for Richardson's[35] position that this is Christ himself; elsewhere angels have been the messengers, and the same seems to be true here. He has in his hand a small open book. He stands with one foot on the land and one on the sea to indicate that his message is for the whole world. He cries with a loud voice like the roar of a lion. The cry was no doubt to attract attention to what he was going to say. Before he can make his announcement, "the seven thunders uttered their voices." Thunder is symbolical of warning. In all other prefatory passages in which thunders occur (8:5; 11:19; 16:18) they form a premonition of judgments of divine wrath; that is probably the significance here. Along with the seven

---

[35]Richardson, *op. cit.*, p. 101.

seals, seven trumpets, and seven bowls there was the warning of the seven thunders. John had been told to write what he saw and heard. In obedience to that injunction he started to write the warnings of the seven thunders. A voice from heaven stopped him and told him to seal up the things which the seven thunders had uttered. The reason for this is given in the next few verses—there was to be no more warning. The angel who had been thus interrupted now lifted his hand and gave the last solemn verdict, "There shall be delay no longer." He continued to reveal the fact that the sounding of the seventh trumpet would usher in the finish of God's mystery. The warning given by the six trumpets had been sufficient; men refused to repent; retribution will be visited without further delay. For that reason John was not allowed to write down the warnings issued by the seven thunders. There is to be no more warning, no more delay.

The little book in the hand of the angel is the second thing of importance in this chapter (10:8–11). The voice spoke again from heaven with instructions to John to go and take the little book from the angel. He received it with instructions from the angel to eat it; he was further assured that it would be sweet in his mouth but bitter in his belly. When he had eaten it, he found that those words were true. Then came a commission for him to prophesy over many people.

Controversy has raged over the content of the book. Some believe it to hold the vision of chapter 11. Others look upon it as containing a second revelation which begins with chapter 12 and goes on to the end of Revelation. Others think it contains simply the commission to preach God's judgment upon men who have rejected him. All these ideas have evidences in their favor and evidences which are against them. From a close study of the entire context, it appears that the content of the book has to do with matters of sorrow and woe—this is true in Ezekiel 2:8 ff. When Ezekiel had swallowed the book, he was required to utter lamentations and woes upon ancient Israel. So with this book, whatever it contained it was a message which meant sorrow for John as he delivered it. It appears, therefore, that the message was rather general: woes upon men under God's judgment for having rejected him, woes upon Christians in the hands of their enemies, woes upon the church in conflict with the great world-power Rome, woes upon Rome and her great destruction. Perhaps it is a combination of all these things since he was to prophesy to "many peoples and nations and tongues and kings."

Scholars are rather generally agreed on the meaning of John's eating the book. His eating it symbolized his thoroughly mastering its message. He was to assimilate it, make it a part of himself. In his mouth the little book would be sweet. This no doubt symbolizes the sweetness, the joy of receiving a revelation from God and the delight of being trusted with the responsibility of his message. Every preacher knows this joy. Every preacher with the right feeling in his heart knows, too, the bitterness that comes in the delivery of God's message of condemnation to men in sin. No matter how much John knew that men under God's wrath must be punished, the delivering of that message brought bitterness and sorrow even as he thought about it. The thought of the dreadful consequences of the revealed wrath of God as it falls upon sinful man is a bitter thought no matter how necessary that judgment may be.

The measuring of the Temple (11:1-2) is the third symbol in this interlude. A measuring rod was given to John and he was told to measure the temple and the altar and the worshipers. The outside court was not to be measured since it had been given over to the nations and the holy city was to be trodden under foot forty-two months.

This should not be taken to mean that the Temple at Jerusalem was still standing, nor that the Temple is to be restored before the end of the world and the second coming of Christ. This language, as elsewhere in this book, is purely symbolical. The Temple is to be measured for special care and preservation.[86] The meaning of the symbolism is that the true spiritual Israel will be protected and preserved by God in the troubles that are ahead—it is a vision of consolation for God's own in contrast to the condemnation threatened for their oppressors. The great bulk of the Gentile world dominated by persecuting Rome will suffer. This is symbolized by the fact that

---

[86]Cf. Zechariah 2:2.

the court of the Gentiles was not measured for protection. This period of distress is pictured as lasting forty-two months. In round numbers that is three and one-half years. Three and one-half was the indefinite number. It symbolized uncertainty, restlessness, turmoil which had its turning point either to the good or to the bad. So here is symbolized God's protection over his own during an indefinite time of turmoil and difficulty while people generally are in the hands of godless Rome; however, this is not always to be. There is a turning point. God will see to that.

The two witnesses (11:3–13). The identity of the two witnesses has been variously interpreted. Larkin[87] as representative of the futurists interprets it literally. He says they are to be men who will be witnesses of the end of the world. They will have supernatural power and divine protection for a while. They will then be killed by the representatives of the ruling Antichrist but after three and one-half days will be brought back to life. He identifies them as Moses and Elijah. He explains that, according to Malachi 4:5–6, Elijah was to come as a forerunner of the great and dreadful day of the Lord. This could not have been fulfilled in John the Baptist, says Larkin, because he announced only the first coming of Christ and judgments. He evades the statements of Jesus (Matt. 17:11–13; Matt. 11:1–14) that John was Elijah by saying Jesus meant that John was Elijah if the world received the kingdom; the world rejected Jesus and the kingdom, therefore, John was not Elijah! Such explanations cannot be taken seriously. The main question is, What possible comfort could there have been to the persecuted Christians in John's day in knowing that several thousand years from then such events as those above described would take place? None whatsoever; it would have been meaningless and comfortless to them.

Carroll,[88] representing the continuous-historical interpretation, applies this vision to the apostasy of the church during the dark period from the third century to the Reformation. He follows the year-day method of interpretation, which makes the 1,260 days of the three and one-half years equal to 1,260 years, thus reaching from

[87]Larkin, *op. cit.*, pp. 84 ff.
[88]Carroll, *op. cit.*, pp. 150 ff.

about the end of the third century to about the Reformation. The two witnesses according to this view are the true church and the preacher who never cease to witness during this dark period. The same question arises as with the literal view. What comfort to the Christians of John's day could have been found in this? They needed something to help them right then. They knew and cared nothing about an apostate Roman Catholic Church in the West nor an apostate Greek Catholic Church in the East. They knew of a beaten and broken church in their own day and needed something to assure them of divine help and strength. Neither of the above interpretations answers that need.

The criterion in every attempt to rediscover John's message must be, What meaning did this message have to Christians in John's day? He was writing in a time of supreme and urgent need. His message had to be intended to meet that need. The passage under consideration must be approached from that viewpoint. When viewed in its proper place in the book, this vision is seen to be a part of an interlude between the sixth and seventh symbols of a series. The interlude is made up of four parts; the other three parts are clearly apocalyptic images. This, too, must be regarded as a symbol rather than a literal prediction. What does it symbolize?

The number "2" in Oriental symbolism carried the idea of strength—two men were much stronger than one man. In this instance the two witnesses appear to symbolize a testimony or witness of great power.[39] In this God seems to be saying, "Be assured of the fact that though the world in which you live is dominated by evil men, you will be protected and the gospel will be preached; the Christian witness will be maintained." Every word that is used to describe the two witnesses and their function shows that John is writing allusively. The task of the church is universal publication of the gospel; this will be carried out even if it is in the face of adversity. The witnesses represent the militant spirit of true Christians and their testimony.

This vision naturally divides itself into three parts in which the remarkable progress of the gospel during the apostolic age is re-

[39]Dana, Kiddle, Richardson, Pieters, D. Smith, Hengstenberg, Swete.

flected. *First,* there was the period when the gospel was preached with remarkable success. It was attested by evident divine approval as seen in the miracles which were performed by the apostles. This period is symbolized in verses 4–6 where the two witnesses are spoken of as being possessed of divine power: nothing it seemed could destroy them; they had power to perform miracles in the material world; they had power to bring evil upon those who opposed them. *Second,* there was a time when a power arose which attempted to crush this testimony of the gospel. It was temporarily successful, and at the time this book was written the gospel was going through this crucial stage. It seemed that imperial Rome would be able to crush Christianity and then rejoice over its destruction. This is symbolized in verses 7–10. The beast, symbolical of Rome embodied in the emperor, made war against the witnesses and put a stop to their remarkable work. They were killed and, to heap indignities upon them, their bodies were left unburied that all people might gape at them. The world against which the two witnesses had preached held great rejoicing over the fact that these men were out of their way and would trouble them no more. It requires no stretch of the imagination to see this as the attitude of the Roman Empire in this period when it seemed that Christianity was being crushed so that it could never rise again. *Third,* there was the period of the progress of the gospel which proved that Rome had not considered the power of God. His power caused Rome to be overthrown and enabled the redemptive message of the gospel to live with greater triumph. This is the period, reflected in verses 11–13, which was just ahead of the Christians. The symbolism shows the restoration of life to the two witnesses. When life returned after they had been crushed for three and a half days, an indefinite period of turmoil and trouble, even their enemies recognized that it must have been divine power which brought it about. They were victorious; the truth of their message was vindicated as their enemies saw them rescued by God's power. In connection with this there was such an evident demonstration of God's power that many were led to acknowledge him and give glory to him. This, too, was evidenced in the triumph of Christianity over its persecution during the Domitianic reign. When it came victoriously through that experience, many were led to turn to embrace Christianity.

Thus ends the interlude, a message of divine retribution. There is to be delay no longer. God's message of judgment is to be proclaimed in all its bitterness. God's people are known and protected by him. There will be a strong witness of the gospel during this period of distress just ahead. When it is all over, Christianity will have been thoroughly vindicated in the sight of men.

(7) *The seventh trumpet, transitional:* God's covenant, 11:14-19. It was stated at the close of the sixth trumpet that two visions of a consolatory nature would be observed before the next general vision. One of these consolatory visions was the interlude (10:1 to 11:13) which consoled the Christians by the assurance of God's righteous retribution upon those who were persecuting them. The second is this vision of the ark of the covenant which is transitional, leading over into the next vision. In verse 14 the third woe is announced; it is introduced by the ark of the covenant and embraces the destructive forces which follow, beginning with chapter 12.

When the trumpet sounded, a host of voices from heaven declared, "The kingdom of the world is become the kingdom of our Lord, and of his Christ: and he shall reign for ever and ever." This is a song of victory and rejoicing. Dark days have been experienced, but Christ was victorious. In the conflict between the Christians and the world, beginning with chapter 12, there will be experienced darker days. The outcome of the struggle is announced before the beginning of the conflict is pictured; the outcome is victory for Christ. As a comfort to his people before the conflict begins, God reveals the ark of his covenant in the temple in heaven. This symbolizes the fact that God has not forgotten his people or his covenant with them. The church will be in conflict with the world, and satanic persecution will rage, but God's covenant with his people is still secure; they will be victorious. This was a very encouraging way to introduce the conflict. Modern journalism uses the same method in relating the story of some great battle. A headline assures us of the victory of our army in some battle; then the action is recounted in detail. Many times it appears that the enemy has the upper hand and will win, but all the time we know that victory is ours because we have seen the headline announcing victory. John used this method many times in Revelation—always very effectively.

CHAPTER VIII

The Lamb and the Conflict

(Revelation 12:1 to 20:10)

At this point Swete[1] divides the entire book of Revelation into two sections. He looks upon chapters 1–11 as the first apocalypse revealing Christ as head of the church and the controller of the destiny of the world, and chapters 12–22 as the second apocalypse revealing the trials and triumphs of the church. He thinks the first drama is complete within itself, and that if the second had been lost, it would never have been missed. It is true that the writer makes a new beginning at 12:1, but the reader was prepared for that by 10:11, where John was told that he was to prophesy many more things to many people. In the light of all the evidence, it appears best to see this as an integral part of the whole message. The seals lead to the trumpets. These in turn culminate in the appearance of a little book which contains the truth of judgment upon men. This message is to be delivered by the prophet. Here is the message.

The characters here are essentially the same; the conflict is the same but is presented under a different aspect; the outcome is the same as has been indicated in the beginning. It is interesting to note that from here to the end of the book the action is much faster than heretofore. In climatic sequence judgment on Rome is followed by judgment on all evil. Finally the conflict emerges into complete victory for God and the forces of righteousness.

The figures of this vision are not uniform as in some of the others; i.e., seven seals, seven trumpets, seven bowls of wrath.

---

[1]Swete, *op. cit.*, pp. xxxix ff.

Neither are they distinctly set apart in the text. They are often discussed in the same paragraph, but one or the other will dominate the interest of that paragraph.

The issue of the conflict is the Radiant Woman and her children. The dragon with his allies—the first beast and the second beast—makes every attempt to destroy the woman and her children. But the forces of God—the Lamb and the sickle (judgment)—are victorious. As the conflict closes in chapter 20, we shall see the dragon and his allies consigned to the lake of fire, never to bother the Lamb and his people. This is the symbolism. All these characters must be identified before we know the meaning. When they have been identified and the action explained, the message of Revelation is clear.

The Issue: the Radiant Woman and Her Children (Israel, Christ, the Christians), 12:1-2, 5-6, 14-17

John saw a great sign in heaven. The sign was that of a woman dressed with the radiance of the sun. She had the moon for a pedestal and twelve stars for a crown. She was with child and in travail of childbirth. The child born to her was a manchild, destined to rule the nations. He was caught up to heaven as a protective measure, and the woman fled to a place of protection in the wilderness. This was necessary because of the danger from the blood-red dragon which threatened her and her child.

Scholars have differed in their view of the identity of the woman. Some[2] identify her as the "church," using the term in the sense of the messianic community out of which Christ was born rather than in the true sense of "church" since it is difficult to see the church producing Christ. The general New Testament picture has Christ producing the church. Others[3] hold that the woman symbolizes Israel who, in the person of the virgin Mary, produced Christ. The children of the woman are viewed in two sections of the chapter: the manchild (Christ), verse 5, and "the rest of her seed" (Christians), verse 17.

---

[2]Pieters, Richardson, Kiddle, S. Smith, Beckwith, Stuart, Swete.
[3]Dana, Moffatt.

The manchild is certainly symbolical of Christ. Some scholars of the continuous-historical school deny this. They view the woman as the church and the manchild as the sons and daughters born of the travail of the church. These sons and daughters become martyrs but are caught up to heaven for eternal safety. This sounds good, but it does not answer the need of those who first received the book. John's readers did not need information about the outcome of the church of the Middle Ages. They got what they needed—a view of Christianity from its beginning to the assurance of ultimate triumph. From its very inception the Christian religion has been the object of satanic opposition, but it is destined to triumph over every foe.

The "rest of her seed" of verse 17 must be a reference to the Christians. Note that they are identified as those who "keep the commandments of God *and hold the testimony of Jesus.*" This last is important. The first part could be a reference to Jews only, but the second part definitely identifies these people as Christians. They, too, taste the frenzied opposition of Satan and his forces, but victory with Christ is their destiny.

The Forces at War

We turn now to the forces which are active in this war upon the woman and her seed. Perhaps a brief identification as a preface to what follows will be helpful. The forces of evil are led by the dragon, who is identified as the devil. His allies are the first beast (13:1), who symbolizes the emperor of Rome, Domitian, and the second beast (13:11), who symbolizes the committee set up in Asia Minor to enforce emperor worship. The forces of good are led by God, who also has two allies: the Lamb (14:1), who symbolizes the *redeeming* Christ, and the sickle (14:14), which symbolizes eternal judgment. The battle is one bitterly fought, but the victory goes to God with his *redeeming* Christ and eternal judgment.

(1) The forces of evil are led by the dragon (12:3-4, 7-17).—He is described in ominous terms. He is red in color, the color of blood. He has seven heads, which symbolize great wisdom. He has ten horns, which symbolize great power. Upon his heads are seven

diadems, such as are worn by royalty—symbolizing great authority. He is so large that with a lash of his tail he can knock down the stars from the heavens. This huge, fierce, and powerful dragon stands before the pregnant woman ready to devour her babe as soon as it is delivered. What chance has a helpless woman and a newborn Child against such opposition? It appears hopeless. But wait! John tells us in verse 5 that this Child is destined to rule the world.

When the Child was born, the dragon made his effort to destroy it, but God's protective care was exercised and the Child was caught up to heaven and safety. Thus in a brief statement we see the providential care which attended Christ during the days of his sojourn upon the earth. From the early days of his childhood the devil tried to destroy him. Through the years of his ministry those efforts continued. At the last the devil appeared to be the victor when Christ was nailed to the cross and placed in the tomb. But the power of God was able to give him the victory even over death. He was raised from the grave and caught up to the very throne of God. The devil lost the first battle in the conflict!

This is apocalyptic imagery. A battle is raging. The scene shifts from earth to heaven, then back to earth in the course of affairs. So in the pageantry we see the devil, unsuccessful in his efforts to destroy the Christ on the earth, as he tries even to invade heaven to destroy the child.

Here (vv. 7–12) is war in heaven. As the devil tries to invade heaven to destroy the Christ, he is met by Michael and his angels. Michael is the fighting angel; he has a sword in hand! So fierce is their defense that the devil and his forces are unable to get even a foothold in heaven; they are cast down to the earth. Heavenly voices proclaim the victory of the people of God over all the efforts of the devil. They are victorious because of their loyalty to the *redeeming* Lamb; even if it meant death, they were loyal.

This paragraph must be interpreted in its context in Revelation rather than in relation to obscure Old Testament passages or Milton's *Paradise Lost*. This is not a historical account of the original state of the devil and his fall from that state; it is apocalyptic imagery to present the picture of the devil's efforts to destroy the Christ and his people. Thus the devil has lost two battles in the conflict. He was unable to destroy the Christ on the earth. He was unsuccessful in his efforts to invade heaven to destroy the Christ. Now he turns to a third part of his campaign. He will exercise his wrath on the woman who produced the Christ.

In verse 6 the woman was seen as she took her flight into the wilderness. She is fleeing the wrath of the dragon. She will be protected for 1,260 days or, roughly speaking, three and one-half years. This same idea is repeated in verse 14 in the symbol "a time, times, and half a time," or three and one-half times. Remember that in Jewish apocalyptic writings this was a number which symbolized indefiniteness, turmoil, trouble. The woman, Israel, is given eagle wings with which she may flee the pursuing dragon, who has doubled his efforts in the realization of the limited time which is his (v. 12). In his efforts to destroy her, the dragon spits out a river to engulf her, but the earth swallows it up, and she is safe. The dragon is unable to destroy her.

Here again is apocalyptic imagery. Some interpreters find in this a symbol of the national disintegration of Israel. The climax of that disintegration came with the destruction of Jerusalem in A.D. 70. Even though Israel is scattered throughout the world, she has been able to preserve her racial integration. All efforts to destroy her as a race have failed. This is an interesting view, and it may be the thing symbolized here. Many inferences of a doubtful nature have been drawn from this idea. It is safe to keep in mind that here in Revelation, as elsewhere in New Testament prophecy, the center of God's plan and purpose is Jesus, not the Jews. The main purpose of this imagery is not to show the destiny of the Jews but to show the efforts of the devil in this raging conflict. This is the third battle which he has lost. He turns now for a fourth battle. This one (v. 17) is directed against the Christians, and he finds some allies ready to help him in the battle.

a. The first beast: Roman Emperor, 13:1-10, 18.—In league with the devil to destroy the Christians is a foreboding beast, a jungle brute. He has ten horns—symbolizing great power. He has seven heads—symbolizing great wisdom; or from verse 3 it appears that this may symbolize great durability. Even when one of his heads received a death stroke, it continued to live. The beast has ten diadems—symbolizing great authority. Upon his heads are names of reviling and blasphemy. He is a vicious fighter partaking of the nature of a leopard, a bear, a lion, and exercising the power given to him by the dragon. One of his seven heads bears the marks of a death stroke, but it goes on living. The inhabited earth—except the Christians (v. 8b), worships the beast and the dragon which gives him his power. He has authority to rule forty-two months (three and one-half years); he utters blasphemies against the name of God; he is victorious, temporarily, over the Christians but is destined for destruction (v. 10). He can be identified by these marks, plus the symbolical number "666" of verse 18.

Of the many debated portions of the book of Revelation, this one has probably received the most varied treatment; perhaps mistreatment is a better word for it. It is known that speculation as to the identity of this beast began as far back as Irenaeus (c. A.D. 180). A multitude of cryptic methods has been used to determine his identity by determining the meaning of his number as given in the eighteenth verse—"666." Some of these will be considered. The safest method of determining the identity of this beast is to study the symbolism in the day in which the book was written.

The first beast is frequently called "Antichrist" because he appears as a rival deity to Christ. The term is not used in the book of Revelation. The futurists expect to find him in some exceedingly wicked ruler at the end of the age just before the second coming of Christ. Such a system calls for a restoration of the Jewish nation, the rebuilding of the Temple, the restoration of sacrificial worship, and then the breaking of the Antichrist's covenant with the Jews. Space cannot be given here to refutation of this bizarre system which is at opposites to the New Testament teaching. Such a presentation would have been meaningless and, hence, comfortless to John's readers.

In 12:17 John saw the dragon go and stand on the sands beside the sea. As he watched the turbulent water, he saw a strange beast come forth. The word used for beast is a wild, savage, jungle brute. Such a beast in Jewish apocalyptic work symbolizes a ruler or his government (compare Dan. 7:2-8). The marks which identify this beast are facts known historically about Domitian, the Roman emperor in John's day.

He blasphemed God, the name of God, and the sanctuary of God (v. 6). Domitian appropriated to himself the titles of deity. He demanded that he be addressed as "Supreme Lord and God." He even refused to receive correspondence directed to him unless it used this salutation. From the Christian's viewpoint such was blasphemy of God and the name of God.

He exercised supremacy over the known world (v. 7). To the Romans the Roman world was the "inhabited earth." They even named their sea to indicate this—"middle of the earth," Mediterranean.

He was worshiped by all except the Christians (v. 8). Even the Jews compromised by praying to their God for the emperor and demonstrated their loyalty to the emperor. Only the Christians refused to do such homage.

Images were set up to make worship of the emperor easier (v. 14). This is a well-known fact in Roman history in the time of Domitian. When Trajan came to be emperor, he had many of the golden images melted and turned to better purposes. People who refused to worship the emperor Domitian were refused the privileges of buying and selling in the market places. This is reflected in verse 17. Those who did worship him received a mark upon their hand or forehead to indicate, according to the custom of some of the pagan cults, that the individual was an adherent of the particular deity. The mark was the name of the emperor. John presents the name in the symbolic number "666."

From early Christian history men have been counting the name of the beast to determine his identity. One of the most frequently used theories is the one presented by David Smith in the *Disciple's Commentary*. It reduces "Nero Caesar" to the Hebrew consonant equivalent "Nron Ksr" and adds up the numerical equivalent for each letter. In the primitive languages a letter was often used for a number as in the Roman system: V for 5, X for 10, C for 100, etc. So in Hebrew the numerical equivalent would be: N = 50, R = 200, O = 6, N = 50, K = 100, S = 60, R = 200. The total is 666. Thus many interpreters have held that the emperor indicated is Nero. David Smith, with a better view of history, adapts this to the Nero redivivus myth. This was an idea current that the wicked Nero was reincarnated in Domitian, who was certainly the ruler at the time this book was written.

The favorite theory of the continuous-historical school was started by Irenaeus and fits well the Roman Catholic apostasy idea of this group. According to this view the first Roman ruler was named Latinus; in Greek his name is spelled Lateinos ($\lambda\alpha\tau\epsilon\hat{\iota}\nu o s$). In the Greek letter evaluation system the following works out nicely: $\lambda = 30, \alpha = 1, \tau = 300, \epsilon = 5, \iota = 10, \nu = 50, o = 70, s = 200$. The total is 666. The mark of the beast is the Latin church; the Roman Catholic system which is opposed to true Christianity. Here as always in this system there is the fatal objection: What possible meaning would this interpretation have had for the Christians of Asia Minor in A.D. 95? They certainly were not being bothered by the Roman Catholic Church! Their trouble was with Domitian.

With a similar result to this Greek system the Roman system has been used.[4] Where a Roman letter had no numerical evaluation, it was made to equal zero. The following is the result: V = 5, I = 1, C = 100, A = 0, R = 0, I = 1, U = 5 (the same as V), S = 0; F = 0, I = 1, L = 50, I = 1, I = 1; D = 500, E = 0, I = 1. Thus the Latin expression, *vicarius filii dei,* "in place of the son of God," is made to be represented by 666. It is reported that this expression is encrusted in jeweled letters on the pope's crown as it is used in the ceremony of his coronation. Thus again the pope is made to bear the brunt of John's accusation.

The following system was suggested by a student in the author's class in New Testament in 1941: Let the English alphabet have the numerical equivalents starting with A = 100, B = 101, C = 102, etc. The following letters will have the values indicated. H = 107, I = 108, T = 119, L = 111, E = 104, R = 117. The total, Hitler

[4]Granger, *The Beast That Was and Is Not.*

= 666. Doubtless many people in the world at that time would have subscribed to this interesting result! Unfortunately the student had no good reason for starting his evaluation at 100 rather than some other number. So it turned out to be only another mathematical mystery.

This *"reductio ad absurdum"* treatment is given to indicate the futility of such efforts to arrive at the truth. By this cryptic method the number has been applied to several popes and a larger number of political personages during the course of the world's history. A pathetic loss of time and thought and mathematical ingenuity has marked the labor of an endless number of men who have tried to solve the riddle of this mystic number and assign it to some contemporary.

The number, and not the name, is the significant thing. Doubtless the name was one which, taken by itself, would be portentous, but the number is the real portent. The number "6" awakened a feeling of dread in the breast of the Oriental who felt the significance of numbers. It fell short of the sacred "7" and was an evil number. To the Oriental there was doom in the number "6" when it stood alone. Raise it to a series—"666"—and there is the representation of a potency of evil than which there can be no greater, a direfulness of fate than which there can be no greater. By symbol the number "666" is evil raised to its highest power.[5] The beast to whom John gave the number represented the combination of malignant work embodied in political power and false religion. The name expresses the inner nature of the one to whom it is applied. Several interpreters[6] have noted that the cryptic number "888" was used in the Sibylline Oracles (1:324) as a symbol for Jesus. He goes as far beyond the perfect "777" as this beast falls short of it. This string of sixes represented to the Christians everything that was distasteful, evil, terrible, and brutal. The persecuting Roman emperor with his forced diabolical emperor worship was that "everything." He was the ally of the devil in an attempt to destroy the Christians. If the number is to be applied to one man, it appears that Domitian,

---

[5]Richardson, Pieters, Dana, Milligan.
[6]Swete, Richardson.

monster of sin, cruelty, and degradation fulfilled that role. David Smith is close to this in his view that the number represents Nero redivivus.

b. The second beast: Committee to enforce emperor worship, 13:11-17. In league with the dragon (devil) and the first beast (emperor) to destroy the Christians is the second beast. The same word for beast is used in his case as that of the first beast. He, too, is an unusual beast. He has two horns like a lamb, but when he speaks it is the dragon's voice which is heard. He exercises the power of the first beast which he, the first beast, received from the dragon. The office work of this second beast was to enforce the worship of the first beast, even making the image set up for people to worship appear to talk. He places a mark, the name of the first beast or the number of his name, on every person who worships the beast. All who refuse to worship the beast and receive the mark of identification are forbidden the right to buy or sell in the markets. Such is the symbolism of this third member of the forces of evil.

There are four characteristics which help to identify this second beast:

Two horns like a lamb indicate an outward religious appearance; the lamb was a religious symbol. His having only two horns may symbolize his limited power as over against the seven horns of the Lamb of God (5:6).

The voice of a dragon indicates that he spoke with the diabolical authority of Satan.

He exercised the power of the first beast; his power was derived from the Roman State or the emperor.

His work was to enforce emperor worship. All these characteristics seem to identify the second beast as the "Communé" or "Concilia"⁷ set up in Asia Minor to enforce the state religion. This was an official body which had charge of the state religion and had as its duty to force all to do homage to the image of the emperor. Christ had his prophets to carry on his religion; Antichrist, too, had prophets, pseudo prophets, to carry on his work. Christ's prophets used miracles; Antichrist's pseudo prophets used pseudo miracles. David

⁷Hardy, *Christianity and the Roman Government*, p. 72.

Smith says concerning this second beast that it was an image of the priesthood which administered the impious cult of the emperor, a blasphemous counterpart of the Lamb which was slain, our Great High Priest.[8] John and his readers knew what the imperial cult meant since it was better organized and enforced in Asia Minor than in any other part of the Roman Empire. It was composed of deputies whose duty was to build images of Domitian, altars at the images, and legislate in any way they considered best to enforce the state religion. Worshiping the emperor was a test at every phase of life. Christians were boycotted in the market for refusal to bear the mark of the emperor. Marriage settlements, wills, transfers of property—none of these were legal without the stamp of the emperor. Such innocent usage came to have a repulsive religious significance with the Christians. It was like brands used in heathen religions to mark the adherents of the religion; this custom seems to be used symbolically by Paul, "I bear in my body the marks of the Lord Jesus" (Galatians 6:17). All these things heaped up the difficulties and increased the power of their persecutors.

Thus we find three members of the forces of evil as they are engaged in battle with the forces of righteousness. First, the dragon who is identified as the devil with all his cunning, power, and evil. Second, the first beast which is identified as the wicked emperor Domitian who receives his power from the devil. Third, the second beast which is identified as the Roman Concilia, an organization, outwardly religious but internally devilish, for the enforcing of emperor worship and the punishing of all who refused to take part in the ceremonies of the state religion. Clearly they represent the ultimate in ferocity and malignancy as they set themselves against the people of God. They appear invincible, but John turns from this scene in the pageant, a scene hopelessly dark, to present a radiant scene which shows the forces of righteousness which will ultimately overcome the forces of evil.

(2) The forces of righteousness led by God (14:1-20).—The scene just closed in the pageant of redemption was a fearsome vision, one which gave little hope to the Christians. There was, of

---

[8] D. Smith, *op. cit.*, p. 663.

course, the assurance that the success of this unholy three was temporary—it was to last only three and one-half years, symbolically—but that reassuring suggestion fell short of making the picture hopeful. For this reason there was mercifully given to the Christians another scene for their comfort and assurance. This one was as bright and glorious as the past one was dark and portentous.

The last scene showed the outlook from the vantage point of the Christians; this scene shows the outlook from the vantage point of God and the heavenly hosts. It leaves no doubt as to the outcome. The devil has two instruments to use in battle: the first beast and the second beast. God also has two instruments to use: the Lamb—Christ, and the sickle—God's judgment.

a. *The Lamb* standing on Mount Zion (14:1-13) is the first of the forces of righteousness which God uses. There is no question as to the meaning of this symbol. It refers to the triumphant Christ. Following the dark and threatening scene of the last two chapters, the curtain is drawn aside to reveal the Lamb, safe on Mount Zion, with a perfect number (144,000) of his redeemed with him. These bear a mark of identity just as the adherents of the devil-emperor worship bore. The mark on their forehead is not an evil one but "his name (the Lamb's) and the name of his Father." This triumphant picture was one calculated to cause the hearts of the Christians to leap for joy. Their Redeemer-Lamb as their champion is marshaling a complete army of righteousness about the crest of Mount Zion. Those with the Lamb sing a song, a new victory song, the meaning of which can be known only by the redeemed with the Lamb. They are with him and victorious because they had kept themselves undefiled "with women," symbolical of freedom from the spiritual fornication of idol worship. "They follow the Lamb wherever he goes" —they have been and are absolutely loyal to him. "In their mouth was found no lie"—no denial of the supremacy of Christ. There can be no doubt about the outcome of the battle when the Lamb is thus pictured safe on Zion with a perfect number of the redeemed with him—they shall not fail; with him they are victorious.

Aside from this assurance of victory there is given another symbol of the victorious campaign of the Lamb. Verses 6 and 7 picture an angel flying through the heavens with an announcement of "eternal good tidings." These tidings are proclaimed to all who dwell on the earth. It is the "good tidings" or "eternal gospel" of God's victory, and is followed by a call to all men to "fear God, and give him glory." He is the Almighty Creator who made heaven and earth and sea and fresh waters. More than this, "the hour of his judgment is at hand." All this indicates that the victory of the Lamb is so certain that an angel messenger announces the triumph and victory before the battle is fought. It has been observed that John uses this method often in Revelation.

Following the angelic announcement of God's triumph, glory, and judgment, there is a second angel who flies along announcing the doom of imperial Rome (v. 8). Babylon, which represented the evil and repulsive to the Jews, is here used to symbolize Rome. Because of her enforcing spiritual fornication, idol worship, she has fallen. The aorist used is the constative aorist, which looks upon the entire process of Rome's fall as one momentary act of falling. So certain is the fall in the mind and purpose of God that it is looked upon as already having taken place.

In verses 9-12 is pictured by the announcement of a third angel the destruction of those who have worshiped the emperor. This is a reflection of the first century Christian horror of emperor worship. The one who has worshiped the beast or his image or received his mark, that one shall taste the undiluted wrath of God—"drink of the wrath of God, which is prepared unmixed in the cup of his anger." This tasting of the undiluted wrath of God consists of torment with fire and burning sulphur. This is not a torment which will soon be over—"the smoke of their torment goeth up forever and ever; and they have no rest day and night." This is a terrible punishment in contrast to that received by the martyrs. The Christian martyr was burned at the stake; but that was over in a few minutes, and he found himself possessed of eternal life in fellowship with God. Those who worshiped the emperor fell before God's judgment and found a life of eternal burning in the sulphurous fumes. Verse 12, "Here is the patience of the saints, they keep the commandments of God [not the Roman Concilia], and the faith of Jesus [not Domitian]," is a praise and an encouragement to the becoming endurance of the Christians.

Verse 13 presents one of John's frequent contrasts inserted for vividness. "A voice from heaven," one with divine authority, gave the commandment to write the beatitude given here. It was God's statement, not just John's. "Blessed are the dead who die in the Lord from henceforth: yea, saith the Spirit, that they may rest from their labors; for their works follow with them." Blessings are pronounced, not upon all those who die, but upon the Christians who die. From the moment of their death they are blessed by a twofold blessing. First, they "rest from their labors." The word for rest, ἀναπαήσονται, literally means "they shall be refreshed." The word for labors, κόπων, literally means "toil under great adversity." They are thus refreshed after great toil. Jesus pictured this in his teachings when he said, "Come unto me, all ye that labor and are heavy laden, and I will give you rest" (Matthew 11:28). Thomas Gray's "Elegy Written in a Country Churchyard" catches the anticipation of refreshment after labors in his line, "The ploughman homeward plods his weary way." He expects, at home, to find refreshment after labor. The Christian finds death an entrance to a home where he is refreshed after his labor in this world. Second, "their works follow with them." Their efforts make up a part of the grand train of achievement which leads to ultimate victory.[9] This is true, but it appears that more than this is involved in this passage. The Christian who dies triumphantly in the Lord finds that he has not lost his works; he is not saved so as by fire. He makes an abundant entrance with all his genuine works for the Lord. He does not go empty-handed as a one-talent servant but as one who has used every opportunity to invest himself profitably for the Lord.

b. The sickle (14:14-20) is the second force of righteousness which God has in opposition to the forces of evil. The statements are such as to leave little doubt as to that symbolized by the sickle; it is divine judgment. The sickle is used elsewhere in the Bible to suggest this idea.[10] Christ appears as King (he wears a golden

[9]Dana, *The Epistles and Apocalypse of John,* p. 138.
[10]Cf. Joel 3:13; Matthew 13:39.

crown) and Judge (he has a sickle in his hand). When the divine signal is given, he thrusts in the sickle to reap the harvest of grain which was ripe and ready for harvesting. At a second signal he thrusts in the sickle to reap the clusters of ripe grapes. The grapes were gathered into the wine press of God's wrath. When they were trodden in the wine press, blood came out in a stream two hundred miles long and deep enough to reach to the bridles of horses.

There is general agreement that this represents judgment. There is disagreement over the two symbols. Some[11] hold that the harvest of grain symbolizes the judgment upon the righteous, and that the gathering of the vintage of grapes symbolizes judgment on the wicked. Others[12] hold that no such differentiation is to be understood and that both symbols picture the fact of judgment in the hands of God as an instrument of defeat for the forces of evil. There are evidences on both sides of the question. The context appears to favor the latter view—judgment as an instrument of defeat for the forces of evil. None of the authorities cited as holding the view which differentiates between the two symbols holds the view that this Scripture teaches two separate judgments. That is in the hands of the futurists, who delight in finding numerous judgments. This symbol is a dramatic way of presenting the fact of divine judgment. The terror of it is reflected in the immense stream of blood pictured in verse 20. The futurists and restorationists have trouble here with their literalism; they cannot find room in Palestine for a river two hundred miles long, whether of water or blood! Some of them try.[13] The forces of evil are strong: the devil and his two allies, Antichrist and Roman Concilia. But the forces of righteousness are stronger: God with his two allies, the Victorious Christ and Divine Judgment. As the curtains close on this scene, there is rejoicing in the hearts of those who watch the pageant.

---

[11]Cf. Richardson, D. Smith, Milligan, and Swete, *in loco*.
[12]Cf. Stuart, Ramsay, Dana, Kiddle, Moffatt, and Beckwith, *in loco*.
[13]Larkin, *op. cit.*, p. 173.

Exultation of the Redeemed, 15:1-8

The interlude between symbols six and seven in this section is very brief. The last symbols pictured the opposing forces of righteousness and evil in readiness for deadly conflict. The next series will picture the bowls of wrath of final retribution poured out on the enemies of the gospel. An interlude of praise and thanksgiving is inserted to picture the exultation of the redeemed as they sing the song of Moses and the Lamb.

John saw "a sea of glass mingled with fire"; such a view perhaps as may be made by the reflection of the rays of the setting sun falling on a body of water and turning it fiery red. David Smith[14] thinks the crystal sea of chapter 4 is here turned red by the reflection of the lurid conflagration of persecution which was raging down on earth. Milligan[15] thinks the sea reflects either the fire of God's judgment or the trials by which God purifies his people. This latter view is about the same as Smith's. Those who had been victorious over the attempts at forcing emperor worship are pictured standing on (ἐπί with the accusative means "on" or "upon"; when it means "by," it is used with the genitive) the sea of glass. In chapter 4 it was observed that the crystal sea symbolized the transcendence of God—he could not be approached by man. Here in chapter 15 the sea is still present; he is still transcendent and cannot be approached by man. But the sea does not keep those who are his and have already died from approaching him—they stand "on" the sea in his very presence. When the consummation has been passed, chapter 21 will reveal that "the sea is no more," and that all God's people are in intimate fellowship with him. Here in chapter 15 the saints who have crossed through martyrdom to be in the presence of God have heavenly harps in their hands—symbolical of praise. They sing the song of Moses and the song of the Lamb, a song which combines praise for the power of God, the deliverance which he gives, and the righteous character which prompts the deliver-

---

[14]D. Smith, *op. cit.*, p. 672. See also Swete, *op. cit.*, p. 194.

[15]Milligan, *op. cit.*, p. 260.

ance. The bowls of wrath soon to be emptied will present a dread experience in the world. The faithful, persecuted Christians have need of fortification for it; they need to see how it is viewed in heaven. Therefore, they are given this vision to show the condition of those who have fallen in the persecution and, hence, their own condition if persecution unto death overtakes them. The exultant saints in heaven are pictured to cheer and comfort the saints on earth as they are in the midst of evil days.[16]

The temple of the tabernacle of testimony was opened. This seems to symbolize the heavenly repository of God's covenant. It is not pictured as the Temple of Solomon or either of its successors. It is the "Tent of Witness" of the wilderness tabernacle.[17] The tabernacle is not opened here to reveal the ark of the covenant as it was in 11:19. It is opened to allow the seven angels to come from the Presence-Chamber to pour out the bowls of God's retributive wrath upon the earth. The angels were dressed similarly to the priests of old and acted as God's agents to pour out these seven last plagues.

One of the four living creatures gave seven bowls of wrath to the seven angels. The complete number "7" symbolizes the completeness of wrath now to be emptied. The time has come. During this time the tabernacle was filled with smoke symbolical of the powerful presence of God. So completely was it filled that "none was able to enter into the sanctuary, till the seven last plagues of the seven angels should be finished" (15:8). This symbolized that the wrath of God was filled—the martyred saints of chapter 6 had been told to wait because the time was not ripe for God's retribution—and there was no room for intercession during this visitation of wrath.[18] All this affords an easy transition over to the pouring out of the seven bowls of wrath.

------

[16]This position is taken by D. Smith, Milligan, Dana, Richardson, Swete, Beckwith and Kiddle, *in loco*.

[17]Cf. Numbers 9:15; 17:7; 18:2.

[18]Cf. 1 Kings 8:11—"The priests could not stand to minister by reason of the cloud."

The Bowls of Wrath, 16:1 to 20:10

This has been called by some a wild and fantastic vision. It is not a figurative setting forth of actual events which the Asian Christians had seen; it symbolizes swiftly executed wrath of God as it falls on the Roman Empire in mighty consummation. The empire was as yet strong and evidently in no danger of falling. But, to one enlightened as John was by the Spirit of God, the State was doomed. So here the apostle leaves history behind and soars in imagination into the yet undiscovered future.[19] When permission is given, the angels go in swift succession to execute the wrath of God on the great enemy of his cause and people.

There are many similarities between these and the trumpet plagues. Like the trumpets, they represent woes upon nature and upon man; and, like the trumpets, a part of their symbolism is parallel with the Egyptian plagues. But there are marked differences between the bowls and the trumpets. The trumpet judgments were calls to repentance; the bowl judgments are visitations of punishment when hope of repentance is passed. The trumpet judgments were partial, touching only a third part of their objects; the bowl judgments are final, touching the whole of the object. The trumpet judgments did not reach man until the sounding of the fifth trumpet; the bowl judgments fall upon man from the very first. The symbolism of the bowls and that of the trumpets are parallel. There is difference in the symbolism of the fifth in each series, but the thing symbolized is the same. As bowl after bowl is emptied, the judgment increases until finally it reaches the imperial city. No attempt to determine the special meaning of the objects thus visited by the wrath of God—land, sea, rivers, sun—has yet been or is ever likely to be successful. The general effect of God's final retributive wrath alone appears to be important. The bowls are grouped four, two, interlude, and one—just as were the seals and the trumpets.

(1) *The first bowl* (16:1-2) was poured out upon the land. It did not scorch the earth as did the blowing of the first trumpet. Rather

---

[19]D. Smith, *op. cit.*, p. 675.

it fell upon men marked with the name of the beast and caused to come upon them grievous and loathsome sores.

(2) *The second bowl* (16:3) was emptied upon the sea. The water was turned to blood, and every living thing in contact with the sea perished.

(3) *The third bowl* (16:4–7) was poured out upon the fresh water, and it, too, became blood. A voice was heard proclaiming the righteousness of God in this act. He visits punishment in accordance with sin: Once the Empire had made the blood of the martyrs run like water; now all the Empire can find to drink is blood—and they deserve it. God's judgments are righteous.

(4) *The fourth bowl* (16:8–9) was emptied upon the sun. It sent out scorching rays to burn wicked men with fire. They were so perverted that they blasphemed God in the midst of the punishment and refused to turn from their perversion.

While the first four plagues were upon nature but brought their effect upon man, the next two are poured out particularly upon man.

(5) *The fifth bowl* (16:10–11) was poured out upon the throne of the beast. The kingdom of the beast was darkened; great pain came upon the people of the kingdom, so that they gnawed their tongues in great anguish; but in their perversion they refused to turn from their idol worship.

(6) *The sixth bowl* (16:12) was emptied upon the Euphrates River. The river was dried up and the way opened for the coming of the great eastern enemies of the Empire.

The Three Frogs: Satan's Recruiting Agents, 16:13–16

This interlude is placed in the vision between the sixth and seventh symbols just as in the other visions. When the sixth bowl was emptied, the way was made open for the coming of the Parthian enemy of Rome. This is, of course, symbolical of the army-host in the hand of God to do battle with Rome. When the three allies of the evil forces see this possibility, they realize that they must gather the kings of the world to defeat these Parthians.

John sees three unclean spirits in the form of frogs make their appearance. They make their appearance out of the mouths of the dragon, the first beast, and the second beast, which is here called the false prophet. No verb is used to show how they came out. The Greek simply states, "I saw *out of* the mouth of the dragon. . . ." Dana[20] takes the position that the frogs were vomited up. Swete[21] thinks they were breathed out—the breath of the three allies changed to frogs. The loathsomeness of the figure inclines one to Dana's views. The idea of breathing out evil influences inclines one to Swete's view. Perhaps it is immaterial. These three frogs are called spirits of demons sent out by the three evil allies to deceive the kings of the world and get them on the side of Rome for the approaching conflict. They fulfil their task of deception and gather the kings to the battlefield, a place called "Har-magedon." The battle is not fought until we reach chapter 19.

This is the symbolism; what is the meaning? The futurist[22] has no difficulty. He sees no need for an interpretation of Armageddon, which ends world history and secures God's throne for him. Neither this nor the view of the continuous-historical method of interpretation has any meaning for those who needed the message most—the persecuted Christians of Asia Minor. The last named group[23] applies the whole thing to the apostasy of the Roman Catholic Church. The drying up of the Euphrates was the counter teaching of the Reformation which stopped the flow of Catholic teaching. The three frogs were (1) the declaration of the Council of Trent, (2) the declaration of the Vatican Council, (3) the papal encyclicals, particularly those completing the system of Mariolatry. The battle is the struggle between Catholicism and the true church. Not by the wildest stretch of the imagination could this have had any meaning to the Christians for whom the book was primarily intended.

This paragraph is symbolical. It pictures the devil, the emperor, and the Concilia rallying their forces to battle against the forces of

---

[20]Dana, *The Epistles and Apocalypse of John*, p. 141.

[21]Swete, *op. cit.*, p. 207.

[22]Larkin, *op. cit.*, pp. 144 ff.

[23]For an example compare Barnes, *in loco.*

righteousness. The three frogs perhaps symbolize some form of evil propaganda since they came from the mouths of the three. They are the offspring of the devil, of godless government, and of false religion. They are the real enemies of Christ. True religion has no worse enemies, and Satan no better allies, than false propaganda. From the witnesses who withstood Moses before Pharaoh, on down to such products of the first century as Simon Magus and on to our own day, there have been those who pretended to work signs which the belief of the age has attributed to superhuman influence. So these recruiting agents of Satan work signs (a characteristic Johannine conception for miracle) to enlist followers. The lust for power and the bitterness of false religion are here pictured in their efforts to strengthen themselves. Behind them is the devil pushing them on. There have been many times when nations have been seized by a dark passion for war which the historian finds difficulty in explaining. Such a conflict is here pictured, but it is spiritual rather than material.

These allies gather their forces on the battlefield called Armageddon. This was a famous Hebrew battlefield. Here Gideon and his three hundred defeated the Midianites. Here King Saul was defeated by the Philistines. Here Barak and Deborah overthrew the hosts of the Canaanite king, Jabin. Here Ahaziah died of Jehu's arrows. And here Pharaoh-Necho overthrew Josiah. The place was burned into the minds of the Jewish people, and the mourning for Josiah in the valley of Megiddo was long afterward quoted as a typical example of national grief. Thus Megiddo fitly symbolized the worldwide distress of righteousness and evil engaged in deadly combat. This is not an actual material sword and spear battle. Such a thing would be at cross purposes with all the teachings of the New Testament, the ideals which Jesus held, his death on the cross, and all God's purposes of grace. Jesus' way was never the way of the sword. His sword is the sword of the Spirit, the Word of God. If one expects this to be a literal, material battle, he must expect the army to be headed by a committee of three frogs. Both figures are symbolical; neither is literal. There is no reason for making one literal and the other symbolical. The Armageddon in the book of

Revelation has no location on the maps of the world; it is logical, not spatial. The battle is not one in which material, physical armaments will decide the issue; the battle is between righteousness and evil, and righteousness is the certain victor.

(7) *The seventh bowl* (16:17 to 20:10) is now poured out, and it is revealed that all the forces of evil cannot defeat the cause of righteousness. When the contents of this bowl were scattered broadcast upon the air, a voice was heard from the throne in the temple saying, "It is done" (perfect tense). With this final instalment of God's wrath, there were manifestations of divine wrath—thunder, lightnings, voices, and an earthquake; the imperial city of Rome was divided into three parts—the divine number indicates that divine work overthrew the city. Babylon (here Rome) was looked upon as the supreme antidivine world power.[24] It is thus remembered in the sight of God. His destructive power falls so effectively that the earthquake levels the mountains and submerges the islands, which are Rome's strongholds. Hailstones weighing a hundred pounds each fell with destructive force upon wicked men, who continued to blaspheme the God who was responsible for these things—a graphic picture of God's judgment.

Here, as in other places, the three things which led to the downfall of Rome are noted: natural calamity, internal rottenness, and external invasion. Rome was doomed. Thus does John picture God's judgment upon the oppressors of his people. It did little good for the allies to send out their recruiting frogs; God's power dashed Rome to pieces just the same.

When John saw the earthquake and giant hailstones combine to dash Rome to pieces, one of the seven angels recently engaged in administering God's retributive wrath told him to come over to another stage and see in detail what he had just seen in the quick fall of the city. What he saw covers the last scene of conflict between the forces of good and the forces of evil. One should beware of weaving the materials of this section (17:1–20:10) into some fantastic eschatological program. This has often been done, with the result of wasted time and energy and a perversion of the true

---

[24]Moffatt, *op. cit.*, p. 449.

teachings of the Scriptures. These scenes do not compose a scene of connected events for the purpose of satisfying our curiosity about the future. All of us possess that curiosity; some control it better than others. These visions are designed to set forth the promise of the ultimate triumph of righteousness over all the evil forces which oppose it. This was its message to the Christians of Asia Minor about A.D. 95. It assured them of the certain victory of Christianity over Rome. In a similar way today it assures us of the certain triumph of Christ's cause over the cause of evil in every age. In this respect the philosophy of the history method of interpretation is correct. The vision is given to us under the symbolism of several pictures setting forth the doom of Rome.

a. The Scarlet Woman: Rome, 17:1–18

Such great importance was attached to Rome as the center of the persecuting power of the first century that three whole chapters are given to portray her doom. This is a series of scenes in the pageant to show the fate of Rome as it had already been foreshadowed in 14:8 and 16:19. Here Rome is pictured as a great harlot who sits upon many waters and practices her fornication with the kings of the earth; she is guilty of spiritual fornication in her idol worship, and she entices the kings of the provinces as she conquers them to partake of the evil with her. The waters upon which she sits are symbolical of the people over whom she reigns. She is thus described to John; but when they reach the stage where the pageant is being shown, she is seated upon a scarlet-colored beast, which is full of blasphemous names, has seven heads, and ten horns. The beast, the color of the dragon-devil in chapter 12, is no doubt the Empire which supports this wicked city. The woman was dressed in luxurious and haughty splendor and held in her hand a cup. The cup held the unclean things of her fornication. This is evidently the same as what is pictured in verse 6, where the woman is drunk all the time (present participle) with the blood of the saints and martyrs of Jesus. "The unclean things of her fornication" are, then, the evils which have come out of her idol worship and persecution. Her "offspring" is quite different from that of the Radiant Woman of chapter 12. Her name is written upon her forehead, "Mystery, Babylon the Great, the Mother of the Harlots and of the Abominations of the Earth." She was a mystery, a wonder. What a woman and what a beast to be ridden by her! She is the great harlot, the main one responsible for the idol-emperor worship, and she is the mother of a family of harlots. She delights to drink the blood of the martyrs. She is intoxicated by it.

Many of the futurists hold that this speaks of the city of Babylon which is to be restored in the last days. The continuous-historical group says that this is the apostate Roman Catholic Church. Perhaps the safest method is to take the explanation which the angel gave to John: "Wherefore didst thou wonder? I will tell thee the mystery of the woman, and of the beast that carrieth her." He explains that the beast "was, and is not; and is about to come up out of the abyss, and to go into perdition." This is a reflection of the Nero redivivus myth. The Roman Empire is thus pictured as personified in Domitian, the reincarnation of Nero. The empire is about to suffer destruction. The heathen world wonders at the history and progress of Rome. Those who are Christian do not wonder at her because they know she is doomed.

Beginning with verse 9, the angel explains that the seven heads of the beast are seven mountains; Rome was built on seven hills. They are also seven kings which have formed the basis of the great empire:[25] Augustus, Tiberius, Caligula, Claudius, Nero, Vespasian, and Titus. There is an eighth who is to have a part in this history, but he is one of the seven already mentioned—he was and is the reincarnation of the evil, persecuting work of Nero. The ten horns of the beast represent the power of the Empire. Her power was in her provinces, so this symbol which the angel identifies as "ten kings, who have received no kingdom as yet; but they receive authority as kings, with the beast, for one hour" must refer to the vassal kings, rulers of Rome's provinces, who receive authority from Rome and enjoy this delegated authority for a very short time

---

[25]For full discussion of this symbol, see the section of this book where this series of kings was discussed under the "date" of the book.

—"one hour." They have only one thought, and that is to obey the Roman Empire which is personified in Domitian. That is the reason they have been so zealous to persecute the Christians. They war with the Lamb, but the Lamb is victorious because he is "Lord of lords, and King of kings." The time will come when these provinces will have their part in her destruction. This was one of the greatest fears that Rome had. Everywhere in the book of Acts there are indications of Rome's fear of any kind of turmoil and unrest which might possibly turn into a revolution. The chapter closes with the statement that the woman, the harlot who met this destruction, was the great city which lorded it over the kings of the earth. The first triumph pictured to the Christians is the certain doom of imperial Rome.

b. The Oracles of Doom: Rome's Allies, 18:1-20

All through this section the main thing in the writer's mind is the fall of Rome. He views it from different points and repeats for emphasis. Much of chapter 18 is Old Testament language in regard to the ancient city of Babylon. In John's day it had already been fulfilled. It is used here to picture the destruction of the Babylon of the New Testament, Rome.

The first angel in the vision announces the fall of Babylon because of her spiritual fornication. This includes the statement of the way the merchants of the world had capitalized on her wantonness and fornication and had thus become her allies in evil. A subsequent paragraph will show their own doom in connection with that of the Empire.

A second voice issued a call to God's people to come out from association with this wanton woman, to have no fellowship with her sins lest some of her plagues (strokes) fall upon them. They are assured that her sins have reached to high heaven and God has taken notice of them. Now (v. 6) she is going to receive punishment in like kind and in proportion to her sin. She has boasted about herself; she has been full of pride; she has said, "I shall never have occasion to mourn." Now she is to receive double punishment for all her evil. In "one hour"—very quickly—plagues, famine, mourning, and death come to visit her, and she shall be utterly consumed. This is a picture of *her* destruction, but how about her allies? They are pictured as standing in two groups to mourn over her. Rome was built upon two things: territorial conquest and trade expansion. Thus do the two groups mourn because they go down with her.

First, the kings of the earth mourn because of her fall. These are her allies who, coming under her power, entered into her spiritual fornication and evil. They turn aside to weep and wail because of such sudden destruction to the great city. Second, the merchants of the earth lament over her destruction because now they have no market for their merchandise. There are about thirty articles of trade mentioned here. To create such a business the merchants have entered into the evil of the Empire. Now they fall with her. Nothing can be economically good if it is morally bad. The same fate awaits any nation guilty of the same sin. The merchants and the mariners who carry their wares stand far off, cast dust on their heads, and weep over such destruction of the city. The burning of Rome under Nero was a small matter compared to God's wrath against the entire Empire and allies. Doom comes to all. The curtain falls on the second triumph of the pageant. It is a desolate scene but one of rejoicing to the Christians as they see another indication of God's power and their certain rescue.

c. The Stone: Destruction of Municipal Rome, 18:21–24

The third triumph pictures graphically the destruction of municipal Rome. First the Empire, then the allies, now with one blow the imperial city falls. Repetition is used for emphasis and assurance. The Christians needed plenty of both. A strong angel lifted a huge stone and cast it into the sea and stated that that illustrated the way Rome would fall and be found no more. Then he pictured the cessation of the three major things in Roman life:

Amusement life (v. 22) shall cease. There shall be no more the sound of music: harper, minstrel, flute-player, or trumpeter.

Business life (v. 22) shall cease. No craftsman of any kind shall be found; the voice of the mill shall be heard no more.

Home life (v. 23) shall cease. There shall be no more the light of festive lamp or the voice of bride and bridegroom.

With the destruction of these three, Rome, the great city, is destroyed. Nothing was to be found in her except the blood of the martyrs which was the cause of her destruction. She was destroyed; the blood of the martyrs stands as an eternal testimony against Rome and to the loyalty of the Christians. Those who oppose this method of interpretation point out the fact that Rome still stands. That is true, but it is not the persecuting Rome of John's day. A combination of many things brought an end to that Rome long ago. The Christian movement which that Rome tried to stamp out still stands and will stand when all other "Romes" have fallen to decay even as that ancient Rome fell.

d. The Rejoicing Saints, 19:1–10

The symbolization of the complete destruction of Rome ushers in the fourth of the triumphs of the consummation. This triumph pictures the exultation of the redeemed saints. The scene opens with a great host in heaven singing a hallelujah chorus. It is a song which attributes deliverance and glory and power to God because of his righteous judgments upon wicked, persecuting Rome. It is not a song of rejoicing over the evil which has fallen upon Rome as much as it is a song of rejoicing over the triumph of righteousness and truth. Above the wails and lamentation of fallen kings, merchants, and mariners, and above the noise of crashing walls and flaming streets is heard the song of the rejoicing saints that righteousness has triumphed over evil. The destruction pictured in the fall of Rome was great. But no greater than would have been the destruction wrought by godless nations and men and women allowed to proceed unchallenged and unhindered along the roads of cruelty, degeneracy, and persecution of the righteous people of God. It is this triumph of righteousness that calls forth the hallelujah chorus.

The chorus repeats the hallelujah and John remarks that the smoke of Rome going up forever and ever is the thing which called forth this second hallelujah. The destruction of Rome was not pictured as that of a city which burns to the ground and where men go in to remove the wreckage. It is pictured as an eternal destruction, an eternal burning. There is always fuel to add to the burning so that the smoke goes up forever and ever, and such a city can never be rebuilt. With this second hallelujah we have the introduction of the four and twenty elders and the four living creatures as they join in the song of triumph and say, "So be it; Hallelujah!"

A voice spoke from the altar with a command for all the Lord's servants to praise him. And at this point John heard the redeemed as a great multitude, as the voice of many waters take up the song, "Hallelujah: for the Lord our God, the Almighty, reigneth." They sing of this joyous occasion, for they consider that the marriage of the Lamb and the bride has come. The bride is the church, and she has kept her robe pure and white for this occasion. The bridegroom is the Lamb, who has been preparing a place for his bride. Now the joyous hour for the union has come. But it appears that the redeemed were premature in their thoughts. The time for the complete union has not come yet. The Lamb has yet another battle to fight before all opposition to the union is removed. One of the messengers assuages the disappointment by telling John to write, "Blessed are they that are bidden to the marriage supper of the Lamb." All the redeemed will be there, but the time is not yet.

The book of Revelation does not reveal to us the marriage of the Lamb and the church. By the time we get to that, perhaps chapter 21, the figure has changed and the marriage is not mentioned again, even though there is perfect union between Christ and the redeemed. John does this often. He did not show the releasing of the winds of retribution (7:1); he changed the figure to the trumpets. He prepared the way for the Parthians to invade Rome (16:12), but he did not use them; he changed the figure and let an earthquake and giant hailstones do the destructive work. In both instances the goal was reached. So it is with the symbol of the marriage.

The vision is symbolical, certainly. A few make it literal and tell when, who, where, what, and all about it. One man was heard to say that it was a real marriage and that the apostle Paul would perform the ceremony because he had so much to do with the betrothal. All such ideas are fantasy and no more. The Oriental marriage was a great and happy occasion. But the public marriage ceremonies in John's day had become so corrupt that the Christians could not attend. Here is one where all may and will attend—they will be the bride when that final happy union with the Lamb comes. The marriage was a beautiful symbol for the union of Christ and his church. This is the reason for the joyous song of the triumphant redeemed.

e. The Victorious Warrior: Christ, 19:11 to 20:10

The next triumph in the series is that of Christ. Up to this point he has been pictured as Lion, Lamb, Judge, and now he is a victorious Warrior. There appears to be little doubt that he is the One symbolized here. The Christians who view the pageant see the curtains drawn to reveal one riding on a white horse, symbolical of victory. The rider is called "Faithful and True," "The Word of God," and on his garment is written "King of kings, and Lord of lords." These names identify him as the Christ. In the beginning of the book he was called "the faithful and true witness" (1:5; 3:7; 3:14). One of John's favorite terms for Christ is the "word of God" —God's utterance to man. The Lamb is identified in 17:14 as "Lord of lords, and King of kings." Aside from the names there are other marks which identify him: "His eyes are a flame of fire" (1:14). "Out of his mouth proceedeth a sharp sword" (1:16). "He shall rule them [the nations] with a rod of iron" (12:5). "He treadeth the fierceness of the wrath of God" (14:20). "He is arrayed in a garment sprinkled with blood" (Isaiah 63:3).

The victorious Warrior is not by himself. He is followed by heavenly armies; all the riders are upon white horses and they wear pure white linen. All this is symbolical of victory. No statement is made as to whether or not they are armed. Their Leader goes before them, and he is armed with the sharp sword which proceeded out of his mouth. With it he is to smite the enemy into subjection and then rule them with the strength of iron. The sword is best identified as "a spiritual weapon of resistless might." Some have called it the Bible since the Bible is spoken of as the "Sword of the Spirit." Others call it simply "Judgment," a similar symbol to the sickle of chapter 14. Whichever or whatever it is, it is a spiritual weapon of resistless might. With it he wins the battle.

The victory is announced before the battle begins. An angel standing in the sun, the direction from which light for a dark world comes, issues an invitation to the birds of the heavens to come together for a feast which God would provide for them. They were invited to eat the flesh of kings, of military captains, of mighty men, of horses, of horsemen, of all men, free and slave, small and great. The carnage of the enemies of God is going to be great. The scene closes with the birds of prey flocking to the battlefield.

(a) Victory over the First and Second Beasts, 19:19–21

The battle is soon over. The beast and his allied kings of the earth and the false prophet were no match for the victorious Warrior and his sharp sword. The beast and the false prophet were cast alive into the "lake that burneth with brimstone." The rest were killed with the sword which came from the mouth of the victorious Christ. The destruction was complete; the battle over; the Christ victorious.

As at various other places in Revelation, there has been much dispute as to the correct interpretation here. The futurists look on this as a literal battle which will usher in the kingdom of God. Just how literal the battle is to be observed when Seiss[26] concludes that both riders and horses are literal. In a similar vein Ottman says, speaking of the birds of prey invited to the feast, that they represent literal vultures that shall fatten on the bodies of the slain.[27] Writers of this group look upon the beast as the personal Antichrist of the

---

[26]J. A. Seiss, *The Apocalypse* (Philadelphia: School of the Bible, 1865), III, p. 250.
[27]F. C. Ottman, *The Unfolding of the Ages* (New York: Publication Office, "Our Hope," 1905), p. 421.

last days and expect his army to be a military force, brought to Palestine for warfare against the Jews; by that time he will have complete possession of the land, and the Lord and his army will have to overthrow him to set up the millennial kingdom.

Those who follow the continuous-historical school, and have viewed the beast as the Roman Catholic Church, must, to remain consistent, find in this passage a great struggle by which that power is overthrown. Since the Roman Catholic Church is still in existence, they teach that Armageddon is yet in the future.[28] A frequent objection to the above methods of interpretation is voiced again: What possible meaning would these ideas have had for the Christians of John's day?

For the proper interpretation of the book, we must always seek for a starting point in the immediate age and circumstances of the writer, and of those for whose instruction, assurance, and comfort he writes. This is a book thoroughly suited to the times in which it was produced. Armageddon is not a place name; it is a symbolic term for a decisive conflict. Christ is pictured as coming down from heaven, but this does not picture the second coming of Christ which we find discussed elsewhere in the New Testament. This scene symbolically represents his coming to the aid of the persecuted Christians with heavenly assistance in their spiritual struggles. If the beast is identified, as it has been in this work, with the emperor as he personified the pagan persecuting Roman Empire, there is no other explanation of this battle. It is a vivid symbolical representation of the final victory of Christ's cause and people over that pagan Empire. The beast (Domitian) and the second beast (false prophet, Roman Concilia, state religion priesthood) were cast into the lake that burns with fire and brimstone. This is symbolical of their destruction. Christ overcomes them; the Christians are bothered with them no more. The conflict pictured is a spiritual conflict.[29]

---

[28]Cf. Barnes, Carroll, Lord, *in loco.*

[29]D. Smith, J. Smith, Pieters, Dana, Richardson, Allen, Beckwith, Milligan, Kiddle, and Swete, *in loco.*

(b) Victory over the Allies of the Beasts, 19:21

It is interesting to note that even among those who hold this position there is much division as to detail. For instance, the scholars are divided over the meaning of the statement "the rest were killed with the sword of him that sat upon the horse, even the sword which came forth out of his mouth." One group[80] holds that this means the conversion of the allies of Rome when they saw Rome fall; in this way they were numbered as casualties. Either they were converted or rendered disinclined or unable any longer to lend their support to the policy of persecution. Others[81] hold that this is indicative of his power in the judgments which he speaks— the death-dealing power of the Messiah uttered against his foes. Some[82] take no definite stand on this detail of the symbolism, while one man[83] very boldly takes the position that it means both. He holds that the sword is that of which Paul speaks in Ephesians 6:17, and that in interpreting, room should probably be allowed for punitive as well as for restorative operations; the Word slays by pronouncing judgment as well as by reducing to the obedience of faith. But, he believes, it is probably the latter process which is chiefly in view. With such good evidence on both sides of the question, this position affords a convenient solution.

Some scholars have objected to this entire method of interpreting this symbolic battle. They have done so on the basis that the language is too warlike and severe in character to allow such an interpretation. All the details are severe: flaming eyes, drawn sword, rod of iron, wine press of wrath, blood-stained garments. These are in better keeping with the destruction of real war than with the idea of spiritual judgment upon men. It must not be forgotten, how-ever, that such battle terms are used in Christian songs of today. "Onward, Christian soldiers, marching as to war," "Press the battle

---

[80]Pieters, J. Smith, *in loco.*
[81]Milligan, Kiddle, and Beckwith, *in loco.*
[82]Dana, D. Smith, *in loco.*
[83]Swete, *op. cit.*, p. 259.

ere the night shall veil the glowing skies," "Lead on, O King Eternal, the day of march has come . . . we lift our battle song"—all these are phrases representing nothing more than spiritual conflict as the gospel is advanced. They are very vivid and realistic. A Christian missionary reports that Japanese police, hearing Korean Christians singing such songs as these, concluded that they were plotting an uprising.[84]

In this chapter of Revelation the familiar military symbolism is pressed to its limit to create the proper impression—certain victory for the cause of righteousness over the beast, the false prophet, and their allies. This meant freedom from persecution for the Christians. The pagan religion and godless government of Rome were doomed to fall. And when they fell, God's cause, God's people, God's purposes would go right on living and growing. It is at such points as this in the book that the philosophy of history school makes its bid for recognition. Their verdict would be: "This symbolizes the complete victory of the Son of God over all hosts of wickedness, not just in John's age but in any age of the world's history." That is true, but the primary emphasis is on the victory over the pagan false religion of Asia Minor about A.D. 95.

(c) Victory over Satan, 20:1-3

This victory is pictured in the chaining of Satan for a thousand years. From chapter 12 to this point three enemies have been allied in their opposition to Christ and his people. Of these three the first two were overcome by the Victorious Christ in 19:19-20. There can be no full, complete victory so long as this third part of the alliance is at large. In this paragraph his fate is indicated. John is not entering upon a new subject at this point; he is continuing the previous discussion. This is another point at which the modern device of chapter divisions is a hindrance rather than a help.

Review again the way these three great enemies of the Christians have been working—the devil, the beast, the false prophet. They were the main opponents of the Lamb, in one way or another stir-

---

[84]Pieters, *op. cit.,* p. 288.

ring up all the efforts that had been made against him by the kings of the earth, their armies, and followers. For a time they appeared to succeed. The saints were robbed, persecuted, exiled, or slain. But this could not continue; it must be shown that the final triumph remains with those who have suffered for the sake of righteousness. This triumph is pictured in various scenes: the fall of imperial Rome, the fall of Rome's allies, the fall of municipal Rome, the rejoicing of the saints, the disposal of two of the great enemies—the beast and the false prophet. The complete disposal of the third, the devil, remains and is finally effected in 20:10. The verses which follow that describe the judgment of those who had listened to the devil, and the complete triumph of the Christians and their union with Christ. These considerations are of themselves sufficient to show that the *overthrow of Satan,* and not the reign of a thousand years, is the main theme of the first ten verses of this chapter.

In this scene there is a symbolic setting forth of the final victory of the persecuted Christians of Asia Minor. The chapter needs to be approached with great humility of spirit, a recognition of its difficulties, an avoidance of dogmatic statements, and respect for the honest interpretation of others. This chapter has been a bitter debating ground for Christians for many centuries. Richardson[35] states that your interpretation of this chapter will determine whether you take your stand with the premillennarians, postmillennarians, or a-millennarians. John, in his visions on the isle of Patmos, never dreamed that his readers would debate and divide over the contents of this chapter. No doubt this is true. John did not record the scene to give us a series of connected events to satisfy our curiosity about the future. He gave it to set forth the promise of the ultimate and certain triumph of the cause of Christ and those who were being so sorely persecuted.

The limitations of this work preclude a detailed discussion of the rival interpretations of this passage. All these rival interpretations center around the "millennium." This word which means "thousand" does not appear in the New Testament; it is derived from the

[35]Richardson, *op. cit.,* pp. 156 ff.

term "a thousand years" which is used in this passage. If verses 4, 5, and 6 of Revelation 20 had been omitted, no one would ever have dreamed of a literal thousand years of Christ's reign upon the earth—his setting up a temporal throne in Jerusalem and inaugurating a millennial reign as an earthly monarch. Yet whole systems of eschatology, theology, and philosophy of history have been constructed on this precarious basis of highly symbolical verses.

Briefly here is the action of the paragraph: An angel came down from heaven with a key to the abyss and a strong chain in his hand. He chained the devil and cast him into the bottomless pit for a thousand years in order that he might not practice his act of deception upon the nations for a thousand years; after this he was to be loosed for a short time. Another scene showed the fate of those who had lost their lives for the testimony of Jesus, those who refused to worship the beast or his image. They are shown alive and reigning with Christ for a thousand years. This is called the first resurrection, and blessings are pronounced upon those who have a part in it. When the thousand years of the devil's being bound were up, he was loosed and entered again upon his old tactics: deceiving the nations and gathering them for an attack on the city of God. Fire came down out of heaven and destroyed them. The devil was cast into the lake of fire where the beast and false prophet had been cast in chapter 19. Judgment from the great white throne followed.

Forgetting premillennialism and postmillennialism and all preconceived interpretations, what was the probable meaning of this scene to John and the persecuted Christians in A.D. 95? We must remember their condition, that two of their enemies have just been deposed, and here is the act of the pageant which reveals the fate of the power behind the other two—the dragon, which is the devil. Sparse comfort would come to them even if they knew that several hundreds or thousands of years from then there would be a restoration of Jewish theocracy, a personal Antichrist, a bloody Armageddon and victory (premillennialism). Sparse comfort would come to them even if they knew that after a few thousand years of

gospel preaching world affairs would be so good and human government so perfect that the efforts of the devil would be of no avail
(postmillennialism). These things would not help them; and the
book was given first of all for them. What did they see in it to comfort and strengthen them? This, if we can find it, will be the safest
interpretation.

They saw their great adversary, the devil, effectively stopped from
deceiving the nations in the matter of emperor worship. This has
been the deception he has been practicing since chapter 13. Now
he is chained and cast into the abyss that he may not practice this
deception for a thousand years. Keep in mind that "deceive the
nations" is not to be applied to all his work. It applies at the particular point of deceiving them into believing that the emperor is
divine and is to be worshiped. The chain is not literal; one would
hardly use a literal chain on a spiritual being. The thousand-year-
period is no more literal than the chain. Numbers in Revelation
are symbolical. "Ten" is a complete number, and "one thousand"
is a high multiple of ten. The number is to be understood as an idea
of completeness. It does not represent a period of years either before
or after the second coming of Christ. It tells John's readers that the
devil is going to be completely restrained from deceiving the nations
into worshiping the emperor. True, just when he appears to be
absolutely bound, he breaks forth in one last effort to continue his
work (20:3, 7–10) but his power is completely destroyed then.

(d) Victory with the Martyrs, 20:4–6

What did John and the Christians see in the scene which had to
do with the saints reigning with Christ a thousand years? They
saw the triumph of the martyrs who had died as a result of the work
of the devil, the first beast, and the second beast. Just as the devil
was completely bound, the martyrs were completely victorious. The
thousand-year-period is not to be taken literally. The martyrs are
not under the throne crying for vengeance as they were in chapter
6. They are on thrones reigning with Christ. The cup of God's
retributive wrath has been filled; it has poured over the sides upon

the oppressors of his people. The oppressors are defeated; the oppressed are glorified; they reign with Christ a thousand years—a
picture of perfect blessedness. There is no question but that these
are the martyrs of the Domitianic persecution; they were such
as refused to worship the beast and his image; they did not receive
his mark on their forehead; they were the ones who had been
beheaded for the testimony of Jesus. Only by twisting the Scriptures
can the symbol be made to fit anyone else. The martyrs who had
suffered so much are completely victorious with Christ. This was the
message which would bring consolation to the bereaved saints in
Asia Minor—a message which assured them of the fate of their
loved ones who had fallen under the axe of the persecutors.

This triumph of the martyrs is called the "first resurrection." The
"second resurrection," which is not mentioned but implied, must
be the general resurrection discussed so often in the New Testament.
The "first death," which is not mentioned but implied, must be
physical death. The "second death" which is mentioned here is
symbolical of eternal separation, eternal punishment in the lake of
fire. The martyrs who are pictured triumphant are blessed because
they have passed the first death (physical), and the second death
(eternal separation from God) has no jurisdiction over them. Their
cause triumphs with them. They are victorious with the Christ for
whom they died.

No basis is found in the symbolism for a literal reign of a thousand-year reign of the saints with Christ on earth either before or
after his second coming. No basis is found in the symbolism for
multiple resurrections and judgments. Theological systems which
have majored on a literal interpretation of these verses and have
interpreted the clear teachings of the New Testament in the light
of the obscure have found several resurrections and several judgments taught. They find a resurrection of believers at what they
call the "rapture," when Christ comes to call his people out of the
earth before the great tribulation which is also interpreted as future.
Seven years later, at the "revelation" (the second stage of the program of the Lord's second coming), they find a resurrection for
those who have become believers and died during the period be-

tween the "rapture" and the "revelation." According to their system, people are converted and die during the millennium which is set up at the "revelation." So there must be a resurrection of this group at the close of the earthly millennium when the heavenly order is set up. If the wicked dead are raised at a separate judgment, the system has at least four (perhaps more) resurrections. In similar fashion they find multiple judgments ranging from two (one before and one after the millennium) to seven, according to the particular interpreter.

This is pure fantasy read into a literal interpretation of these highly symbolical verses. By the "proof-text" approach one can prove practically any proposition by perverted use of Scripture passages. When the entire New Testament is studied, it teaches *one* general resurrection (of both good and evil) and *one* general judgment (of both good and evil), both of which are directly related to the second coming of Christ which brings to an end this world order and ushers in the eternal heavenly order. A full study of this and related subjects on eschatology is in prospect but cannot be given at length in this book.

(e) Victory Complete: the Overthrow of Satan, 20:7–10

In verses 1–3 of this chapter a picture was presented of the binding of the devil so he could not deceive the nations into believing that the emperor was divine and to be worshiped. But the Christians were not to expect that he would give up without a struggle. Just when he appears to be forever bound, he breaks out in a new effort at deceiving the nations into lining up with the emperor rather than the Christ. The nations are given under the term Gog and Magog. These names recall ancient enemies of God's people. They were much discussed in apocalyptic writings, and the Talmud speaks of them as the enemies of the Messiah. In Ezekiel 38, Gog is a name for Antiochus Epiphanes, and Magog a name for the nation over which he was prince. He was the hated enemy of the people of God in the interbiblical period. He polluted their temple by having swine flesh sacrificed upon the altar. His evil work was finally put to an end by the revolt which gave Israel her only taste of national freedom from the Babylonian captivity to the present day. The terms Gog and Magog serve well as symbols for the barbarous people who rally with the devil about the camp of the saints. The devil's efforts are unsuccessful. Lightning falls from heaven to destroy his evil work. So it is not worldly power but heavenly power which finally brings to an end the evil work of this archenemy of God's people. He is cast into the lake of fire and brimstone to writhe with Domitian and the leaders of the state worship; eternal, ceaseless torment is their lot. Thus do the cause of righteousness and the persecuted Christians of Asia Minor triumph. The forces of evil and the forces of good have met; the battle has been fought; the forces of good have won. God with his two allies (the redeeming Lamb and eternal Judgment) has triumphed over the devil and his two allies (the emperor and the emperor worship committee). These three enemies have been cast into the lake of fire.

From a study of the Scriptures alone, without the aid (?) of preconceived systems of eschatology, it appears that John knew nothing about a "millennium" in any sense in which the word is used as a theological term. Premillennialists[36] say that Christ will come and usher in a thousand-year period of Utopian peace and righteousness. Postmillennialists say that the gospel will usher in a thousand-year period of peace and righteousness, at the end of which Christ will come. A-millennialists say that there is no such thing as a millennium taught in the New Testament. Preterists say that the millennium began when Christianity was made free of danger from heathenism about A.D. 300 (some place its beginning with the death of Christ) and that we are in it now. Because

---

[36]Many people have erroneously identified "premillennialism" with the New Testament teaching regarding the imminence of the second coming. The New Testament does teach that the Lord's return may be at any moment. This view of expectancy was held by Paul, John, Peter, James, and others. But one may accept this without accepting the ideas of the premillennial system regarding the setting up of an earthly kingdom, etc. Many have called themselves premillennial when all they really meant was that they believed in the imminence of the second coming. The two things are *not* synonymous.

of a conflict between these views, many evils have resulted in Christian history. Fanatical zeal has been generated which has caused communities and churches to be torn asunder and fellowship and friendship destroyed. The cause of the kingdom of God has often been retarded because of an insistence on a literal meaning for a passage which is highly symbolica. Altogether it has been largely an unprofitable experience. It appears that the best thing to do is to study the passage in its context and against its background and thus determine its meaning for John and those for whose benefit it was first given—the persecuted Christians of first century Asia Minor. Such has been the purpose of this study. Perhaps the solutions suggested do not explain all the little details. Unanimity of opinion can never be reached on these details. In spite of this, I believe this interpretation comes close to the truth which Christ wanted the broken, persecuted, discouraged Christians to see.

Revelation is a series of apocalyptic images given for the assurance of the people of God that Christ is going to be victorious over all opposition. For the Christians of John's day the assurance was given by showing the victory of Christ over the system of emperor worship because that was the greatest enemy of Christ in that day. The same assurance is given to Christians in every age. Find the greatest enemy of Christ (whether corrupt religion, godless government, social anarchy, or any other), put it in the place of emperor worship, and see its eventual failure as the living Christ, the redeeming Lamb, marches to victory over chaotic world conditions— Worthy Is the Lamb.

CHAPTER IX

The Lamb and Eternal Destiny

(Revelation 20:11 to 22:5)

The last act in the pageant of redemption pictures God's judgment and the final destiny of man. Just how this was related to the total picture in John's conception we are not told. The writers of the New Testament, following the Lord's injunction to "watch," expected his second coming and kingdom consummation in their own day. This is the proper Christian attitude in every age. Perhaps with this in mind and viewing the triumph of Christ over emperor worship, John expected the final judgment and the setting up of the eternal order to come with the victory of Christ over Domitian and his system. The fact that this was not true does no violence to the integrity of the Scriptures. The time of the end is a matter for God's sole knowledge and must be hidden even from those who were inspired of God to write about it. It will come in God's own time and in accordance with his purpose. He has not told us when that is to be. He has told us something of the nature of it. That is the content of this act in the pageant.

The structure of this vision is in keeping with the message to be given. When the time of eternal judgment comes, men will stand in two classes: redeemed and unredeemed. This vision is divided on this basis. The two are discussed side by side, but there is a broad general division between them. The earth-stage of the pageant has been closed; the curtain is drawn on the celestial stage to reveal eternal destinies.

The Destiny of the Unredeemed, 20:11–15; 21:8, 27; 22:15

John saw a great white throne and the one who sat upon it. The white throne symbolizes sovereign and holy justice; no one can question the verdicts rendered from this judge. He has all the evidence, he knows how to pronounce a just verdict, and he knows how to execute the sentence. In a manner of speaking, he is jury, judge, and sheriff all in one. John saw the dead, small and great, standing before the throne ready to receive their sentence. No statement is made as to the identity of the small and great as some special group. It appears that they symbolize the dead generally. Judgment is measured out on the basis of the records of two books. First, "books" were opened—books which contained the works or deeds of these who are being judged. The idea of God's keeping a record of the deeds of man is often found in the Scriptures. It is no doubt a figurative way of saying that God is keeping an accurate record of the deeds done in the flesh—none escape his eye, but he does not necessarily have to write them in a set of books to remember them. Second, "the book of life" was opened. This is a "life kind of book" in contrast to the "work kind of books" before mentioned. The dead were judged according to the things written in the books. If any man's name was not found in the book of life, the records in the books of works condemned him and he was cast into the lake of fire. It is not stated but seems to be implied in connection with the other New Testament teachings that if a man's name was found in the book of life, he was safe from condemning judgment and found his place with the great body of the redeemed discussed in the next chapter.

About the most difficult thing in the New Testament to work into a harmonious system is the body of Scriptures having to do with death, the interim between death and the resurrection, the resurrection, and the judgment. Jesus talked about a "sheep and goat" judgment; John here writes about a "great white throne" judgment. Some New Testament scholars hold that the two are separate judgments[1] and that one who believes otherwise is a heretic who is

---

[1] The distinction often made is that the "sheep and goat" judgment is on nations

untrue to "plain Scripture teaching." Other scholars hold that the two are simply different ways of speaking about the same judgment. In fairness to all the Scripture teachings, this seems to be the better interpretation. When one sees all the confusion that arises in trying to work out the eschatology of the New Testament, he is inclined to believe that the Lord has a reason for leaving it that way. Man needs to know that there is going to be a resurrection, a judgment, an eternal life after death. It is not necessary to his spiritual progress that he know all the details of those matters. If it had been, God would surely have revealed it in a plainer way. It is in line with the economy of God's revelation that he shows to man what he sees that man needs to know for his spiritual progress. Other things must be left for God's own knowledge. There are some things man does not need to know, and he must be satisfied to let it remain in the knowledge of God alone. The vision before us was given for the same purpose as the other varied teachings on the judgment: to warn man of the fact and terror of judgment but to assure him that the terror is erased for the man whose name is in the book of life—the man redeemed by the blood of Christ.

This brief paragraph does not exhaust the teaching of the destiny of the wicked. They appear at other places where a descriptive verse is thrown in by means of contrast to bring out the blessed condition of the redeemed. These verses identify those who have their part in the lake of fire: the fearful, the unbelieving, the abominable, murderers, fornicators, sorcerers, idolators, liars, unclean, dogs, and "everyone that loveth and doeth a lie." This is not an index to those who find their eternal destiny one of eternal separation and punishment; it is rather a series describing the quality or character of those who are eternally condemned.

Destiny of the Redeemed, 21:1 to 22:5

In contrast to the few verses which describe the destiny of the wicked, John gives a lengthy passage to describe the destiny of the

and that it comes before the millennium to decide which nations will continue during the millennium; the decision is based on the treatment they have given Christ. In this system the "great white throne" judgment comes at the close of the millennium and is a judgment of individuals.

redeemed. This was the main thing which the Christians of that day as well as those of subsequent days desired to know. This destiny is pictured in three symbols to show the perfect condition of the redeemed. Heaven is revealed from three different angles.[2]

(1) Fellowship with God, 21:1-8

The tabernacle which is symbolical of perfect fellowship is the first symbol. Just as God's place of abode with his people in the wilderness was the tabernacle, so the new heaven and the new earth will be his abode with them throughout eternity. He will have perfect fellowship with them. There will be no more separation from them because in the new heaven and new earth "the sea is no more." To John on Patmos the sea was the thing which separated him from the things dearest to him, the churches of Asia. In his vision of God in chapter 4, a transcendent sea kept the people away from God, but when all the destiny of man has been worked out, "the sea is no more"; man is in intimate fellowship with God.[3] John heard a voice proclaiming "the tabernacle of God is with men, and he shall dwell with them, and they shall be his people." This voice came immediately after the Holy City, New Jerusalem, was seen coming down glorious and beautiful in appearance. So the New Jerusalem is a tabernacle where God dwells with his people. He wipes away their tears and erases forever crying, mourning, pain, and death. They have had their share of these things on earth. Now all things are new. As a guarantee that they can depend on this, God instructed John to write that these things were true and dependable because he, the Alpha and Omega, is the power bringing it about.

(2) Protection by God, 21:9-26

The city which is symbolical of perfect protection is the next figure. The new heaven and new earth must have a capital city in accordance with their splendor. The vision which is given to John

---

[2]This view is offered with some variations by Richardson, Pieters, D. Smith, Dana, J. Smith, Beckwith, and Swete, *in loco*.

[3]Swete, Peters, Beckwith, D. Smith, Dana, and Richardson, *in loco*.

leaves nothing lacking. He saw the New Jerusalem glorious as a bride, and with the light of God's favor upon her. The city has a wall great and high. Walls of the cities in that ancient day were for protection. This great high wall symbolized perfect protection. There were twelve gates to the city—symbolizing an abundant entrance. The ancient cities had one gate, which was closed at night or when the enemy approached. If one was caught outside, it meant destruction. The New Jerusalem has not one gate but twelve—a perfect number. Moreover, these gates are never closed—there is an abundant entrance. Each gate is made of one huge pearl—symbolizing the fact that the entrance to heaven is by the way of suffering—the pearl is the only jewel which is produced by suffering and pain in overcoming difficulty.

The city had twelve foundations; so perfect a foundation could not be shaken. The city is perfectly square; height, breadth, and length measures 12,000 furlongs. To make this into a literal number destroys the symbolism. Twelve thousand furlongs is equivalent to 1,500 miles in present-day measurements, but that has no meaning. The efforts of many to determine the number of people who could live in a city this size and how much room each would have are futile. The number "12,000" is a multiple number from two perfect numbers, "12" and "1,000." It is used to create the impression of perfection and completeness. There will be perfect room for all the redeemed; nor can one determine how populous heaven will be by deciding how much room each person will have to have and then dividing it into the cube of 1,500 miles reduced to cubic feet.

The entire description is intended to present a strong, spacious, perfect, and beautiful city where God's redeemed will dwell with him in perfect fellowship. To try to make this a literal city does violence to the scheme. Some have done this and have arrived at absurd conclusions. They find that the city is 1,500 miles square; and Palestine, where it is to be located, in their view, is not more than about 150 by 70 miles. Therefore, they think that the city will stand high above Palestine, and perhaps stationary, as the earth revolves under it. This is a symbolical picture of a city with walls of jasper placed on foundations of sapphire, chalcedony, emerald, sardonyx, beryl, topaz, amethyst, etc. Each of its twelve gates is a huge pearl, and the streets are pure gold. No lamp is needed because the Lamb is the light of the city. There is no temple in the city. The temple was the place where God met his people, where sacrifice for sin was made, where intercession was made. It is not needed in the New Jerusalem, because there is no sin to be atoned for and because the people are in the immediate presence of God. This glorious city is inhabited by people of all nations, and it lends its protection to them all.

(3) Provisions from God, 22:1-5

The garden, which symbolizes perfect enjoyment and the supply of all needs, is the third symbol in picturing the destiny of the redeemed. Here is a garden with a beautiful river the crystal water of which is the water of life which issues from the throne of God and of the Lamb. On either side of the river grows the tree of life, which bares its fruit twelve months out of the year and the leaves of which have healing power. There are three basic things necessary to the sustaining of life: water, food, and health. This picture symbolizes the provision of all three. The water of life and the perpetual fruit of the tree of life furnish the food and drink; the leaves with their healing powers furnish health. Together they symbolize God's nurture and care for his own. How can a man live forever? Here is the answer, and it comes from "the throne of God and of the Lamb"—God has all that is needed to sustain eternal life in man.

In this garden, with life divinely sustained, man shall serve God forever. He tried it on earth, but his efforts were imperfect because there were so many handicaps. There will be no handicaps in heaven, and "his servants shall serve him." Another beautiful thought is found in the expression, "they shall see his face." Often in this world men have this longing. It is expressed in poem and song and often in the deep anguish of the heart when no one else can know about it. But when this earth is passed and man finds himself in the eternal presence of God, then he will look on the face of his Redeemer-God and serve him forever. What greater pleasure could one ask?

This is God's answer to the longing of man to know about the future life. In symbol God says, "Heaven is a place of perfect fellowship, perfect protection, perfect provision of needs, perfect service to God." Great contrast is noted here between the destiny of the wicked and the destiny of the redeemed.

Conclusion

(Revelation 22:6–21)

The pageant is over, and the final curtain has been drawn. John has seen and has shown to his audience the picture of God's care over them in their conflict, the certainty of their triumph over the terrible conditions of the day, and the glory which is beyond the grave which is opening before them. All that remains is the necessity of impressing upon their minds once again the importance of this message. Now the Redeemer steps in front of the curtain to issue his final word.

In verses 6–7 he assures the hearers that this is a message of divine authority. It is a message which announces upon the authority of God a speedy rescue for his distressed people. Blessings are pronounced upon those who in obedience to him live the overcoming life set out in this book. In verses 8–9, John adds his personal testimony to the authority of the book. His testimony would mean much to the Christians of Asia Minor.

In verses 10–15 the importance of the book for the immediate needs of the people is indicated. John is told not to seal the book up for some distant generation. It is first of all for the Christians of John's own day (v. 10). God's period of probation for the enemies of his cause has ended (v. 11). His judgment upon them is imminent (v. 12). Preparation for meeting the conditions is to be desired (v. 14).

Verse 16 brings to their attention again the fact that this is not just some man's message. It comes from Jesus himself.

Verse 17 issues the invitation for men to accept the bounty which God offers. The Spirit invites; the bride[1] invites; individual participants invite. The invitation is extended to any who will accept its terms.

Verse 18 is a warning for the protection of the book. Apocalyptic books were treated with great freedom in John's day. Men cut out the part they wanted and discarded the rest. But this is no ordinary apocalypse. To add to it or to take from it is to incur the displeasure of God with its consequences—strong language to assure the preservation of the book as John sent it to them.

Verse 20 voices a final promise of the Lord's purpose to come quickly to the aid of his persecuted people. In acceptance of the promise and in the attitude of patience and trust, John bows his head with his audience to whisper the reverent prayer, "Even so, come, Lord Jesus."

Who can read this book which breathes the atmosphere of victorious faith and courageous trust in God, with the unfailing assurance in the fulfilment of his purpose and the victory of the Christ of the cross and the empty tomb, without shouting with the people of the book—

> Worthy is the Lamb that was slain,
> And has redeemed us to God by his blood,
> To receive power, and riches, and wisdom,
> And might, and honor, and glory,
> And blessing, and dominion,
> Forever and ever.
>
> Amen.

---

[1]The bride may be the church as in 19:7, or it may be heaven as in 21:9. Either is an effective view.

Bibliography

BOOKS

General

Addis, W. E. *Christianity and the Roman Empire.* London: The Sunday School Association, 1893.

Allen, Cady H. *The Message of the Book of Revelation.* Nashville: Cokesbury Press, 1939.

Brown, David. *The Apocalypse.* New York: The Christian Literature Company, 1891.

Case, Shirley Jackson. *The Millennial Hope.* Chicago: The University of Chicago Press, 1918.

———. *The Revelation of John.* Chicago: The University of Chicago Press, 1919.

Charles, R. H. *A Critical History of the Doctrine of a Future Life in Israel, in Judaism, and in Christianity.* 2d ed. London: Adam and Charles Black, 1913.

———. *Religious Development Between the Old and the New Testaments.* New York: Henry Holt and Company, n.d.

———. *The Apocrypha and Pseudepigrapha of the Old Testament.* Vol. II. Oxford: At the Clarendon Press, 1913.

Dana, H. E. *New Testament Criticism.* Fort Worth: The World Book Company, Inc., 1924.

———. *Searching the Scriptures.* New Orleans: Bible Institute Memorial Press, 1936.

———. *The Ephesian Tradition.* Kansas City: The Kansas City Seminary Press, 1940.

219

————. *The Epistles and Apocalypse of John*. Dallas: Baptist Book Store, 1937.

Eckman, George P. *When Christ Comes Again*. 2d ed. New York: The Abingdon Press, 1917.

Eusebius, Pamphilus. *The Ecclesiastical History*. Translated by C. F. Cruse. Philadelphia: J. B. Lippincott and Company, 1869.

Feinberg, Charles. *Premillennialism or A-millennialism?* Grand Rapids: Zondervan Publishing House, 1936.

Gettys, J. M. *How to Study Revelation*. Richmond: John Knox Press, 1946.

Gibbon, Edward. *The Decline and Fall of the Roman Empire*. 5 vols. Chicago: Thompson and Thomas Publishers, n.d.

Goodspeed, Calvin. *Messiah's Second Advent*. Toronto: William Briggs, 1900.

Gregory, Caspar R. *Canon and Text of the New Testament*. New York: Charles Scribner's Sons, 1920.

Hamilton, Floyd E. *The Basis of Millennial Faith*. Grand Rapids: William B. Eerdman's Publishing Company, 1942.

Hardy, E. G. *Christianity and the Roman Government*. New York: The Macmillan Company, 1925.

Hendricksen, W. *More Than Conquerors*. Grand Rapids: Baker's Book Store, 1940.

Jones, Russell Bradley. *The Things Which Shall Be Hereafter*. Nashville: Broadman Press, 1947.

King, William Peter. *Adventism*. New York: Abingdon-Cokesbury Press, 1941.

Kuyper, Abraham. *Chiliasm, or the Doctrine of Premillennialism*. Translated by G. M. Van Pernis. Grand Rapids: Zondervan Publishing House, 1934.

Lipsey, P. I. *Revelation: an Interpretation*. Jackson, Mississippi: Purser Brothers, Printers, 1946.

Lockhart, Clinton. *Principles of Interpretation*. 2d ed., revised. Fort Worth: S. H. Taylor, Printer, 1915.

Morgan, G. Campbell. *A First Century Message to Twentieth Century Christians*. New York: Fleming H. Revell Company, 1902.

Moulton, R. G. *The Modern Reader's Bible for Schools: the New Testament.* New York: The Macmillan Company, 1920.

Mullins, E. Y. *The Christian Religion in Its Doctrinal Expression.* Philadelphia: The Judson Press, 1917.

Newman, A. H. *A Manual of Church History.* Vol. II. Philadelphia: The American Baptist Publication Society, 1899.

Ottman, F. C. *The Unfolding of the Ages.* New York: Publication Office, "Our Hope," 1905.

Palmer, Frederic. *The Drama of the Apocalypse.* New York: The Macmillan Company, 1903.

Pieters, Albertus. *The Lamb, the Woman, and the Dragon.* Grand Rapids: Zondervan Publishing House, 1937.

Polhamus, W. R. *The Unveiling of Jesus Christ.* New York: Fleming H. Revell Company, 1936.

Ramsay, W. M. *The Church and the Roman Empire.* New York: G. P. Putnam's Sons, 1912.

———. *The Letters to the Seven Churches.* New York: Hodder and Stoughton, 1904.

Rand, H. B. *Studies in Revelation.* Haverhill, Massachusetts: Destiny, 1941.

Richardson, Donald W. *The Revelation of Jesus Christ.* Richmond: John Knox Press, 1939.

Roberts, Alexander, and Donaldson, James. (Editors) *The Ante-Nicene Fathers.* Vols. I, III, and IV. New York: The Christian Literature Company, 1890.

Robertson, A. T. *Epochs in the Life of the Apostle John.* New York: Fleming H. Revell Company, 1935.

Scott, E. F. *The Book of Revelation.* New York: Charles Scribner's Sons, 1940.

Stalker, James. *The Two St. Johns of the New Testament.* New York: The American Tract Society, 1895.

Strong, A. H. *Systematic Theology.* 3d ed. New York: A. C. Armstrong and Son, 1890.

Venable, C. L. *Reading of Revelation.* Philadelphia: Muhlenberg, 1947.

Warfield, B. B. *Biblical Doctrines*. New York: Oxford University Press, 1929.

Weigall, Arthur. *Nero, the Singing Emperor of Rome*. New York: G. P. Putnam's Sons, 1930.

Westcott, B. F. *A General Survey of the History of the Canon of the New Testament*. 6th ed. Cambridge: Macmillan and Company, 1889.

Wishart, C. F. *The Book of Day*. New York: Oxford University Press, 1935.

Commentaries

Alford, Henry. *The Greek New Testament*. Vol. IV. London: Rivingtons, Waterloo Place, 1862.

Barnes, Albert. *Notes on the Book of Revelation*. New York: Harper and Brothers, Publishers, 1864.

Beckwith, Isbon T. *The Apocalypse of John*. New York: The Macmillan Company, 1919.

Benson, E. W. *The Apocalypse*. London: Macmillan and Company, 1900.

Bultema, H. *The Apocalypse*. Muskegon, Michigan: Bereer Publishing Company, 1921.

Carroll, B. H. *The Book of Revelation* ("An Interpretation of the English Bible"). Edited by J. B. Cranfill. New York: Fleming H. Revell Company, 1913.

Charles, R. H. *The Revelation of St. John*. 2 vols. ("The International Critical Commentary") New York: Charles Scribner's Sons, 1920.

Elliott, E. B. *Commentary on Revelation*. London: Seeley, Burnside, and Seeley, 1844.

Erdman, Charles R. *The Revelation of John*. Philadelphia: The Westminster Press, 1936.

Hengstenberg, E. W. *The Revelation of St. John*. Translated by Patrick Fairbairn, 2 vols. New York: Robert Carter and Brothers, 1852.

Kiddle, Martin. *The Revelation of St. John*. ("The Moffatt New

Testament Commentary") London: Hodder and Stoughton, 1940.

Kuyper, Abraham. *The Revelation of St. John.* Translated by John Kendrik de Vries. Grand Rapids: William B. Eerdman's Publishing Company, 1935.

Larkin, Clarence. *The Book of Revelation.* Philadelphia: Moyer and Lotter, 1919.

Lord, David N. *Exposition of the Apocalypse.* New York: Harper and Brothers Publishers, 1847.

Milligan, William. *The Book of Revelation.* ("The Expositor's Bible") New York: A. C. Armstrong and Son, 1889.

Moffatt, James. *Revelation of St. John the Divine.* ("The Expositor's Greek Testament") Grand Rapids. William B. Eerdman's Publishing Company, n.d.

Seiss, J. A. *The Apocalypse.* 3 vols. Philadelphia: School of the Bible, 1865.

Simcox, W. H. *The Revelation of St. John the Divine.* ("Cambridge Greek Testament for Schools and Colleges") Revised by G. A. Simcox. London: Cambridge University Press, 1909.

Smith, David. *The Disciple's Commentary on the New Testament.* Vol. V. New York: Ray Long and Richard R. Smith, Inc., 1932.

Smith, Justin A. *An American Commentary on the New Testament.* Vol. VII. Philadelphia: The American Baptist Publication Society, 1888, Reprinted, 1942.

Stuart, Moses. *Commentary on the Apocalypse.* Vol. II. Andover: Allen, Morrill and Wardwell, 1845.

Swete, H. B. *The Apocalypse of St. John.* 2d. ed. London: Macmillan and Company, 1907.

Weiss, Bernhard. *A Commentary on the New Testament.* Vol. IV. New York: Funk and Wagnalls Company, 1906.

Articles

Encyclopaedia Britannica. Chicago: Encyclopaedia Britannica, Inc., 1940.

Burkitt, Francis Crawford. "Apocalypse." Vol. II, pp. 99–101.

Charles, R. H. and Oesterley, W. O. E. "Apocalyptic Literature." Vol. II, pp. 101–105.

The International Standard Bible Encyclopaedia. (James Orr, editor) Chicago: The Howard-Severance Company, 1930.

Orr, James. "Revelation of John." Vol. IV pp. 2582–2587.

Thomson, J. E. H. *"Apocalyptic Literature."* Vol. I pp. 161–178.